'For Freedom's battle'

BYRON'S LETTERS AND JOURNALS
VOLUME 11
1823–1824

For Freedom's battle once begun,
Bequeathed by bleeding Sire to Son,
Though baffled oft is ever won.
THE GIAOUR, lines 123–125

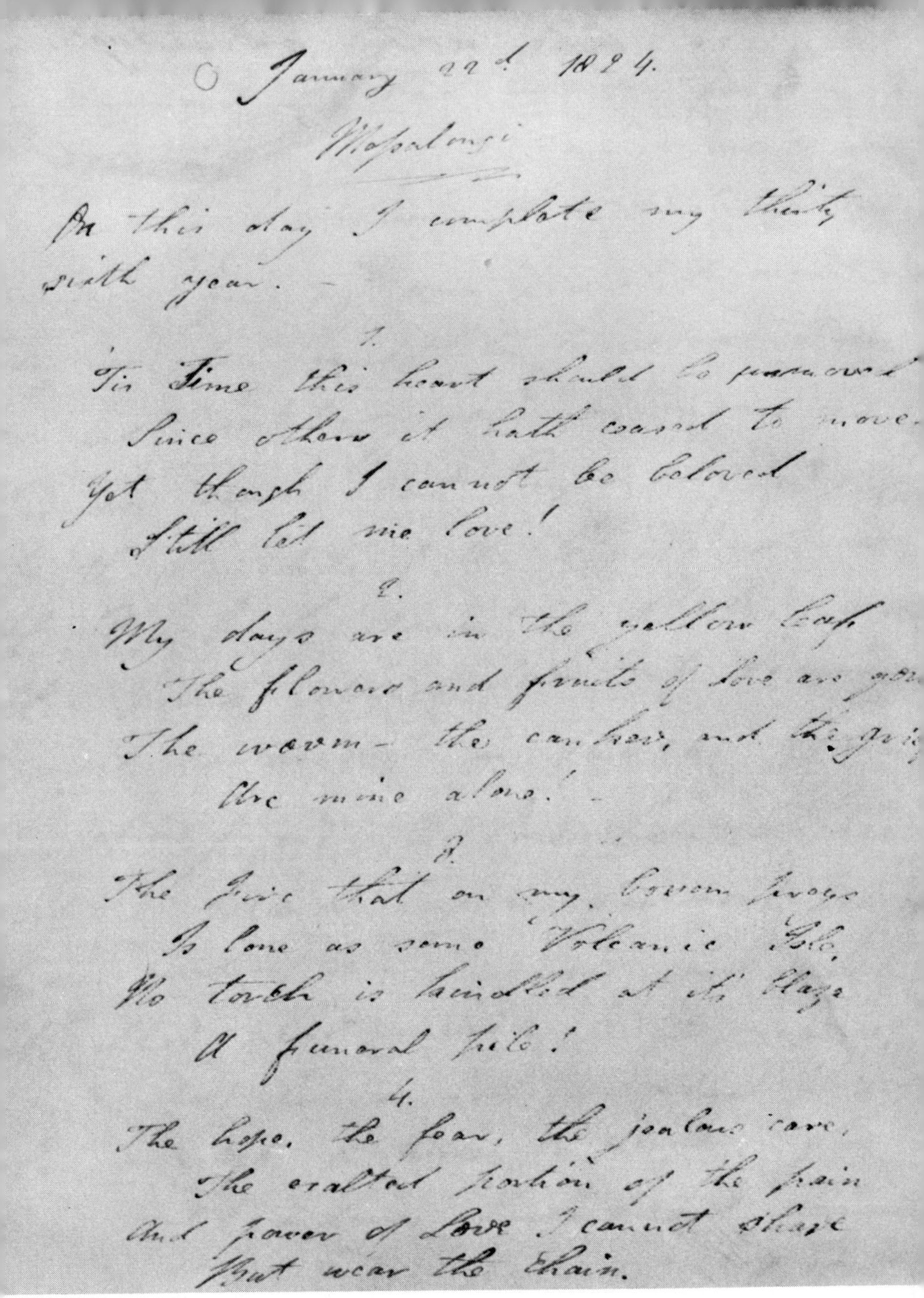

January 22d 1824.

Messalonghi

On this day I complete my thirty sixth year. —

1.

'Tis time this heart should be unmoved
Since others it hath ceased to move.
Yet though I cannot be beloved
Still let me love!

2.

My days are in the yellow leaf
The flowers and fruits of love are gone
The worm — the canker, and the grief
Are mine alone! —

3.

The fire that on my bosom preys
Is lone as some Volcanic Isle,
No torch is kindled at its blaze
A funeral pile!

4.

The hope, the fear, the jealous care,
The exalted portion of the pain
And power of Love I cannot share
But wear the chain.

First page of Byron's poem written into his last Journal on his 36th birthday (printed in full on p.11)

'For Freedom's battle'

BYRON'S LETTERS AND JOURNALS

Edited by
LESLIE A. MARCHAND

The complete and unexpurgated text of all the letters available in manuscript and the full printed version of all others

VOLUME 11
1823–1824

JOHN MURRAY

VOLUMES ALREADY PUBLISHED

1. 'In my hot youth' (1798–1810)
2. 'Famous in my time' (1810–1812)
3. 'Alas! the love of Women!' (1813–1814)
4. 'Wedlock's the devil' (1814–1815)
5. 'So late into the night' (1816–1817)
6. 'The flesh is frail' (1818–1819)
7. 'Between two worlds' (1820)
8. 'Born for opposition' (1821)
9. 'In the wind's eye' (1821–1822)
10. 'A heart for every fate' (1822–1823)

First published 1981 by
John Murray (Publishers) Ltd
50 Albemarle Street, London W1X 4BD

British Library Cataloguing in Publication Data
Byron, George Gordon, *Baron Byron*
Byron's letters and journals.
Vol. 11: 1823—1824: 'For freedom's battle'
1. Byron, George Gordon, *Baron Byron*—Correspondence
2. Byron, George Gordon, *Baron Byron*—Diaries
3. Poets, English—19th century—Correspondence
I. Marchand, Leslie Alexis II. 'For freedom's battle'
821'.7 PR4381.A3
ISBN 0–7195–3792–4

Printed in Great Britain by
Latimer Trend & Company Ltd, Plymouth

CONTENTS

This volume contains Byron's letters from Greece, written during his last residence there, first from Cephalonia, and then from Missolonghi, where he strove against great odds to aid the Greeks in their war for independence. A new set of correspondents appears and a new tone is apparent. Though his old facetiousness breaks through occasionally, his letters reflect his serious concern with the business of the revolution and his efforts to unite the Greeks in a common cause despite their dissensions. His chief correspondents were his business agents in the islands, Barff and Hancock, and his banker friend in Genoa, Charles Barry, to whom he wrote his frankest accounts of daily affairs. His letters to Hobhouse and to John Bowring, secretary of the London Greek Committee, attempted to give a realistic picture of the Greek struggle. To Teresa Guiccioli he wrote only short dutiful postscripts in English to the longer letters of her brother, Count Pietro Gamba. Included in this volume are a number of additional letters which became available too late to take their chronological place in the earlier volumes. Among these is the outstanding sequence of fifteen letters discovered in the vaults of Barclay's Bank locked in a trunk deposited in 1820 by Scrope Davies, Byron's witty friend, drinking companion and Fellow of King's College, Cambridge.

EDITORIAL NOTE

This eleventh and last volume of *Byron's Letters and Journals* brings to a conclusion a labour of more than ten years. I can truthfully say that during that time my interest never lessened in the task or the man, for Byron is never dull and his letters and journals reflect a personality that is many-faceted but fundamentally ever the same. That quality of "Sincerity and Strength" which Matthew Arnold found in Byron's poetry, shines through his letters in equal measure and is clearly apparent in those from Greece. I am as convinced as when I began that his letters and journals contribute as much as his poetry to his literary reputation.

In any work so extensive there are certain to be errors and shortcomings for which the editor must take responsibility. Some of these are due to my own human fallibility, and some to circumstances over which I had little control such as the economic realities of modern publishing. But it has been my aim to present an accurate text of all Byron's extant and available letters, with sufficient annotation to make the context clear. My prediction (in Johnson's words) that it is impossible not to explain too much for some and not enough for others has been fully justified if I may judge by reviews and private correspondence relating to earlier volumes.

The total number of letters in this edition now stands at about 2,900 (my earlier estimate of 3,000 was not reached, though no doubt more letters will come to light after the final printing). There were 1,198 in the last collected edition, edited by Rowland E. Prothero. More than eighty-five per cent of those in this edition are published from manuscripts or facsimiles. More than a hundred are first published in this edition (it is difficult to determine precisely, for many had obscure periodical publication). And several hundred are here first published without omissions.

As in previous volumes, the Editorial Principles are repeated below to make this as self-sufficient as possible. In addition to an index, of proper names there is an appendix of "Additions and Corrections" to the text and notes in previous volumes, some of my own later finding and some called to my attention by numerous knowledgeable readers and reviewers. I am deeply grateful to those readers who have pointed out errors and have identified quotations and allusions which escaped me.

The final volume (12th) of this edition is in preparation. It will consist of an index of Byron's aphorisms and *bons mots*, including most of his facetious and memorable phrases, and a combined subject and general index covering the 11 volumes of Letters and Journals.

ACKNOWLEDGMENTS (Volume 11). The National Endowment for the Humanities has since almost the beginning of this project given support with generous grants which have facilitated my work immeasurably. The sense of my indebtedness to many people is overwhelming as I contemplate these eleven volumes and write *finis* to the task. Perhaps I can best indicate those to whom I owe most by referring the reader to the repetition of the same names in the acknowledgments of previous volumes. I can but again express my gratitude here and add a few names of those who have lately come to my assistance. Stewart Perowne and Sir Rupert Hart-Davis have read proofs with keen critical eyes and have made many helpful suggestions for the notes. My wife, Marion, has spent countless hours checking proof and index and has saved me from many errors. Her understanding and admiration of Byron, and her insights, have lightened my task throughout the long labour. Antony Peattie has been most helpful in checking the text and notes in copy and proof. I am indebted again to Ricki B. Herzfeld for transcriptions and translations of the Italian letters in this volume. And I am grateful to Professor M. Byron Raizis for transcribing and translating a letter in Greek signed by Byron. Finally I cannot give adequate thanks to my publisher and friend John Murray for his perpetual enthusiasm and the active assistance he has rendered me throughout this long task; to his colleague John Gibbins I am deeply indebted for his careful editing and proof reading.

For permission to get photocopies of letters in their possession and to use them in this volume I wish to thank the following libraries and individuals: Arents Tobacco Collection, New York Public Library; Barclays Bank; Roger W. Barrett; Benaki Museum, Athens; Biblioteca Classense, Ravenna; The British Library; The Rt. Hon. Lord Brocket; Buffalo and Erie County Public Library; C. E. Clarabut; G. M. Clive; Martin Davies; Gene De Grusen; University of Delaware Library; Harry S. Dickey Collection; Dyce Collection, Victoria and Albert Museum; Milton S. Eisenhower Library, The Johns Hopkins University; Fales Collection, New York University Library; Fitzherbert Papers, Derbyshire Record Office; Gennadius Library, Athens; Harrow School Library; Henry E. Huntington Library; Humanities Research Centre, University of Texas; Lord Kinnaird;

The Viscount Knebworth; Ivan Londos; Longman Group, Ltd.; Lovelace Papers, Bodleian Library; The Mitchell Library, the Library of NSW, Sydney, Australia; Mugar Memorial Library, Boston University; John Murray; National Historical Museum, Athens; National Library, Athens; Nottingham Archives; Carl H. Pforzheimer Library; Pierpont Morgan Library; Harry Oppenheimer; the late Francis Lewis Randolph; Roe-Byron Collection, Newstead Abbey; Scripps College Library; Stark Library, University of Texas; Brigadier D. E. Taunton; Robert H. Taylor Collection, Princeton University Library; Texas Christian University Library; D. Tolstoy; Vigo County Library, Terre Haute, Indiana; Watson Library, University College London; Widener Collection, Harvard University; Robert A. Wilson.

For assistance of various kinds I wish to thank the following: Betty T. Bennett; Norman Brennan; Tim Burnett; John Buxton; Joseph Byrnes; The Earl of Cawdor; Cecil Clarabut; Patrick Cruttwell; Martin Davies; Roy A. Dehn; William Donati; Wilfred S. Dowden; Mrs. E. E. Duncan-Jones; Mrs. Mervyn Ellison; Paula R. Feldman; Paul Fussell; Mihai H. Handrea; Margaret Howell; Verlyn Klinkenborg; Paul Magnuson; Jerome J. McGann; Mrs. Doris H. Meriwether; Andrew Nicholson; Mrs. Annabella M. Oliver; Gordon N. Ray; Charles E. Robinson; William St. Clair; Ian Scott-Kilvert; Margot Strickland; Mrs. J. Voignier-Marshall; Lindsay Waters; George Watson; Sir Francis Watson; Carl Woodring; Robert Yampolsky.

* * * * * *

EDITORIAL PRINCIPLES. With minor exceptions, herein noted, I have tried to reproduce Byron's letters as they were written. The letters are arranged consecutively in chronological order. The name of the addressee is given at the top left in brackets. The source of the text is indicated in the list of letters in the Appendix. If it is a printed text, it is taken from the first printed form of the letter known or presumed to be copied from the original manuscript, or from a more reliable editor, such as Prothero, when he also had access to the manuscript. In this case, as with handwritten or typed copies, or quotations in sale catalogues, the text of this source is given precisely.

When the text is taken from the autograph letter or a photo copy or facsimile of it, the present whereabouts or ownership is given, whether it is in a library or a private collection. When the manuscript is the source, no attempt is made to indicate previous publication, if any. Here I have been faithful to the manuscript with the following exceptions:

1. The place and date of writing is invariably placed at the top right in one line if possible to save space, and to follow Byron's general practice. Fortunately Byron dated most of his letters in this way, but occasionally he put the date at the end. Byron's usual custom of putting no punctuation after the year is followed throughout.

2. Superior letters such as S^{r} or 30th have been lowered to Sr. and 30th. The & has been retained, but &^{c} has been printed &c.

3. Byron's spelling has been followed (and generally his spelling is good, though not always consistent), and *sic* has been avoided except in a few instances when an inadvertent misspelling might change the meaning or be ambiguous, as for instance when he spells *there* t-h-e-i-r.

4. Although, like many of his contemporaries, Byron was inconsistent and eccentric in his capitalization, I have felt it was better to let him have his way, to preserve the flavour of his personality and his times. With him the capital letter sometimes indicates the importance he gives to a word in a particular context; but in the very next line it might not be capitalized. If clarity has seemed to demand a modification, I have used square brackets to indicate any departure from the manuscript.

5. Obvious slips of the pen crossed out by the writer have been silently omitted. But crossed out words of any significance to the meaning or emphasis are enclosed in angled brackets ⟨ ⟩.

6. Letters undated, or dated with the day of the week only, have been dated, when possible, in square brackets. If the date is conjectural, it is given with a question mark in brackets. The same practice is followed for letters from printed sources. The post mark date is given, to indicate an approximate date, only when the letter itself is undated.

7. The salutation is put on the same line as the text, separated from it by a dash. The complimentary closing, often on several lines in the manuscript, is given in one line if possible. The P.S., wherever it may be written in the manuscript, follows the signature.

8. Byron's punctuation follows no rules of his own or others' making. He uses dashes and commas freely, but for no apparent reason, other than possibly for natural pause between phrases, or sometimes for emphasis. He is guilty of the "comma splice", and one can seldom be sure where he intended to end a sentence, or whether he recognized the sentence as a unit of expression. He does at certain

intervals place a period and a dash, beginning again with a capital letter. These larger divisions sometimes, though not always, represented what in other writers, particularly in writers of today, correspond to paragraphs. He sometimes uses semicolons, but often where we would use commas. Byron himself recognized his lack of knowledge of the logic or the rules of punctuation. He wrote to his publisher John Murray on August 26, 1813: "Do you know anybody who can *stop*—I mean point—commas and so forth, for I am I fear a sad hand at your punctuation". It is not without reason then that most editors, including R. E. Prothero, have imposed sentences and paragraphs on him in line with their interpretation of his intended meaning. It is my feeling, however, that this detracts from the impression of Byronic spontaneity and the onrush of ideas in his letters, without a compensating gain in clarity. In fact, it may often arbitrarily impose a meaning or an emphasis not intended by the writer. I feel that there is less danger of distortion if the reader may see exactly how he punctuated and then determine whether a phrase between commas or dashes belongs to one sentence or another. Byron's punctuation seldom if ever makes the reading difficult or the meaning unclear. In rare instances I have inserted a period, a comma, or a semicolon, but have enclosed it in square brackets to indicate it was mine and not his.

9. Words missing but obvious from the context, such as those lacunae caused by holes in the manuscript, are supplied within square brackets. If they are wholly conjectural, they are followed by a question mark. The same is true of doubtful readings in the manuscript.

Undated letters have been placed within the chronological sequence when from internal or external evidence there are reasonable grounds for a conjectural date. This has seemed more useful than putting them together at the end of the volumes. Where a more precise date cannot be established from the context, these letters are placed at the beginning of the month or year in which they seem most likely to have been written.

ANNOTATION. I have tried to make the footnotes as brief and informative as possible, eschewing, sometimes with reluctance, the leisurely expansiveness of R. E. Prothero, who in his admirable edition of the *Letters and Journals* often gave pages of supplementary biographical information and whole letters *to* Byron, which was possible at a time when book publishing was less expensive, and when the extant and available Byron letters numbered scarcely more than a third of those in the present edition. Needless to say, I have found Prothero's notes of inestimable assistance in the identification of persons and quotations in the letters which he edited, though where possible I have double checked them. And I must say that while I have found some errors, they are rare. With this general acknowledgment I have left the reader to assume that where a source of information in the notes is not given, it comes from Prothero's edition, where additional details may be found.

The footnotes are numbered for each letter. Where the numbers are repeated on a page, the sequence of the letters will make the reference clear.

In an appendix in each volume I have given brief biographical sketches of Byron's principal correspondents first appearing in that volume. These are necessarily very short, and the stress is always on Byron's relations with the subject of the sketch. Identification of less frequent correspondents and other persons mentioned in the letters is given in footnotes as they appear, and the location of these, as well as the biographical sketches in the appendix, will be indicated by italic numbers in the index. Similarly italic indications will refer the reader to the principal biographical notes on persons mentioned in the text of the letters.

With respect to the annotation of literary allusions and quotations in the letters, I have tried to identify all quotations in the text, but have not always been successful in locating Byron's sources in obscure dramas whose phrases, serious or ridiculous, haunted his memory. When I have failed to identify either a quotation or a name, I have frankly noted it as "Unidentified". When, however, Byron has quoted or adapted some common saying from Shakespeare or elsewhere, I have assumed that it is easily recognizable and have passed it by. I have likewise passed by single words or short phrases (quoted or not quoted) which may have had a source in Byron's reading or in conversation with his correspondents, but which it is impossible to trace. And when he repeats a quotation, as he frequently does, I have not repeated the earlier notation except occasionally when it is far removed from its first occurrence in the letters, hoping that the reader will find it in the index in the last volume. No doubt readers with special knowledge in various fields may be able to enlighten me concerning quotations which may have baffled me.

Since this work will be read on both sides of the Atlantic, I have explained some things that would be perfectly clear to a British reader but not to an American. I trust that English readers will make allowance for this. As Johnson said in the Preface to his edition of Shakespeare: "It is impossible for an expositor not to write too little for some, and too much for others . . . how long soever he may deliberate, [he] will at last explain many lines which the learned will think impossible to be mistaken, and omit many for which the ignorant will want his help. These are censures merely relative, and must be quietly endured."

I have occasionally given cross references, but in the main have left it to the reader to consult the index for names which have been identified in earlier notes.

SPECIAL NOTES. The letters to Thomas Moore, first published in his *Letters and Journals of Lord Byron* (1830), were printed with many omissions and the manuscripts have since disappeared. Moore generally indicated omissions by asterisks, here reproduced as in his text.

Beginning with Volume 7, I have divided some of Byron's longer letters into paragraphs, where a pause or a change of subject is indicated. This helps with the proof-correcting, and makes easier the reading of the text, without distracting significantly from the impression of Byron's free-flowing and on-rushing style of composition.

BYRON CHRONOLOGY

1823 Aug. 3—Arrived at Argostoli, Cephalonia, in brig *Hercules*.
Aug. 11—Left for visit to Ithaca.
Aug. 17—Returned to Cephalonia—night at monastery above Samos.
Aug. 18—Returned to Argostoli.
—Marco Botzaris wrote to invite Byron to Acarnania.
Aug. 19—Botzaris killed in battle.
Sept. 2—Left the *Hercules*.
Sept. 4—Moved to Metaxata.
Sept. 6—Trelawny and Browne left for the Morea.
Sept. 28—Began journal.
Sept. 30—Discontinued journal on receiving news of daughter's illness.
Oct. 5—Series of earthquakes on Cephalonia.
Oct.—George Finlay arrived in Cephalonia and called on Byron.
—Letter from Frank Hastings.
Oct. 28—Lord Sidney Osborne came from Corfu to visit Byron.
Nov.—Dr. Julius Millingen arrived in Cephalonia.
Nov. 10?—Browne arrived from Morea with Greek Deputies Orlando and Luriottis.
Nov. 13—Signed agreement for loan of £4,000 to Greek Government.
Nov.—Finlay left for Peloponnessus.
Nov. 22—Col. Leicester Stanhope, agent of the London Greek Committee, arrived.
Nov. 30—Byron wrote to the General Government of Greece, warning of dangers of their dissensions.
Dec. 6—Stanhope left for Missolonghi.
Dec. 8—Millingen left for Missolonghi.
Dec. 11—Mavrocordatos landed in Missolonghi.
Dec.—Greek squadron arrived and captured some Turkish vessels.
Dec.—Legislative Body invited Byron to join Mavrocordatos.
Dec. 17—Resumed journal.
Dec. 29—Embarked on the "mistico"; Gamba on "bombard"
Dec. 30—Arrived in Zante in morning—sailed for Missolonghi at 6:00 p.m.

Dec. 31—Mistico chased by Turkish ship; bombard seized and taken into Patras.

—Sent Lukas ashore near Anatolico with letter to Stanhope.

1824 Jan. 1—Mistico fled up coast and took refuge at Dragomestre.

Jan. 3—Bombard released by Turks and arrived in Missolonghi.

—Mistico arrived in Missolonghi with Greek escort and anchored.

Jan. 4—Came ashore to great reception.

Jan.—Consented to take 500 Suliotes into his service and pay.

Jan. 14—*Hellenica Chronica*, Greek newspaper, started by Col. Stanhope.

Jan. 20—Town blockaded by Turkish fleet; Greek squadron fled.

Jan. 22—Wrote verses on his 36th birthday.

Jan. 23—Returned four Turkish prisoners to Patras.

Jan. 25—Byron commissioned by Mavrocordatos to lead expedition against Lepanto.

Feb. 1—Visit to Anatolico.

Feb. 5—Parry, the fire-master, arrived with storeship *Ann*.

Feb. 10—Finlay arrived with invitation from Trelawny and Odysseus to meeting of Greek leaders at Salona.

Feb. 14—Disillusioned by greed of Suliotes.

Feb. 15—Seized by violent fit, supposed epileptic.

Feb. 16—Leeches applied and bleeding could not be stopped for some hours.

Feb. 21—Col. Stanhope left for Athens.

—Earthquake shook Missolonghi.

Feb.—Byron gradually recovered.

March—*Telegrafo Greco*, Italian newspaper, started.

March 21—Finlay returned to Athens.

March—News of conclusion of Greek Loan in London reached Missolonghi.

—Journey to Salona delayed by floods.

April 9—Wrote last letters to Barff and Barry.

April 19—Died of fever—weakened by bleeding, only remedy known to doctors.

On This Day I Complete My Thirty-Sixth Year

'Tis time this heart should be unmoved,
  Since others it hath ceased to move:
Yet though I cannot be beloved,
    Still let me love!

My days are in the yellow leaf;
  The flowers and fruits of Love are gone;
The worm—the canker, and the grief
    Are mine alone!

The fire that on my bosom preys
  Is lone as some Volcanic Isle;
No torch is kindled at its blaze
    A funeral pile!

The hope, the fear, the jealous care,
  The exalted portion of the pain
And power of Love I cannot share,
    But wear the chain.

But 'tis not *thus*—and 'tis not *here*
  Such thoughts should shake my Soul, nor *now*
Where Glory decks the hero's bier
    Or binds his brow.

The Sword, the Banner, and the Field,
  Glory and Greece around us see!
The Spartan borne upon his shield
    Was not more free!

Awake (not Greece—she *is* awake!)
  Awake, my Spirit! think through *whom*
Thy life-blood tracks its parent lake
    And then strike home!

Tread those reviving passions down
  Unworthy Manhood—unto thee
Indifferent should the smile or frown
    Of Beauty be.

If thou regret'st thy Youth, *why live*?
  The land of honourable Death
Is here:—up to the Field, and give
    Away thy Breath'.

Seek out—less often sought than found—
  A Soldier's Grave, for thee the best;
Then look around, and choose thy Ground,
    And take thy Rest!

Missolonghi,
January 22, 1824

Byrons last entry in his journal

BYRON'S LETTERS AND JOURNALS

[TO EDWARD BLAQUIERE]

Brig Hercules—Capt. Scott—Cephalonia. August 3d. 1823

Dear Sir,—Here am I[1]—but where are *you*?—at Corfu they say—but *why*?—I have received all yr. letters—with many thanks—what ought I to do?—I have some good will—about nine thousand pounds in Credits or Cash—with the command of more—and all from my own Income.—Of the Committee I only can say that they are full of good ⟨will⟩ intentions—are impatient to hear from you—and that I am a member—the Greek news is here anything but Good.—

ever yrs.
N B

P.S.—Excuse haste I write on the binnacle of a ship by the light of a lanthorn and a Squall blowing.—

[TO COUNTESS TERESA GUICCIOLI]

Argostoli di Cefalonia 4 Agosto—1823

[Postscript to Pietro Gamba's letter to Teresa]

P.S./—My dearest Teresa—I cannot write long letters as you know—but you also know or ought to know how much and entirely I ever am yr.

A. A. in E.[1]
N B

[TO COUNTESS TERESA GUICCIOLI]

Argostoli di Cefalonia—10 Agosto 1823

[Added to Pietro Gamba's letter to Teresa]

My dearest T[eres]a—We are here all very well and extremely well used by all the English here.——Of Greece and of the Greeks—I can say little—for every thing is as yet very uncertain on that point.—I pray you to remain tranquil, and not to believe any nonsense that you

[1] Byron and his party arrived at Argostoli, on the Ionian island of Cephalonia on August 3, having been advised to stop there rather than at Zante by James Hamilton Browne, a Scotsman who had been dismissed from the military service because of his Philhellenic sympathies. Browne had joined Byron in Leghorn. He had been in Greece before and knew that Colonel Charles James Napier, the English Resident on Cephalonia, was favourable to the Greek cause.

[1] Amico ed amante in eterno (friend and lover for ever) became the regular closing of letters of both Byron and Teresa to each other.

may hear; for the present we remain in this island—till we have better intelligence.—Tomorrow we are going to make a tour in the Island—for a day or two—

ever yrs. most affectly. A. A. in e.
N B

[TO CHARLES F. BARRY] *Cephalonia. August 10th. 1823*[1]

Dear Sir—We have been some days in harbour here to collect information on the state of the neighbouring countries before I proceeded there.—There is great uncertainty in the reports—but on the whole they are unfavourable.—The Turkish fleet is in sight from the heights of these Islands—and the greater part of the nearest coast in a state of declared and partly efficient blockade.—The Greek Government is [word illegible] (it is believed) and the Turks are trying to penetrate into the Morea.—The Greeks appear to want every thing—even *union*—for they are divided again it seems among themselves.—All this I state as stated to me—Mr. Blaquiere has left the Morea—and has been at Corfu [on] his way to England.[2]—Notwithstanding all this I shall remain as long as I can to seek an opportunity of reaching the Main—though the hazard is considerable—and perhaps useless.—Every one has been very kind and attentive here—but of course without compromising themselves—which was not to be expected—nor would I wish it.——I speak of the English.——

Of your two Correspondents to whom you gave me letters of Credit—Sr. Carrithi is unwilling—and Mr. Corialegno[3] (is that the name?—) willing—but hardly competent to advance money on even the best bills of exchange. Mr. Carrithi not only declined—but declared that he had no connection with the house of Webb at Genoa—and when referred to the letters for the proof that it was of the *same firm* with that of Leghorn—he replied that it was all the same—he had no connection with either.—As it is probable that the same reply may

1 Barry has written on the manuscript: "Lord N. Byron Cephalonia Augt 18 Recd Sept. 6". But he misread the date. An extra curl on the "0" makes it look slightly like an "8", but since the letter mentions nothing of his journey to Ithaca from which Byron had just returned on the 18th, the 10th is the more probable date.

2 Byron had expected to meet Blaquiere and get news from him concerning the situation on the mainland before proceeding, and was chagrined that he left for England so precipitately.

3 Geronimo Corgialegno, banker at Argostoli, became Byron's source of exchange until he discovered Charles Hancock in Cephalonia and his partner Samuel Barff (at Zante), who thenceforth handled all his business.

be made at Zante—and as it is not only extremely inconvenient but even hurtful to the Credit of your house—as well as to myself—I hope that you will take some step to remedy this—otherwise I do not see what is to be done—as my English letters (which are also very Essential) only refer to Constantinople—Smyrna—Venice—and Trieste—and to your houses at Genoa and Leghorn.——Carrithi made no distinction or difficulty about Messrs Ransom's house—but merely declined acting for your own in any way—and pretended to wonder why you should expect that he should.——This might be remedied by your sending me up my Credits (English and on your house also) in dollars *here*—but with whom here could I trust a sum of thirty five thousand dollars (more or less) with a Greek I could not leave it in safety—and there are no English houses here that I know of—and yet somewhere in these Islands the Credits must be negociated—as being the nearest point to the place where I want them.—The ten thousand dollars which I have on board—are safe—but I have recurred to them—and lucky that I had them—since these fellows would not recognize your firm.—You can address to me here—to the Care of your Correspondent Corialegno (I think the name) who is extremely civil—and will advance what he can—but the truth is—I fancy—that Specie in these islands is nearly as scarce as on the Main—or at any rate that from political or other reasons—they are reluctant to accept your bills—or unused to trade as bankers.——I have engaged about forty Suliotes here (the place and people I knew formerly) but the English Government in violation of a solemn promise on their landing—*now* refuses to restore them their arms.——But nothing can be kinder than the Officers &c. have *been individually* to us—as far as their duty will permit. I say this the more readily as I neither expected—nor had cause to expect it.—Of the Greeks I shall say nothing till I can say something better—except that I am not discouraged—and am

always yrs.
N B

P.S.—If you think any part of this letter worth communicating to Mr. Kinnaird you may—as I have not yet written to England——I shall stay out as long as I can—and do all I can for these Greeks;—but I cannot exaggerate—they must expect only the truth from me both of—and to them. You may also tell Mr. K[innair]d that about the beginning of the year I may probably require an addition to my letters &c. as if these fellows give me an opportunity I will stand by them as I said before.—

[TO COUNTESS TERESA GUICCIOLI]

St. Euphemia—Cephalonia—A[gost]o 11 o 1823

My dearest Teresa—All Well!—and doing well.—We are on the point of embarking for Ithaca[1]—after a warm ride in the Sun from Argostoli.—Pietro your brother will have told you the rest.——Do not be alarmed, as our present voyage is merely for pleasure in the Islands.—Ever and entirely

A. A. in e. + + +
N B

P.S.—We have received great kindness and hospitality from the English here both military and Civil.—

[TO COUNTESS TERESA GUICCIOLI] *Cefalonia—Ag[ost]o 20 o 1823*

[Added to Pietro Gamba's letter to Teresa]

My dearest Teresa—Pietro will have satisfied you with the account of our health and safety.—We have been travelling in this Island and in Ithaca and have visited the places to which the remembrances of Ulysses and his family are attached.—Of political news we can say but little as little is actually known—and even that is partly contradictory——Let me hope that you keep up your spirits and that you will continue to do so.—I write in English as you desired, and I suppose that you are as well acquainted with that language as at Genoa.——We have already written three or four times and will continue to do so by every good opportunity.—I am just going to take a ride on shore with Colonel D[uffie][1] and take advantage of the fresco for that purpose.—Ever dearest T.

A. A. in e. + + + +
N B

[TO COUNTESS TERESA GUICCIOLI]

Argostoli Cefalonia 23 Agosto 1823

[Added to Pietro Gamba's letter to Teresa]

My dearest T.—I have opened Pietro's letter just to add a few

[1] The trip to Ithaca took about six days. The party consisting of Byron, Trelawny, Count Gamba, Dr. Bruno, and Browne, stayed with Capt. Wright Knox, the English Resident in Vathy, the capital of the island.

[1] Lieutenant-Colonel John Duffie was second in command under General Edmund Stevens of the 8th Regiment (King's) of Foot, then stationed in Cephalonia. Byron and Col. Duffie frequently rode together.

words—not having [at] present time for more as the Post goes this evening.—We are all well—and I am ever as usual

yrs. a. a. in e.
N B

P.S.—I feel sure that you will rather be glad to hear from us briefly but frequently—than at length but rarely.—

[TO CAPTAIN WRIGHT KNOX] *Cephalonia, August 26, 1823*

My dear Sir,—I have to acknowledge your very kind and flattering letter, and am truly glad that you and Mrs. K[nox] have not been so tired of my company as I feared. The few days which I passed with you in your beautiful island, are amongst the whitest in my existence; and as such I shall recollect them,—not without the hope of our meeting again, some time, and somewhere.

I have given directions to Messrs. Kornologni (or Corialegno) [Corgialegno] to furnish the Moreote refugees[1] with every necessary for their decent subsistence at my expense—as before proposed by myself; and I have also (as he may, or should have apprized you) directed two hundred and fifty dollars to be placed at your disposal, for the other families now in Ithaca, to be distributed to the most deserving, or the most necessitous, in such proportions as your better experience and knowledge of their circumstances may suggest. The various demands upon me have made me limit the sum lower than I could wish, but it may be a little help to some in the meantime, and we may perhaps do more by-and-bye.

I hope that Mrs. K[nox] has not suffered from her travels, . . . she is the best and most intrepid craigs-woman (as the Scotch call it) I have met with. Count P. Gamba, and the rest of the party, beg their best thanks and respects both to her and to you; and uniting [with them] in every good wish, I ever am,

Your obliged and faithful servant,
NOEL BYRON

P.S.—I do not include the Moreote family's debt in the subscription. I intend to pay that on a separate account; but I forget the amount.

[1] Byron had seen on Ithaca, when staying with Capt. Wright Knox, the British Resident or Governor, a number of Greek refugees from the islands and the mainland, who had escaped from the Turks after the revolution broke out and who were near destitute, and he tried to alleviate their condition. One family from the Morea, named Chalandritsanos, he brought to Cephalonia and furnished with a house and maintenance. The son, Lukas, then fifteen, later joined Byron as his "page" and was with him until his death in Missolonghi. See Biographical Sketch in Appendix IV.

[TO WILLIAM FLETCHER] *Metaxata*[1]—*Septr. 4th. 1823*

Fletcher—You have forgotten or mis[placed?] the *letters* received to-day which [I] told you to put up with the others [in] the basket in my Cabin—you [must] seek for and send them immediately by the bearer.—

NOEL BYRON

P.S.—There is a man sent on purpose—so be quick.———

[TO LT.-COLONEL CHARLES JAMES NAPIER][1]

Metaxata. Septr. 9th. 1823

My dear Colonel,—I return you your somewhat desponding correspondent's epistle with many thanks for that as for other and many kindnesses.———I have had two from Blaquiere (dated Ancona and addrest to me at Genoa) in the old style—but more sanguine than Signor Pavone's—All this comes of what Mr. Braham pronounced "*Entusymusy*"—expecting too much and starting at speed,—it is lucky for me so far—that fail or not fail I can hardly be disappointed—for I believed myself on a fool's errand from the outset—and must therefore like Dogberry "spare no wisdom".[2]—I will at least linger on here or there till I see whether I *can* be of *any* service in *any* way,—and if I doubt it—it is because I do not feel confidence in my individual capacity for this kind of bear-taming, and not from a disbelief in the powers of a more active or less indifferent character to be of use to them—though I

[1] On arriving in Argostoli Byron and his party had continued to live on board the *Hercules*, but early in September he moved to a small house in the village of Metaxata about seven miles from the capital. He remained there until he left for Missolonghi at the end of December. Gamba (p. 37) gives the date of moving as Sept. 6, but the date of this note indicates that he was already at Metaxata on Sept. 4.

[1] Napier had distinguished himself in the Napoleonic wars. He was appointed Governor and Military Resident of the Island of Cephalonia in 1822 under Sir Thomas Maitland, the Lord High Commissioner of the seven Ionian Islands whose headquarters were in Corfu. Napier was an able soldier and colonial administrator, who, like Byron had a "tempered enthusiasm" for the Greeks, knowing their weaknesses and foibles. Byron recommended him to the London Greek Committee as one most capable of forming a "foreign corps" to help the Greeks, but nothing came of the proposal. Napier later had a distinguished career as soldier and administrator in India, his most spectacular feat being the conquest of Sind with a small force which he announced to London with the one word "Peccavi" (I have Sind).

[2] "We will spare for no wit, I warrant you."—*Much Ado about Nothing*, Act III, scene 5.

feel persuaded that that person must be a military man.——But I like the Cause at least and will stick by it while it is not degraded nor dishonoured. You have been so kind to me (as indeed all our compatriots have been) that any additional trouble—I should give would be in the Gospel phrase—another "coal of fire" upon my head.——The first time I descend into the valley I will call—& I hope whenever you come up this way—you will look in and see how comfortable we are under your auspices.—

ever yrs.
NOEL BYRON

[TO COUNTESS TERESA GUICCIOLI] *Septr. 11th. 1823*

My dearest T.—We have received yr. letters safely—and I am rejoiced to hear so good an account of yr. health.—We are still in Cephalonia waiting for news of a more accurate description for all is contradiction and division in the reports of the state of the Greeks &c. —I shall fulfil the object of my mission from the committee—and then probably return into Italy—for it does not seem likely that as [an] individual I can be of use to them.——At least no one other foreigner has yet appeared to be so—nor does it seem likely that any will be at present.——Pietro will have said more perhaps on this subject.—— Pray, be as cheerful and tranquil as you can—and be assured that there is nothing here that can excite anything but a wish to be with you again—though we are very kindly treated by the English here of all descriptions. Of the Greeks I can't say much good hitherto and I do not like to speak ill of them though they do so of one another.—We are here in a very pretty village—with fine scenery of every description—and we have kept our health—&c.—very well.—Pray—remember me to Costa and his wife—and to Papa and all our acquaintances and allies. ——When we meet again (if it pleases God) I hope to tell you several things that will make you smile.—I kiss your Eyes (*occhi*) and am ever most affectly.

a. a. in e. + + + +
N B

[TO JOHN CAM HOBHOUSE] *Metaxata. Septr. 11th. 1823*

My dear Hobhouse—This letter will be delivered by Capt. Scott of the Hercules—who brought me up into these parts—and has behaved very well—he is a fine tough old tar—and has been a great amusement during our voyage—he is moreover brother to two of yr. constituents and as such to be treated with all due respect—also some Grog with which he regularly rounds off most hours of the four and twenty.——He is a character I assure you as you will perceive at a single glance.

I have received yours and the Committee's letters—to both of which this will serve for present answer.—I will endeavour to do my duty by the Committee and the Cause.—On our arrival here early in August we found the opposite Coast blockaded by the Turkish fleet—all kinds of reports in circulation about divisions amongst the Greeks themselves—the Greek fleet not out (and it is not out yet as far as I know) Blaquiere gone home again or at least on his way there—and no communications for me from the Morea or elsewhere.—Under these circumstances added to the disinclination of Capt. Scott (naturally enough) to risk his vessel among the blockaders or their vicinity without being insured for the full value of his bastimento—I resolved to remain here for a favourable opportunity of passing over—and also to collect if possible something like positive information.——In the mean time I made a tour over the hills here in our old style—and then crossed over to Ithaca—which as a pendant to the Troad—a former Greek traveller would like to see.—I was much gratified by both—and we have moreover been treated in the kindest manner by all the authorities military and civil—from Colonel Napier the resident (whose name and fame you are aware of) the officers of the 8th. and in short by all our own countrymen.——Their hospitality both here and in Ithaca was indeed rather oppressive—for dinners kill a weakly stomached Gentleman.—They also insisted on lodging us—but I would not so far abuse their good nature and am here in a very pretty village between the Mountains and the sea—waiting what Napoleon calls the "March of Events".—These Events however keep their march somewhat secret,—but it appears nearly certain that there be divisions—and that Mavrocordato[1] is *out* (some say *in* again) which were a pity—since he is the only civilized person (on dit) amongst the

[1] Prince Alexander Mavrocordatos (see Biographical Sketch in Appendix IV), an educated Phanariot who had served in administrative posts under the Turks, had been elected President of Greece under the Constitution of Epidaurus in January, 1822, after the early Greek successes in the Revolution. But in February, 1823, when the National Assembly met, there were divisions and jealousies. Two parties were formed, the military led by Kolokotrones in Tripolitza, and the civil headed by Petrobey and Mavrocordatos. When the Prince was summoned to preside over the Legislative Council in Tripolitza in July, he was so alarmed by the threats of Kolokotrones that he fled to Hydra.

liberators.—The Turkish fleet has sailed leaving fifteen Algerine vessels to cruise in the Gulph.—

Mr. Browne and Mr. Trelawny are since then gone over in a boat to a part of the Coast out of the blockade with letters from me to the Greek Government at Tripolitza[2]—and to collect information.—There is little risk for small boats but it is otherwise with larger vessels which cannot slide in everywhere—as the Mussulmans are not very particular. —Count Gamba—a young man about twenty-three—is here with me—and is very popular amongst the English—and is I assure you a fine fellow in all respects.——I have written to apprize the G[reek] Government of the possible approach of the vessel indicated by the Committee—and to prepare them to receive it's Continents.—I caused [had someone] write soon after my arrival to Marco Botzari[3]—in Acarnania and at a considerable expence sent the letter by a small boat which ran through the blockade.—He answered desiring me to come over—and stating that he meant to give battle to the Turks next day—(after the date of his epistle) which he did and was killed—but his party gained the victory—and he behaved most gallantly by all accounts till mortally wounded.——This was very vexatious on all accounts as well for the general loss as the individual—for I was particularly recommended to him (the Chief of the Suliotes) and I cannot have the same confidence in his successor who is less known.——I took forty Suliotes here into pay—got their arms (through Col. Napier's intercession with General Adam) and sent them to join their Countrymen a few days ago—when the blockade was partly done away with——they have cost me a tolerable number in dollars—and the price of their passage (somewhat high) &c. but it was thought best that I should wait for direction from Tripolitza—before I fixed on the place where I ought to proceed with the approbation of the G[reek] Gov[ernmen]t.——I have also spent some hundred dollars in assisting the Greek refugees in Ithaca—and providing for a Moreote family who were in great distress.——

The Turks are in force in Acarnania—but you cannot depend upon *any accounts*—the report of the day is contradicted on the morrow.—Great divisions and difficulties exist—and several foreigners have

[2] Trelawny and Hamilton Browne left for the seat of the provisional government of Greece on September 6. They carried some queries to the Greek leaders from Byron, who hoped to get some more definite information about the situation on the mainland through them. Trelawny was soon won over to the side of Odysseus and retired with him to Athens. Browne returned in November to Cephalonia and then to England.

[3] Botsaris had been recommended to Byron by the Metropolitan Ignatius of Arta at Leghorn, and also by Mavrocordatos as "one of the bravest and most honest of the Greek captains".

come away in disgust as usual——it is at present my intention to remain *here* or *there* as long as I see a prospect of advantage to the cause—but I must not conceal from you and the Committee that the Greeks appear in more danger from their own divisions than from the attacks of the Enemy.—There is a talk of treachery—and all sorts of parties amongst them—a jealousy of strangers and a desire of nothing but *money*—all improvements in tactics—they decline—and are not very kind it is said—to the foreign officers &c. in their service.——I give you this as report—but certainly I cannot say much for those I have seen here——the Slave is not yet improved by his Saturnalia. ——As you are aware what they were before—I need say very little on the subject.—

Of the things sent by Murray (you say) none arrived at Genoa—but the Canteen—and that broken by negligence in packing—*it* is to be sent on—but the other things as I said have not yet been heard of—so my bankers write from Italy.—You will remember me to Douglas K[innair]d from whom I have not yet heard—and to all friends.—I hear that the publisher got an injunction in favour of the new Cantos—I wish him to publish the remainder (four in each volume their [sic] are eight more—i.e. sixteen in all) and tell him to Correct the proofs from the M.S.S. and not be sending his lumbering packets up here—where I have other matters to attend to.——I have had a letter from Hanson requesting the balance of his bill (*£635*) which I will not pay—for the present 1stly.—because I wish to know what it is for—2dly. he has had too many thousands of my money already—and ought to be ashamed to dun—having had *£500* this very blessed year,—and 3dly. because I wish to have all my ready at present in bank to answer my credits;—please to instruct the Hon[oura]ble Douglas K[innair]d to this effect. ——It is also time that Murray should make some settlement or other for "Werner".—I understand that he behaves infamously—circulating facsimiles of my letters &c.—with other matters which will go nigh to give him a place by Curll and Osborne[4] if he don't mind what he is about.——As to his losing by Werner—that may be partly ascertained by comparing his account of ye. number sold—and J. Hunt's of *his publications* at the *comparative* prices—M. said at *first* that he had sold 6000—if so—where were the loss?[5]—It is lucky for John of Albemarle that I have other things on hand—or I would have a buff at him for his delinquencies.—Parchment [Hanson] talks of lending money on Mortgage to Ld. Mountnorris—tell Douglas to allow no

[4] Booksellers whose practices caused Pope to satirize them in the *Dunciad*.
[5] For Murray's details of sales see Vol. 10, pp. 70–71 n 1.

such thing—with my monies—Ld. M. is a shuffler—and well known for such—in Cash affairs—at least his own friends say so.—Hanson talks too of urging the appeal against Deardon—but I had hoped that Crabtree had come to some arrangement with said Deardon about Rochdale by this time—I would part with it for a trifle to be rid of the bore and the expence.———Pray write and say how you are—I am better for my voyage and stood the hot Sun on the hills of this island and of Ithaca like a Dial.—

ever yrs. most truly
N B

Septr. 14th. 1823

P.S.—I have sent over to Missolonghi some medical stores for the wounded there.—Metaxa (the Commandant of the town)[6] is very pressing that I should go over there—but I must first have an answer from the Tripolitza Gov[ernmen]t—and also keep a look out for the arrival of the Committee's vessel.—When these things are settled I may as well be in one place as another I suppose—though I have as little cunning in fortifying a besieged town as "honour hath skill in Surgery".[7]———Col Napier told me yesterday that there is a story in the Islands—Corfu &c.—"that he and I had a quarrel about *arms* on board my vessel—that it was seized—after some resistance or opposition &c. &c. &c." in short a damned lie—which I merely mention that you may contradict and laugh at it—if you hear anything of the kind.—Napier says if his Commission could be saved to him that he would go over too[;] you know he is a famous soldier—one of Sir John Moore's "Well done my Majors!"—left for dead at Corunna[8] and all alive and martial at this moment.—He is besides an excellent fellow—greatly liked—and a thorough Liberal.—He wishes me to state to the Committee *quietly* recollect—his wish to have some communication with them. He would be just the man for a *Chef*—if it could be managed.———

[TO D. GRANT & CO.][1] *Cephalonia, Sept. 12th, 1823*

I have only a moment to acknowledge your obliging letter. I will

[6] Constantine Metaxa was military governor of Missolonghi.
[7] *Henry IV*, Part I, Act I, scene 1.
[8] Napier had been severely wounded and taken prisoner at the battle of Corunna in 1809, but was later released.
[1] David Grant, a merchant at Malta, had agreed to cash Byron's bills of exchange when he encountered difficulty with the exchange in Cephalonia.

write more fully by another opportunity. In the mean time I beg you to accept my acknowledgments for your early communication. I shall also send a copy of Messrs. Webb's circular letter in my possession by which you will perceive that besides my credit on their house in Genoa they will negociate my bills on Messrs. Ransom & Co., Pall Mall, London, in case you should not prefer the bills direct on that house in the Metropolis. My present credits altogether on Genoa and England amount to about seven thousand pounds sterling, including a thousand in circular notes of Ransom & Co. I brought up ten thousand dollars besides, and luckily too, for I have found the difficulties you mention in yr. letter in negociating with the Greeks except at an unfair discount which of course I declined accepting. I will let you know as soon as I have settled the sum I mean to draw for in dollars, and in the meantime have the honour to be,

Yr. obliged and obedt. Servt.
NOEL BYRON

P.S.—You will be pleased whenever I draw to pay on my account and deduct the insurance on the dollars whatever the sum may be that I wish remitted.

[TO JOHN CAM HOBHOUSE] *Septr. 15th. 1823*

Dear H[obhous]e—I add to my former letter the enclosed—which will "prate" to you of our "whereabouts" and *what*abouts—one [curious one?] being the last which Marco Bozzari ever dictated or signed—as he fell on the following day.—The Second is from Metaxa—and the third a mere note announcing the landing of my letter-bearer (Mr. H. Browne) at Pirgo.——

yrs. ever
N B

P.S.—Until I have an answer from Tripolitza—or some further intelligence of the Committee's storeship—I shall hardly go to Messolonghi—address to *Genoa* (to Messrs. Webb) who will forward my letters to Cephalonia or Zante. The Government at Tripolitza are so divided at present and so jealous of foreigners that if I were to land without their directions at any particular place—as "one in authority" —it would form a cause or pretext for taking umbrage, since Mavrocordato is out of office.—

[TO CAPTAIN CLIFFORD, R.N.] *Septr. 18th. 1823*

I should have accepted Captain Clifford's invitation with great pleasure but Col. Napier as well as the Officers of the 8th. have already fed me into such a plethora with good cheer—that I am undergoing a species of Lent necessary to prepare me for shorter commons in The Morea—whenever I may be called there.—I hope however that Captain Clifford will believe me not the less his

obliged and obedt. Servt.
NOEL BYRON

[TO JOHN CAM HOBHOUSE]

Metaxata—Isle of Cephalonia Septr. 27th. 1823

My dear Hobhouse/—By the Hercules I wrote at some length—as you probably will know before the arrival of this which will be delivered by Mr. Peacock[1] a Gentleman who has been in the Morea on business respecting a proposed loan to the soi disant Government.—I beg you to introduce him to Mr. Bowring—his information may be very useful—as also his influence with the Society which he represented here—he is withal Gentlemanly and intelligent.——Perhaps his friends might combine with the Committee on the score of the loan to the Greeks.—

By the inclosed—(or rather *annexed*) mass of papers—you will see the present state of things.——There is private matter mixed up with the correspondence—but you and Mr. Bowring can extract the useful and public part for the information of those interested on the subject.——The fact is that matters are in great disorder.—No less than three parties—and one conspiracy going on at this moment amongst them—a few steps further and a civil war may ensue.——On all sides they are (as you perceive) trying to enlist me as a partizan—but I have hitherto declared that I can recognize only the Greek Government—without reference to the *persons* who may compose it—and that as a foreigner I have nothing to do with factions or private preferences of individuals.—I have not yet gone to the Main—because to say the truth—it does not appear that I could avoid being considered as a favourer of one party or another—but the moment I can be of any real service I am

[1] Robert Peacock apparently represented a syndicate in which a Montenegrin calling himself Count General de Wintz was the chief promoter. The Count was suspected of representing the Knights of Malta. See William St. Clair, *That Greece Might Still Be Free*, pp. 130, 207.

willing to go amongst them.——Mavrocordato is out—and his friends are mustering people for him wherever they can—he has now agents in the Islands &c.—but the enclosed papers will show you the state of affairs,—without further comment of mine.—When the Committee's stores come out—I will direct them to where they may be *really* wanted—which is no easy point to ascertain—for all the Agents of the G[ree]k Gov[ernmen]t are said to *peculate* to the extent of their opportunities——in short—you will learn from all quarters—but an unfavourable account of their proceedings.—For all this I do not despair—and shall continue up here watching opportunities to serve the cause—but little will be done till there is a regular force of some kind.—

ever yrs.
N B

P.S.—Tell Douglas K[innaird]—that except the payments to keep up the *insurances*—he must not let any monies of mine be converted to Hanson's or others purposes——(the fellow has had thousands already) but to keep everything in bank for the Credits of mine of the present and ensuing year.——Of all things to do anything amongst these fellows *money* is the most essential—and I have no wish to spare mine—though I will not allow a sixpence to be expended except to a public purpose—and under my own eye.

List of things said to be sent but not yet arrived—and which I am anxious to have.—

Epsom Salts—
Magnesia—Calcined.
Waite's toothpowder.
Smith's tooth brushes—
Acton's Corn rubbers—
Soda powders.—

JOURNAL IN CEPHALONIA

June 19th. 1823

The Dead have been awakened—shall I sleep?
  The World's at war with tyrants—shall I crouch?
The harvest's ripe—and shall I pause to reap?
  I slumber not—the thorn is in my Couch—
Each day a trumpet soundeth in mine ear—
  It's Echo in my heart——[1]

Metaxata—Cephalonia—Septr. 28th. 1823

On the sixteenth (I think) of July I sailed from Genoa on the English Brig Hercules—Jno. Scott Master—on the 17th.[2] a Gale of wind occasioning confusion and threatening damage to the horses in the hold—we bore up again for the same port—where we remained four and twenty hours longer and then put to sea—touched at Leghorn—and pursued our voyage by the straits of Messina for Greece—passing within sight of Elba—Corsica—the Lipari islands including Stromboli Sicily Italy &c.—about the 4th of August[3] we anchored off Argostoli, the chief harbour of the Island of Cephalonia.——

Here I had some expectation of hearing from Capt. B[laquiere] who was on a mission from the G[ree]k Committee in London to the Gr[eek] Provisional Gov[ernmen]t of the Morea—but rather to my surprise learned that he was on his way home—though his latest letters to me from the peninsula—after expressing an anxious wish that I should come up without delay—stated further that he intended to remain in the Country for the present.——I have since received various letters from him addrest to Genoa—and forwarded to the Islands—partly explaining the cause of his unexpected return—and also (contrary to his former opinion) requesting me not to proceed to

[1] These lines, with the above date, are written at the head of the first page of the manuscript of the Journal. Byron told Dr. Henry Muir, the health officer at Argostoli, that he began to keep a journal when he first arrived in Cephalonia, but that he left off because he could not help abusing the Greeks in it.

[2] With so many false starts, Byron did not remember the date. They left Genoa finally on the 16th of July.

[3] On August 3 Byron wrote to Blaquiere from Argostoli.

Greece *yet*—for sundry reasons, some of importance.—I sent a boat to Corfu in the hope of finding him still there—but he had already sailed for Ancona.—

In the island of Cephalonia Colonel Napier commanded in chief as Resident—and Col. Duffie the 8th. a King's regiment then forming the Garrison. We were received by both those Gentlemen—and indeed by all the Officers as well as the Civilians with the greatest kindness and hospitality—which if we did not deserve—I still hope that we have done nothing to forfeit—and it has continued unabated—even since the Gloss of new acquaintance has been worn away by frequent intercourse.——We have learned what has since been fully confirmed—that the Greeks are in a state of political dissention amongst themselves—that Mavrocordato was dismissed or had resigned (L'Un vaut bien l'autre) and that Colocotroni with I know not what or whose party was paramount in the Morea.—The Turks were in force in Acarnania &c. and the Turkish fleet blockaded the coast from Missolonghi to Chiarenza—and subsequently to Navarino——the Greek Fleet from the want of means or other causes remained in port in Hydra—Ipsara and Spezas[?]—and for aught that is yet certainly known may be there still. As rather contrary to my expectations I had no advices from Peloponnesus—and had also letters to receive from England from the Committee I determined to remain for the interim in the Ionian Islands—especially as it was difficult to land on the opposite coast without risking the confiscation of the Vessel and her Contents—which Capt. Scott naturally enough declined to do—unless I would insure to him the full amount of his possible damage.——

To pass the time we made a little excursion over the mountains to Saint Eufemia—by worse roads than I ever met in the course of some years of travel in rough places of many countries.—At Saint Euphemia we embarked for Ithaca—and made the tour of that beautiful Island—as a proper pendant to the Troad which I had visited several years before.—The hospitality of Capt. Knox (the resident) and his lady was in no respect inferior to that of our military friends of Cephalonia.—That Gentleman with Mrs. K. and some of their friends conducted us to the fountain of Arethusa—which alone would be worth the voyage—but the rest of the Island is not inferior in attraction to the admirers of Nature;—the arts and tradition I leave to the Antiquaries,—and so well have those Gentlemen contrived to settle such questions—that as the existence of Troy is disputed—so that of Ithaca (as *Homer's Ithaca* i.e.) is not yet admitted.—Though the month was August and we had been cautioned against travelling in the Sun—yet as I had during my former experience never suffered from the heat as long as I continued in *motion*—I was unwilling to lose so many hours of the day on account of a sunbeam more or less—and though our party was rather numerous no one suffered either illness or inconvenience as far as could be observed, though one of the Servants (a Negro)[4]—declared that it was as hot as in the West Indies.—I had left our thermometer on board—so could not ascertain the precise degree.—We returned to Saint Eufemia and passed over to the monastery of Samos on the opposite part of the bay and proceeded next day to Argostoli by a better road than the path to Saint Eufemia.—The land Journey was made on Mules.——

Some days after our return, I heard that there were letters for me at Zante—but a considerable delay took place before the Greek to whom they were consigned had them properly forwarded—and I was at length indebted to Col. Napier for obtaining them for me;—*what* occasioned the demur or delay—was never explained.—I learned by my advices from England—the request of the Committee that I would act as their representative near the G[ree]k Gov[ernmen]t and take charge of the proper disposition and delivery of certain Stores &c. &c. expected by a vessel which has not yet arrived up to the present date (Septr. 28th)[5]—Soon after my arrival I took into my own pay a body of forty Suliotes under the Chiefs Photomara—Giavella—and Drako—and would probably have increased the number—but I found them not quite united among themselves in any thing except raising their demands on me—although I had given a dollar per man more each month—than they could receive from the G[ree]k Gov[ernmen]t and they were destitute[,] at the time I took them[,] of every thing.——I had acceded too to their own demand—and paid them a month in advance.——But set on probably by some of the trafficking shopkeepers with whom they were in the habit of dealing on credit—they made various attempts at what I thought extortion—so that I called them together stating my view of the case—and declining to take them on with me—but I offered them another month's pay—and the price of their passage to Acarnania—where they could now easily go as the Turkish fleet was gone—and the blockade removed.—This part of them accepted—

[4] Benjamin Lewis, an American Negro, was employed briefly by Trelawny, but Byron took him into his service. He had a smattering of French and Italian and understood cooking and horses. See Doris Langley Moore, *Lord Byron: Accounts Rendered*, p. 374.

[5] The *Ann*, with the London Greek Committee's stores and the fire-master Parry and a number of mechanics, left England on November 10, 1823, and did not arrive at Missolonghi until Feb. 5, 1824.

and they went accordingly.—Some difficulty arose about restoring their arms by the Septinsular Gov[ernmen]t but these were at length obtained—and they are now with their compatriots in Etolia or Acarnania.——

I also transferred to the resident in Ithaca—the sum of two hundred and fifty dollars for the refugees there—and I had conveyed to Cephalonia—a Morlote family who were in the greatest helplessness—and provided them with a house and decent maintenance under the protection of Messrs. Corgialegno—wealthy merchants of Argostoli—to whom I had been recommended by my Correspondents.——I had caused a letter to be written to Marco Bozzari the acting Commander of a body of troops in Acarnania—for whom I had letters of recommended [sic];—his answer was probably the last he ever signed or dictated—for he was killed in action the very day after it's date—with the character of a good Soldier—and an honourable man—which are not always found together nor indeed separately.——I was also invited by Count Metaxa the Governor of Missolonghi to go over there—but it was necessary in the present state of parties that I should have some communication with the existing Gov[ernmen]t on the subject of their opinion *where* I might be—if not *most* useful—at any rate *least* obnoxious.——

As I did not come here to join a faction but a nation—and to deal with honest men and not with speculators or peculators—(charges bandied about daily by the Greeks of each other) it will require much circumspection ⟨for me⟩ to avoid the character of a partizan—and I perceive it to be the more difficult—as I have already received invitations from more than one of the contending parties—always under the pretext that *they* are the "real Simon Pure"[6].——After all—one should not despair—though all the foreigners that I have hitherto met with from amongst the Greeks—are going or gone back disgusted.—

Whoever goes into Greece at present should do it as Mrs. Fry went into Newgate—not in the expectation of meeting with any especial indication of existing probity—but in the hope that time and better treatment will reclaim the present burglarious and larcenous tendencies which have followed this General Gaol delivery.—When the limbs of the Greeks are a little less stiff from the shackles of four centuries—they will not march so much "as if they had gyves on their legs".[7]——At present the Chains are broken indeed—but the links are still clank-

[6] Mrs Centlivre, *A Bold Stroke for a Wife*. In the play, Col. Feignwell pretends to be Simon Pure.

[7] *Henry IV*, Part I, Act IV, scene 2.

ing—and the Saturnalia is still too recent to have converted the Slave into a sober Citizen.—The worst of them is—that (to use a coarse but the only expression that will not fall short of the truth) they are such d----d liars;—there never was such an incapacity for veracity shown since Eve lived in Paradise.—One of them found fault the other day with the English language—because it had so few shades of a Negative—whereas a Greek can so modify a No—to a yes—and vice versa—by the slippery qualities of his language—that prevarication may be carried to any extent and still leave a loop-hole through which perjury may slip without being perceived.——This was the Gentleman's own talk—and is only to be doubted because in the words of the Syllogism—"Now Epimenides was a Cretan".[8] But they may be mended by and bye.—

Sept. 30th.

After remaining here some time in expectation of hearing from the G[ree]k G[overnmen]t I availed myself of the opportunity of Messrs B[rowne] and T[relawny] proceeding to Tripolitza—subsequently to the departure of the Turkish fleet to write to the acting part of the Legislature. My object was not only to obtain some accurate information so as to enable me to proceed to the Spot where I might be if not most safe at least more serviceable but to have an opportunity of forming a judgement on the real state of their affairs. In the mean time I hear from Mavrocordato—and the Primate of Hydra—the latter inviting me to that island—and the former hinting that he should like to meet me there or elsewhere.

1823
10bre. 17th.

My Journal was discontinued abruptly and has not been resumed sooner—because on the day of it's former date I received a letter from my Sister Augusta—that intimated the illness of my daughter—and I had not then the heart to continue it.——Subsequently I had heard through the same channel that she was better—and since that she is well—if so—for me all is well. But although I learned this early in 9bre.—I know not why—I have not continued my journal, though many things which would have formed a curious record have since occurred.—I know not why I resume it even now except that standing at the window of my apartment in this beautiful village—the calm though cool serenity of a beautiful and transparent Moonlight—

[8] The line, attributed to Epimenides, is in the New Testament (*Titus*, 1: 12): "The Cretans are always liars, evil beasts, slow bellies."

showing the Islands—the Mountains—the Sea—with a distant outline of the Morea traced between the double Azure of the waves and skies—have quieted me enough to be able to write—from [sic] which (however difficult it may seem for one who has written so much publicly—to refrain) is and always has been to me—a task and a painful one——I could summon testimonies were it necessary—but my handwriting is sufficient—it is that of one who thinks much, rapidly—perhaps deeply—but rarely with pleasure.——

But—"En Avant!"—The Greeks are advancing in their public progress—but quarrelling amongst themselves.——I shall probably bon grè mal grè be obliged to join one of the factions—which I have hitherto strenuously avoided in the hope to unite them in one common interest.—Mavrocordato—has appeared at length with the Idriote Squadron in these seas—which apparition would hardly have taken place had I not engaged to pay two hundred thousand piastres (10 piastres per dollar being the present value—on the Greek Continent) in aid of Messolonghi—and has commenced operations somewhat successfully but not very prudently.—Fourteen (some say Seventeen) Greek Ships attacked a Turkish vessel of *12* guns—and took her——This is not quite an Ocean-Thermopylæ—but n'importe—they (*on dit*) had found on board 50000 dollars—a sum of great service in their present exigencies—if properly applied.—This prize however has been made within the bounds of Neutrality on the Coast of Ithaca—and the Turks were (it is said) pursued on shore—and some slain.—All this may involve a question of right and wrong with the not very Tolerant Thomas Maitland[9]—who is not very capable of distinguishing either. I have advanced the sum above noted to pay the said Squadron—it is not very large—but it is double that with which Napoleon the Emperor of Emperors—began his campaign in Italy, withal—vide—Las Cases—passim vol 1 (tome premier).[10]

The Turks have retired from before Messolonghi—nobody knows why—since they left provisions and ammunition behind them in quantities—and the Garrison made no sallies or none to any purpose—they never invested Messolonghi this year—but bombarded Anatoliko—(a sort of village which I recollect well having passed through the whole of that country with 50 Albanians in 1809 Messolonghi included) near the Achelous—some say that S[irota?] Pacha heard of an insurrection

[9] Sir Thomas Maitland, High Commissioner of the Ionian Islands, maintained a strict neutrality.

[10] According to Las Cases (*Mémorial* . . . , tome I, p. 173) Napoleon could raise no more than two thousand louis for his Italian campaign.

near Scutari—some one thing some another—for my part I have been in correspondence with the Chiefs—and their accounts are not unanimous.—The Suliotes both there—here—and elsewhere—having taken a kind of liking *to*, or at least formed or renewed a sort of acquaintance *with* me—(as I have aided them and their families in all that I could according to circumstances) are apparently anxious that I should put myself forward as their Chief—(If I may so say) I would rather not for the present—because there are too many divisions and Chiefs already—but if it should appear necessary—why—as they are admitted to be the best and bravest of the present combatants—it might—or may—so happen—that I could would—should—or shall take to me the support of such a body of men—with whose aid—I think something might be done both *in* Greece and *out* of it—(for there is a good deal to put to rights in both)[.] I could maintain them out of my own present means (always supposing my present income and means to be permanent) they are not above a thousand—and of those not six hundred *real* Suliotes—but they are allowed to be equal (that seems a bravado though but it is in print recently) *one* to 5 European Moslems—and *ten* Asiatics—be it as it may—they are in high esteem—and my very good friends.——

A soldier may be maintained on the Mainland—for 25 piastres (rather better than two dollars a month) monthly—and find his rations out of the Country—or for *five dollars*—including his paying for his rations—therefore for between two and three thousand dollars a month—(and the dollar here is to be had for 4 and 2 pence instead of 4 and 6 pence—the price in England) I could maintain between five hundred and a thousand of these warriors for as long as necessary—and I have more means than are—(supposing them to last) [sufficient] to do so—for my own personal wants are very simple (except in horses for I am no great pedestrian) and my income considerable for any country but England—(being equal to the President's of the United States—the English Secretaries' of State's or the French Ambassador's at Vienna and the greater courts—150000 Francs—I believe) and I have hope to have sold a Manor besides for nearly 3000000 francs more—thus I could (with what We should extract according to the usages of war—also) keep on foot a respectable clan or Sept or tribe or horde—for some time—and as I have not any motive for so doing but the well-wishing to Greece I should hope with advantage.—

[TO PRINCE ALEXANDER MAVROCORDATOS]

Cefalonia—1 Ottobre 1823

[In Count Pietro Gamba's hand—signed by Byron]

Principe,—Le cortesi vostre lettere mi giunsero gratissime sì perchè da un Personaggio che gode tanta stima per tutta Europa, e sì perchè mi davano grata lusinga, che l'opera mia potrebbe essere di qualche vantaggio alla sfortunata e gloriosa vostra Patria. Ma per i'incarico impostomi dal comitato Inglese, del quale io son membro fui obligato [sic] d'indirizzarmi al Governo Greco, comunque era e dove si trovava. Nulla può dolermi maggiormente che in vedere l'E. V. divisa dalla condotta degli affari publici [sic], e in tal situazione da potere scarsamente impiegare i suoi talenti e la sua attività in pro della sua Patria: ma uno Straniero parmi che debba guardarsi con cautela da ogni atto che potesse suscitar partiti e nutrire la discordia. Tale è il mio fermo avviso—e son certo, che la lealtà della E. V. mi vorrà far ragione.

Nessuna maraviglia per certo, che si destino discordie in un Paese Rivoluzionato e scappato appena ad una sì lunga e sì barbara tirannià; ma non posso dissimularne il mio dispiacere—ed anche la speranza che avevo, confortata dagli onorevoli esempi degli anni scorsi, che in una guerra in cui dai Greci non si combatte per Teorie Politiche, ne per la Indipendenza solo, ma per la esistenza stessa potessero tenersi lontani da quei gravissimi mali, che si sono sempre manifestati in tutte le Rivoluzioni. La decaduta mia speranza si volge in spavento quando penso agl'effetti che può menare questa discordia—ai vantaggi e alle opportunità che può offrire ai Barbari vostri opressori [sic]—al raffredamento che produrra in tutti gl'interessati per la vostra Causa, cioè tutti gli amici dei lumi e della Umanità—e ai pretesti che potrebbe prepare ai nemici naturali di ogni libertà di meschiarsi [sic] negli affari della Grecia con rovina di tutte le belle speranze dei buoni. Nonostante ogni deplorabile circostanza il mio animo per la vostra Causa non si cangerà certo—e quando l'occazione mi si offra di rendermi veramente utile alla vostra Patria no mi terrò per pericoli o per sacrifizi o per altra meno nobile cagione di farlo. Prima che mi giungessero le vostre lettere io aveva spedito due Signori Inglese miei compagni al Governo in Morea, dal quale sto sempre attendendo risposta. Nulla mi sarebbe più caro, che di agire in vostra compagnia in questa causa—ma vi ho spiegate le ragioni che mi ritengono: e poi lo stato delle cose finora mi sembra tale, che non vedo come o che uno Straniero possa fare, che torni ad utilità della Grecia, e ad onore per lui. Perciò è molto probabile che io mi decida a rimaner quì in osservazione finchè mi si offra migliore opportunità.

Ho scritto ai Primati Idrioti ringraziandoli delle cortesi loro offerte: e per non replicar lettere la prego di voler presentare i miei rispetti ai Si[gno]ri Lurioti e Tricoupi, che si compiacquero di scrivermi pel mezzo del Sig[no]r Praidi. Nella confidenza che le circostanze si faranno più favorevoli, e che i generosi sforzi dei vostri compatriotti, ai quali Voi avete preso una sì gloriosa parte—con ogni più profondo sentimento di stima e di Rispetto mi dichiaro

di V[ostra] E[ccellenza il?] Dev[otissi]mo Servo
[Signature cut out]

P.S.—Dalle ultime notizie ricevute dal Comitato ho saputo, che una Brigata di Artigleria da campagna compita—con ufficiali esperti—con razzi alla Congreve, e Persone esperte a trattarli e a fabricarli [sic]—erano spediti alla mia direzione per la Grecia. Se i vostri deputati fossero giunti prima in Inghilterra avrebbero concluso un' imprestito senza grandi difficoltà, che ora possono esser molto aumentate dalla conoscenza delle vostre dissensioni—e probabilmente sariano state accettate anche le cambiali del Governo Greco—perciò è sempre di somma urgenza che si affrettino. Gordon non verrà in persona—ma concorrerà coi suoi mezzi a crescere i fondi del comitato.

Altri mi scrivono pure che molti ufficiali non attendono che un [rap]porto da me per venire a soccorso della Grecia—ma nelle presenti circostanze io stimerei un' inganno colpevole il lusingarsi a venire—dove non solo regna tanta discordia, ma dove pare che si abbia una sì grande gelosia degli Stranieri. Io sarei molto contento, che mi si porgesse l'occasione di fare la di lei pregevolissima conoscenza—e se non gli dispiacesse di scrivermi qualche volta di che e come più gli aggrada io l'avrò sempre per un favore—e mi farò un pregio di rispondergli con quella franca sincerità che mi è conosciuta e che ella tanto merita. Mi creda di nuovo con più profondo rispetto

Suo Dev[otissi]mo Servo
N B

[TRANSLATION] *Cephalonia—1 October 1823*

Prince,—Your kind letters were gratefully received by me since they come from a person who enjoys so much esteem throughout Europe and also because they brought the welcome flattery that my efforts might be of some benefit to your unfortunate and glorious Country. But as to the task imposed upon me by the British Committee, of which I am a member, I was obliged to address myself to the Greek Government, no matter how it may have been composed or where it may have been situated. Nothing can give me more pain than to see your Excellency separated from the management of public affairs, or in such a situation as scarcely to be able to use your talents and your industry for the benefit of your Country: but a foreigner, it seems to me, must refrain with certain caution from every act that might sustain parties and foster discord. Such is my firm opinion—and I am certain that the fairness of your Excellency will admit that I am right.

No one is surprised, certainly, that discords are awakened in a country that has undergone a revolution and only just escaped from so long and so barbarous a tyranny; but I cannot conceal my displeasure—and also the hope that I had, encouraged by the honourable examples of the past years,—that in a war in which the Greeks did not fight for Political theories, nor for Independence only, but for their very existence, they would be able to keep themselves far away from those very serious evils that always manifest themselves in all Revolutions. My fallen hope changes to dread when I think of the consequences that this discord can bring—of the advantages and of the opportunities that it can offer to those Barbarians your oppressors—to the coolness that it will produce in all those interested in your cause, that is, all friends of Enlightenment and Humanity—and to the pretexts that it might lend to the natural enemies of every liberty to meddle in Greek affairs, with the collapse of all the noble hopes of the good people. In spite of every deplorable circumstance, my feeling for your cause will certainly remain unchanged—and when the opportunity presents itself to me to be really useful to your country, I will not hold myself back from doing so because of dangers or sacrifices or for any other less noble reason. Before your letters reached me I had sent two Englishmen, my comrades, to the Government in the Morea, from whom I am still awaiting a reply. Nothing would be dearer to me than to work with you in this cause—but I have explained the reasons to you that hold me back. And then the state of things up to now seems such, that I do not see how or what a foreigner might do that could be of benefit to Greece and to the honour of himself. Therefore, it is very likely that I may decide to remain here watching until a better opportunity is offered to me.

I wrote to the Primates of Hydra thanking them for their kind offers, and in order not to duplicate the letters, I beg you to give my respects to Signor Luriotti and Signor Tricoupi, who were so kind as to write to me by means of Signor Praidi. Confident that circumstances will be more favourable, and that the generous efforts of your compatriots, in which you have taken such a glorious part [will triumph]—with every most profound sentiment of esteem and respect, I declare myself

Your Excellency's most devoted servant

[Signature cut out]

P.S.—From the most recent news received from the Committee, I have learned that an Artillery Brigade with experienced campaigners—with expert officers—with Congreve rockets and persons trained in using them and in constructing them—have been sent to Greece under my direction. If your deputies had arrived in England sooner, they would have arranged a loan without great difficulties, which now may be greatly augmented by the knowledge of your dissensions—and probably the Greek government's bills of exchange might also have been accepted. Therefore, it is always of the utmost urgency to make haste. Gordon[1] will not come in person but will contribute from his means to increase the funds of the Committee.

Others write me also that many officers are waiting only for a report from me to come to the aid of Greece, but in the present circumstances I would consider it a culpable trick to entice them to come—where not only does so much discord reign, but where there seems to be such a great jealousy of foreigners. I would be very happy, if the opportunity presented itself to me, to make your most valued acquaintance. And if it would not displease you, to write to me occasionally of whatever and however you most like, I will always consider it a favour——and I will be pleased to reply to you with the frankest sincerity that is known to me and which you so much deserve. Believe me once again, with most profound respect,

Your most devoted servant

N B[2]

[TO JOHN CAM HOBHOUSE] *Metaxata.—Cephalonia. Octr. 6th. 1823*

My dear Hobhouse—I write a few lines by a private conveyance to inform you that I have sent you two packets—whence you will extract information for the Committee—one by Capt. Scott of the Brig Hercules—and the other by Mr. Peacock agent for a Society on his

[1] Thomas Gordon (1788–1841), a wealthy Scotsman who had been in the British army, came to Greece in 1821 and was an adviser of Ypsilanti in the early days of the revolution, but left in disgust after the Greek massacre of the Turks at Tripolitza. He was reluctant to return though urged by Byron and others, but he did come back in 1826 and commanded the expedition to relieve Athens in 1827. He published his *History of the Greek Revolution* in 1832.

[2] Transcribed and translated by Picki B. Herzfeld.

return from his mission to the G[reek] G[overnmen]t——The documents are in considerable number—and will tell you all that is requisite up to their respective dates.——The Greek disputes amongst themselves are in statu quo——the fleet is at length said to be at sea—but has done nothing—indeed there has been (except in the case of Bozzari [Botzaris] who was killed in Rumelia—) a kind of contest of *inaction* on both sides Greek and Mussulman during the present year. —But the Turks have at length come down in force (sixteen thousand they say) on Messolonghi—which however is stronger than it was last year—when they were repulsed in a similar attempt.—There is a squadron of some sort in sight from our windows in the village here at this present writing—but whether Greek or Turk—is not easily made out—two sail one three masted vessel—and apparently ships of war. We are very anxious for your Committee Argo with it's continents—and Congreve rockets—which I will direct to the place where they seem needful.—I have not had any answer yet from the G[ree]k G[overnmen]t but I have heard of a packet directed to me by their order some time ago—which is said to have been searched or destroyed by some of the factions or their adherents at Zante. When Mrs. Fry has done with Newgate it would not be amiss if the Committee would send her into Greece—she would find plenty of exercise for her *re*-moralizing talents by all accounts.—It is my duty and business to conceal nothing either of my own impressions or of the general belief upon the score of the Greeks from the Committee—but when I add that I do not despair—but think still every exertion should be used in their behalf—in the hope that time and freedom will revive for them what tyranny has kept under but perhaps not extinguished—I conceive that you will not despond nor believe me desponding because I state things as they really are.—They want a regular force to support a regular System quite as much as to repel their enemies—in the interim every man that can pay or command from one hundred to a thousand Gillies is independent—and seems to act for himself.—When I state to you that I have had half a dozen offers of different kinds and from different parties to put myself at the head of some hundred boys of the belt and of the blade——all of whom might be maintained for any purpose—with less means than those which I can at present command —you may judge for yourself—how far there is any actual order or regularity.—I have hitherto steered clear of such matters—and avoided committing myself with any of the parties—being a peaceable man—but really if they go on in this way—and I get up in a bad humour some morning there is no saying what one may be provoked into.——

I have got over most of the Suliotes (their best παλι καρια [soldiers]) who were here, to recruit the ranks in Acarnania—one of their bravest Chiefs (Drako) went a few days ago—and is to let me know (he as well as Kosta Bozzari (Marco's surviving brother) the exact state of *their* affairs.—They have lately lost another Chief in action—Giavella—whose widow is here—she sent her little boy a child of four years old to pay me a visit the other day—who is a sturdy little Lion's whelp with an immense head—and neither cries nor laughs like other children—but sits still and blows out his lips and snorts as the Highlanders do when they are angry.—He already talks of revenging his father's death on the followers of Mahomet—according to the good old custom which of course his mother carefully patronizes.—His organ of Combativeness seems considerably developed—and he will doubtless if he lives be a Credit to the Courage line of business.—Of my present position here I have little further to say—I hear that the Canteen has got as far as Zante—but I neither know the name—nor the probable time of Arrival of that same Caraval [sic] or Argosie which is to waft Mr. Parry and his fire-enginry to the seat of warfare.—Blaquiere has probably got back amongst you; he had evaporated before I arrived here.—My own motions will partly depend upon the arrival of your Brigade—or it may be on the answer I may have from the actual G[ree]k G[overnmen]t now in Congress at Salamis (Colouri hodie) or Egina——I have two correspondents there awaiting a reply.—Another English Gentleman volunteer is gone over to Mesolonghi this day—or going.—It is not yet sure that it *is* besieged—and to say the *truth*—no *truth* or very little is to be extracted from the Greek accounts of any kind till *long* after any given occurrence.—

I have had a letter from Bowring (to whom make me remembered) dated August 18th.—in which he mentions (among other matter) the possible or even probable prospect of a loan for the Hellenes but at the same time imposes on me to impress on them the necessity of the most *santa-sacred* (an Italianism of mine—pardon it) observance of engagements—and of a speciality their regular payment of *interest*.—As Henry Morton says to Cuthbert Headrigg—I doubt "that the *penny fee* will be a hard chapter"[1] for the actual members of the G[overnmen]t do not pass for being great dilettanti in the matter of pecuniary punctuality.—But this by the way.—But I doubt that the news of Mavrocordato's being out—and their other slight discrepancies—will enhance the scruples of our monied people.—Besides the deputies to treat for the said loan—are *not yet* embarked! I have written and

[1] In Scott's *Old Mortality*.

railed to urge their *immediate* departure—but no!—they are not gone—nor for aught I know—going.—Mr. Peacock (an important personage for he was authorized to offer large sums) came away much disgusted with them—as almost all foreigners have hitherto done.—I laboured to put him in better humour with them—and perhaps partly succeeded.—I mean (unless something out of the way occurs to recal[l] me) to stay up in the country itself or the neighbourhood of Greece—till things are either better or hopeless—and in every case will take advantage of circumstances to serve the *Cause* if the patriots will permit me—but it must be *the Cause*—and not individuals or *parties* that I endeavour to benefit.—

yrs. ever

N B

P.S.—Remember me to D[ouglas] K[innaird]—from whom I have not heard—tell him as usual—to muster all my possible monies—as well for the present—as for the ensuing year—that I may take the field in force in case it should be proper or prospective of Good that I should do so.—I send you a minute of my answer to Mavrocordato's epistle.——Tell Douglas K[innair]d that I cannot make out from his statement whether the 950—deducted in the first year (1822) from the Kirkby Mallory rental on account of Ly N[oe]l *is* to return to Lady B[yron] and to me or no—but whether it is or not—there was still better than 5000 £ to divide between Ly B. and myself the rental being 6336 £ of which in all I have as yet received but *nine* hundred in two separate payments.—There is therefore or ought to be in any case still due to me from the *1822* rental fully sixteen hundred pounds being my balance of two thousand five hundred—without adverting to the present year—so that I have the better part of two years to receive.—My *own* income is I take it paid more regularly;—as to anything from publications I do not calculate on much but Murray ought to have settled for Werner before this time. Tell Lord E[rskine] that I have at length received his brochure on the G[ree]ks for which many thanks—I shall try and get it translated into Romaic.—

[TO COUNTESS TERESA GUICCIOLI] *8bre. 7mo. 1823*

[Added to Pietro Gamba's letter to Teresa]

My dearest T.—Pietro has told you all the gossip of the Island—

our earthquakes[1]—our politics—and present abode in a pretty village. —But he has not told you the result of one of his gallantries—which I leave to him to describe.—As his opinions and mine on the Greeks are nearly similar—I need say little on the subject.——I was a fool to come here but being here I must see what is to be done. If we were not at such a distance I could tell you many things that would make you smile—but I hope to do so at no very long period.—Pray keep well—and love me as you are beloved by yrs. ever

a.a. + + + in e.
N B

[TO CHARLES F. BARRY] *Oct. 9, 1823*

[Part of letter quoted in auction catalogue]

I have only time to add a postscript to G[amba]'s letter, I have received several of yours duly. The Greeks are marching and have turned out Mavrocordato, who is at Hydra, on board the fleet. I am waiting for a communication from the Greek Government to know how to proceed myself. We have had shocks of earthquake here, but little damage; everybody tolerably well. Various attempts made to extract my monies, but to these I demur, until sure that they are to be applied to the public weal, which is not at present the first consideration of the patriots, according to all accounts. . . .

[TO COLONEL JOHN DUFFIE] *October 9, 1823*

Dear Colonel,—The pelisse fits as if it had been made for me, excepting that it is a little too short in the sleeves, which is not of any consequence.

I shall therefore, with many acknowledgments, accept and wear it,—somewhat, I fear, in the mode of the ass in the lion's skin in the fable; or, rather in the hope which the Indians entertain when they wear the spoils of a redoubted enemy, viz. that his good qualities may be transferred to the new possessor with his habiliments. But these being the garments of a friend, may, I trust, be still more propitious.[1]

[1] On October 5 a series of earthquakes struck Cephalonia. Byron gave an amusing account of the scramble to get out of the building in his letter of Oct. 12, 1823, to Augusta. In 1953 a severe earthquake destroyed the house in which Byron had lived in Metaxata.

[1] Prothero speculates that this was the uniform Byron wore when he landed in Missolonghi.

I send you some papers, but I doubt that you have later ones; however, they can serve the mess as duplicates: the 29th and 30th are among them; but the 26th and 27th (28th being Sunday) are not yet arrived. Believe me ever and truly,

Yours affectionately
NOEL BYRON

[TO AUGUSTA LEIGH] *Cephalonia, 8bre. 12th. 1823*

My dearest Augusta—Your three letters on the subject of Ada's indisposition have made me very anxious to hear further of her amelioration.—I have been subject to the same complaint but not at so early an age—nor in so great a degree.—Besides it never affected my eyes—but rather my hearing and that only partially and slightly and for a short time.—I had dreadful and almost periodical headaches till I was fourteen—and sometimes since—but abstinence and a habit of bathing my head in cold water every morning cured me—I think—at least I have been less molested since that period.—Perhaps she will get quite well—when she arrives at womanhood—but that is some time to look forward to, though if she is of so sanguine a habit—it is probable that she may attain to that period earlier than is usual in our colder climate;—in Italy and the East—it sometimes occurs at twelve—or even earlier—I knew an instance in a noble Italian house—at ten—but this was considered uncommon.—You will excuse me touching on this topic *medically* and "en passant" because I cannot help thinking that the determination of blood to the head so early unassisted—may have some connection with a similar tendency to earlier maturity.—Perhaps it is a phantasy.—At any rate let me know how she is—I need not say how *very* anxious I am (at this distance particularly) to hear of her welfare.——

You ask me why I came up amongst the Greeks?—it was stated to me that my so doing might tend to their advantage in some measure in their present struggle for independence—both as an individual—and as a member for the Committee now in England.—How far this may be realized I cannot pretend to anticipate—but I am willing to do what I can.—They have at length found leisure to quarrel among themselves—after repelling their other enemies—and it is no very easy part that I may have to play to avoid appearing partial to one or other of their factions.—They have turned out Mavrocordato—who was the only *Washington* or *Kosciusko* kind of man amongst them—and they have not yet sent their deputies to London to treat for a loan—nor in short done themselves so much good as they might have done.—I have written to Mr. Hobhouse three several times with a budget of documents on the subject—from which he can extract all the present information for the Committee.—I have written to their Gov[ernmen]t at Tripolizza and Salamis[1]—and am waiting for instructions *where* to proceed—for things are in such a state amongst them—that it is difficult to conjecture where one could be useful to them—if at all.—However I have some hopes that they will see their own interest sufficiently not to quarrel till they have secured their national independence—and then they can fight it out among them in a domestic manner—and welcome.—You may suppose that I have something to *think* of at least—for you can have no idea what an intriguing cunning unquiet generation they are—and as emissaries of all parties come to me at present—and I must act impartially—it makes me exclaim as Julian did at his military exercises—"Oh Plato what a task for a Philosopher!"[2]——

However *you* won't think much of *my philosophy*—nor do I—"entre nous".——

If you think this epistle or any part of it worth transmitting to Ly B[yron] you can send her a copy—as I suppose—unless she is become I know not what—she cannot be altogether indifferent as to my "whereabouts" and *what*abouts.

I am at present in a very pretty village (Metaxata in Cephalonia) between the mountains and the Sea—with a view of Zante and the Morea—waiting for some more decisive intelligence from the provisional Gov[ernmen]t in Salamis.——But here come some visitors.

I was interrupted yesterday—by Col. Napier and the Captain of a King's ship—now in the harbour—Col. N. is resident or Governor here and has been extremely kind and hospitable—as indeed have been all the English here.—When their visit was over a Greek arrived on business about this eternal siege of Mesalonghi (on the coast of Acarnania or Etolia) and some convoys of provisions which we want to throw in—and after this was discussed, I got on horseback (I brought up my horses with me on board and troublesome neighbours they were in blowing weather) and rode to Argostoli and back—and then I had one of my *thunder* headaches (*you* know how my head acts

[1] The Executive and Senate were temporarily seated in Salamis. In October they moved to Nauplia. Kolokotrones, who headed the other faction and proclaimed himself Commander-in-Chief of the Morea, remained in Tripolitza.

[2] Gibbon, *Decline and Fall of the Roman Empire,* Chap. 19.

like a barometer when there is electricity in the air) and I could not resume till this morning.—Since my arrival in August I made a tour to Ithaca—(which you will take to be Ireland—but if you look into Pope's Odyssey—you will discover to be the antient name of the Isle of Wight) and also over some parts of Cephalonia.——

We are pretty well in health the Gods be thanked! by the way, who is this Dr. Tipperary or Mayo or whatever his name is?[3] I never heard of anything of the name except an Irish County?—Laurence the Surgeon if he be the man who has been persecuted for his metaphysics—is I have heard an excellent professional man—but I wonder Ly. B[yron] should employ (so tell her) a Papist or a Sceptic.—I thought that like "douce David Deans"[4] she would not have allowed "a Goutte of physic to go through any of the family" unless she was sure that the prescriber was a Cameronian.——

There is a clever but eccentric man here a Dr. Kennedy[5]—who is very pious and tries in good earnest to make converts—but his Christianity is a queer one—for he says that the priesthood of the Church of England are no more Christians than "Mahmoud or Termagant"[6] are.—He has made some converts I suspect rather to the beauty of his wife (who is pretty as well as pious) than of his theology. —I like what I have seen of him—of *her* I know nothing—nor desire to know—having other things to think about. *He* says that the dozen shocks of an Earthquake we had the other day—are a sign of his doctrine—or a judgement on his audience—but this opinion has not acquired proselytes.—One of the shocks was so prolonged—that though not very heavy—We thought the house would come down—and as we have a staircase to dismount *out* of the house (the buildings here are different from ours), it was judged expedient by the inmates (all *men* please to recollect—as if there had been females we must have helped them out or broken our bones for company) to make an expeditious retreat into the courtyard.—*Who* was *first* out the door I know not —but when I got to the bottom of the stairs I found several arrived before me—which could only have happened by their jumping out of the windows—or down *over* or from the stairs (which had no balustrade or bannisters) rather than in the regular way of descent.—The Scene was ludicrous enough—but we had several more slight shocks in the night but stuck quietly to our beds—for it would have been of no use

[3] A doctor Lady Byron had consulted on Ada's health.

[4] In Scott's *Heart of Midlothian*.

[5] Dr. James Kennedy, Army medical officer stationed in Argostoli. See Biographical Sketch in Appendix IV.

[6] See Scott's *Quentin Durward*, Chap. 17.

moving—as the house would have been down first—had it been to come down at all.—

There was no great damage done in the Island (except an old house or two cracking in the middle), but the soldiers on parade were lifted up as a boat is by the tide—and you could have seen the whole line waving (though no one was in motion) by the heaving of the ground on which they were drawn up.—You can't complain of this being a brief letter.——

I wish you would obtain from Lady B[yron] some account of Ada's disposition—habits—studies—moral tendencies—and temper—as well as of her personal appearance[,] for except from the miniature drawn four years ago (and she is now double that age nearly) I have no idea of even her aspect.—When I am advised on these points I can form some notion of her character—and what way her dispositions or indispositions ought [to be] treated—and though I will never interfere with or thwart her mother—yet I may perhaps be permitted to suggest—as she (Lady B.) is not obliged to follow my notions unless she likes—which is not very likely.—Is the Girl imaginative?—at *her* present age—I have an idea that I had many feelings and notions—which people would not believe if I stated them *now*—and therefore I may as well keep them to myself.——Is she social or solitary—taciturn or talkative—fond of reading or otherwise?—and what is her *tic*?—I mean her foible—is she passionate?—I hope that the Gods have made her any thing save *poetical*—it is enough to have one such fool in a family.—You can answer all this at yr. leisure—address to *Genoa* as usual—the letters will be forwarded better by my Correspondents there.—

yrs. ever
N B

P.S.—Tell Douglas K[innair]d I have only just got his letter of August *14th.* and not only approve of his accepting a sum not under ten or twelve thousand pounds for the property in question[7]—but also of his getting as much as can be gotten *above* that price.

[TO CAPT. HILL[1]] [*Cephalonia*] *8bre 13 1823*

My dear Capt.—Our new (I took a pencil and broke it—& must

[7] For the sale of Rochdale. Kinnaird wrote on Nov. 2, 1823, that it had been sold to James Dearden for £11,225.

[1] An officer of the 8th (King's) Regiment, stationed in Argostoli.

now take to the pen) our new lady of the laundry sends her daughter *alone* among my serving men one half of whom are p---d and the other likely to be so. If her parents do not want to make her a w---- and a thief they had better employ another messenger—for the poor girl seems half a child and to merit a better fate.—I assure you I have no interest saying this one way or the other—for if *I* wanted to get hold of her I could not devise a better school than among these fellows of mine, than whom a greater set of rascals never existed—you had as well tell her father to come *himself* or to send her *mother* with the things—otherwise we shall have some complaint or other probably, and it were [torn] that any damage should [torn] upon those who are in [torn] used to it—on the [torn] ample rather than on this [?Hebe] of the washing tub—It is because *you* recommended this poor family to our business that I am anxious nothing unpleasant should occur to the Girl—and I hope you will do me the justice to think so—believe me

ever yr. obliged

N B

[TO COUNTESS TERESA GUICCIOLI]

Metaxata de Cef [*aloni*]*a 14 Ottobre—1823*

[Added to letter of Pietro Gamba to Teresa]

My dearest T—We have not heard from you for some time why do not you write? we have sent several letters—ever and entirely yrs.

a.a. in e. +

N B

[TO DOUGLAS KINNAIRD] *Cephalonia 8bre. 14th. 1823*

Dear Douglas—I received yr. letter of the 14th August a day or two ago.—I approve of your accepting on my account a sum for the price of Rochdale—"*not under ten* or *twelve thousand pounds* sterling"—and as much *above* as may be consistent with a fair purchase.—It is probably less than a more skilful or lucky personage than myself might have obtained—but any thing is better than such a litigation—and as you have full powers of Attorney to act for me—you can settle as soon as you please.—You ask what I would have you do with the monies on my behalf—supposing "that we succeed"? They had better be invested for the present—(I presume)—in Exchequer bills—which are easily reconvertible into capital—and bear also a moderate interest.—What

I may decide eventually will depend upon circumstances—I could either purchase an annuity—invest in some of the safer foreign funds—or buy land in Italy—France—America—or perhaps Greece.—Such a sum though of no very lofty sound in English denominations—hath a formidable echo in French livres—and Spanish dollars—and Italian Scudi—and in Italy—would (I know) particularly for *ready money*—purchase land to an extent and of a rental—which you have little idea of in Britain for the same amount.———

The reason of this is obvious—scarcity of cash—debts of families—and the system of dividing properties among several children—instituted by Napoleon and still continuing———and when they *do* sell—(which they try frequently) there is not one instance in fifty of their being paid in ten years—but by installments. You could hardly find in Italy ten people to pay 40000 dollars (eight thousand pounds) in one payment—and when they do they allow much in favour of the purchaser. I trust that our purchaser will pay the whole speedily.—You can stop the lawsuit—and above all—let me have no bother with Messrs. Hanson—who will raise difficulties—and try to continue the suit—but *you* have the permanent power of Attorney—and this letter is also further warrant for you to act as we have both agreed upon.——Were there another Chancellor I might appeal but this man will never do justice to a suitor of opposite politics—and is besides (I believe)—the greatest rogue that was sate on a bench since Scroggs and Jefferies.[1] —I am sure he has been so in all concerns of mine—and I will tell him one day in the house of Lords—"if I come over the Sea."[2]———It *is* my intention to pay Hunt's law expences—and there we are also agreed. ———I say nothing of Greek affairs having sent three packets to Hobhouse on that subject lately.—

ever and truly yrs.
N B

P.S.—Address to ye. care of Messrs. Webb & co. Genoa.—The Canteen has arrived I did not want so much *white* but more *red* toothpaste—some things are broken in the Canteen—but it is complete nevertheless. I hear the V[ice] Chancellor dissolved Hunt's injunction in matter of course. Let him publish however the remaining 8 Cantos in two volumes.—We won't give way for "a' that and a' that and

[1] Sir William Scroggs (1623?–1683) as Lord Chief Justice of England had the reputation of a brutal judge. He was impeached before the House of Commons and removed from office in 1681. He was succeeded by the famous "hanging judge", George Jeffreys (1648–1689), who presided over the "bloody assize" after the suppression of Monmouth's rebellion.

[2] Unidentified.

twice as muckle's a' that."——I suppose you will settle something with M[urray] for "Werner" be it little or great.—Are the Kirkby Mallory people paying their arrears?——I may probably wish for further credits in the beginning of the year (for the ensuing season) as a reserve—but I have hitherto been cautious in expending monies on the Greeks and their cause till I see better if they really deserve them. ——Hanson wrote to propose Ld. Mountnorris as a person to lend money to on mortgage—but he is not a customer that I approve of. I desired Hobhouse to give you my opinion on that subject.

[TO JOHN CAM HOBHOUSE] *Cephalonia. 8bre. 16th. 1823*

My dear H[obhous]e—Enclosed is a further report from the Morea —it is full and supposed to be authentic on the state of parties there. You and Mr. Bowring can form your own judgements and use yr. discretion in laying it before the Committee. The enclosed is a Copy— only altered into *better* Italian—the original not being very pure— but the sense and the tenor of the expressions are still retained as nearly as possible.—We have a difficult part to play—in the mean time —the deputies have *not* sailed—so there will be little likelihood of a loan to the Greeks—when once their discords are bruited abroad.—— We want a military foreign force—and a *military* man to head them— Gordon has not done wisely in not coming—he is reckoned a good soldier and with a thousand men at his back—and a little patience might have done much—but *alone* he would do little—they won't obey a stranger—unless he has a force of his own sufficient to make himself respected—so say all the foreign officers who are returning by dozens. —A *Greek Engineer* (an Elevè [sic] of Lord Guilford's) told me a little time ago that they minded *him even* no more than a post—and that otherwise he could have taken Patras.—The Captain of an English ship of war told me that with a couple of *brigs—he* would undertake to reduce the Castles of the Gulph of Lepanto—i.e. those at the entrance. ——I shall continue here till I see when and where I can be of use—if such a thing indeed be practicable—I have hitherto only contradictory accounts.——If you send out a military man—he will have every cooperation from me—or if you send out any other person—I have no objection to act as either his coadjutor—or subordinately—for I have none of those punctilios.

yrs. ever

N B

P.S.—Tell Douglas K[innair]d that "I *do approve* of his obtaining and accepting on my behalf of any sum *not* under ten thousand pounds for the Rochdale property"—this is in answer to a question of his. I have also written this much to him—of course he may get for us as much more as he fairly can.—

[TO DOUGLAS KINNAIRD] *Cephalonia. 8bre. 17 o 1823*

Dear Douglas—I add a few lines by way of duplicate to my answer of the 14th inst. to yours of the 14th. August—merely to repeat that I *do* approve of your proposal of accepting "any sum *not* under ten thousand pounds for Rochdale" and of course as much above it as can be fairly obtained.—To your other question—I reply that the produce for the present may be invested in Exchequer bills—as more easily re-convertible into capital—and also as bearing a moderate interest.—I suppose that you have done as well as could be done in the circumstances—having full confidence in your sagacity and friendship.—You have my power of Attorney—and this letter also for your warrandice to conclude in my behalf the settlement of this and other affairs.—

yrs. ever
N B

P.S.—Address to Genoa as usual—my letter of the 14th. instant is fuller than this on particulars.

[TO COUNTESS TERESA GUICCIOLI] *[October 21st, 1823]*

My dearest T.—I shall merely add two words to Pietro's letter—to scold you for not having written.—We arc all tolerably well—and tranquil—and except an earthquake or two daily—(one of which broke the Lambico for filtering the water—last night) which rock us to and fro a little—things are much as when we wrote before. I hear you are turned moral philosopher—and are meditating various works for the occupation of your old age—all which is very proper.—

ever yrs. a + a + in e +
N B

[TO COL. JOHN DUFFIE] *October 23, 1823*

Dear Colonel,—I have to pray you to permit the regimental smith to shoe my horses, when he can be spared from duty.

I was very sorry that I missed you the other day, and yet I know not how, for I rode out on the road to Argostoli. The day before yesterday I was in town, and with the intention of intruding on you; but I was detained by business till too late.

The Greek provisional government has sent over one of their agents to conduct me to the residence of the said government.[1] Brown and Trelawny, having been better treated than others, probably give a much more favourable account than we have yet had, from other quarters, of the state of the government and country. For my own part, I shall endeavour to judge for myself, and expect to set out early in November, according to the desire of the President and his brethren.

We have had another earthquake here (somewhat smarter than the former,) in the night. It threw down and broke a "lambico," or filtering-machine for water, (I really have forgotten the proper term in our language but it is for a drip-stone to clear water,) and we are bounden to Providence for not having our bones broken instead of crockery. Believe me

ever and truly, your obliged and sincere friend and servant,

NOEL BYRON

P.S.—Count Pietro Gamba salutes you, and is doing his best to get well again; with what success, the doctors know best.

[TO CHARLES F. BARRY] *8bre. 25th. 1823*

Dear Barry—A barrel containing three thousand dollars to my address has been consigned to S.S. Corgialegno—and as I choose to keep my Genoese Credit intact for the present I shall remit to yr. house by some early opportunity bills on Messrs Ransom for six hundred and twenty or thirty pounds which I conjecture to be about the equivalent more or less—but in case there be any balance for or against me you can rectify it from my own accompt with your house.—I have still between 7 and 8000 dollars of those which I brought up with me—so that the reinforcement though not unacceptable was for the present unnecessary.——

Messrs Corgialegno—at first—either had not or pretended not to

[1] The Greek messenger from the Executive Body (controlled by Kolokotrones) was named Anarghiro. According to Pietro Gamba (*Narrative*, p. 50) Byron prepared to leave. But in the middle of November, Browne and the Greek deputies for the Loan arrived bringing a letter from Mavrocordatos asking for a loan of £4,000 to enable him and the fleet to proceed to Missolonghi, and Byron changed his plans.

have funds to supply above a certain sum per month—and for this they required two and a half per cent—as I believe—because they were not aware of the monies I had in hand—and wished to profit by the letters of *Credit*—not much to their *own.* I told them that I had several thousand dollars in hand—and that even were it otherwise I would see them d——d before I agreed to such terms of exchange for the bills of and on respectable houses in Italy and England.—I further added that I had enough for my own occasions for a year to come and that as my *extra*-expenditure was to have been for the Greeks—he might settle it with his compatriots—for whom if I spent my monies—it must naturally be on equitable terms.—They have since changed *their note*—and offer to change *my notes* and to advance whatever I require on fair terms of exchange—but I made their proposition (the original one) pretty public—and the Greeks (as might be expected when their own interest was concerned—) clamoured pretty loudly against this Hebrew proceeding of the Sieurs Corgialegno—so that they grew ashamed of it themselves—and explained it away—something about the scarcity of dollars &c.—and I have allowed them the benefit of their explanation.——They have however been very *civil*—and have opened a correspondence with Napoli di Romania—so that I may draw there too for what I want.—I am invited over by the Greek Gov[ernmen]t who have received Messrs Browne and Trelawney with great hospitality.——They have sent an Agent to conduct me to that city—for which I expect to set out early in November.—Continue to address to Cephalonia however, till I direct otherwise.——The various letters of Credit from Messrs Webb—the Corgialegnos declare to be superfluous—as they wish to be the intermediate agents in our business.—So that all seems very well so far.——

The states of parties in Greece are still the same—I have transmitted by private hands several packets of documents and Correspondence to Mr. Hobhouse M.P. to be laid by him before Mr. *Bowring* for his inspection and the Committee's.—If you write to that Gentleman say—that I do not address directly to him especially by the *post*—as *his* letters are liable to be looked into by the curious in correspondence on the Continent—ever since his adventure in France[1]—but the letters to Mr. H[obhouse] are in fact meant for his perusal with their enclosed papers.—It is very expedient that the Committee should support me

[1] On Oct. 5, 1822, John Bowring was arrested by order of the French Government at Calais and he was imprisoned for a time in Boulogne. His papers, which were seized, included a letter to a Peruvian agent in London and to the Portuguese Ambassador. This link to revolutionary governments made him anathema to the Bourbon regime in France.

with their authority—and if they were to frame a memorial to the Greek Gov[ernmen]t on the subject of their existing differences and the expulsion or secession of Mavrocordato—it would probably have more effect than any *individual* attempt of mine to reconcile the parties—and until they *are* reconciled—it seems to be allowed very generally—that their internal affairs will be in an unpleasant state of weakness—I would of course present such a memorial and enforce it by all lawful means in my power.——

All the stories of the Greek victories by sea and land are exaggerated or untrue—they *have* had the advantage in some skirmishes—but the Turks have also had the same in others—and are now before Mesalonghi in force—and as for the fleet—it has never been to sea at all until very lately—and as far as can be ascertained has done little or nothing to the purpose.—The deputies for the loan are not yet set out —though I have written (to urge their departure) to the G[ree]k G[overnmen]t.—I neither despond nor despair of the Cause—but it is *my* business to state things as they are to the Committee—were it only to show the expediency of further exertion.—I offered to advance a thousand dollars per month for the succour of Mesalonghi—and the Suliotes under Bozzari (who was since killed) but the Gov[ernmen]t have answered me (through Count Delladecima[2] of this island) that they wish to confer with me previously—which is in fact saying that they wish me to spend my money in some other direction.——Now—I will take especial care that it *is* for the public cause—otherwise—I will not advance a parà.—The Opposition say they want to cajole me—and the party in power say the others want to seduce me—so between the two I have a difficult part to play—however I will have nothing to do with their factions—unless to reconcile them if possible.—I know not whether it be true that "Honesty is the best policy"—but it is the only kind that I am disposed to practice or to sanction.—

The Committee should hasten their brigade as it's announcement has been gratefully received by the G[ree]k Gov[ernmen]t who are also profuse in their civilities and acknowledgements to the Committee &c. and are preparing to receive me with all regard.——It is not of their ill-usage (which I should know how to repel or at least endure perhaps) but of *their good* treatment that I am apprehensive—for it is difficult not to allow our private impressions to predominate—and if

[2] Millingen (*Memoirs*, p. 18) called Count Demetrius Delladecima "a Cephaloniot nobleman of considerable shrewdness, sound judgment, and deep acquaintance with Greek character." He was in close contact with many mainland Greeks and gave Byron his appraisal of their recommendations and of their reliability. (Byron generally spelled his name Della Decima.)

these Gentlemen *have* any undue interest and discover my weak side—viz—a propensity to be governed—and were to set a pretty woman or a clever woman about me—with a turn for political or any other sort of intrigue—why—they would make a fool of me—no very difficult matter probably even without such an intervention.———But if I can keep passion—at least that passion—out of the question—(which may be the more easy as I left my heart in Italy) they will not weather me with quite so much facility.———

If the Committee expect to do much good—they must increase their funds—to which I will add all that I can spare of my own———and they should appoint at least *three* persons in whom they have confidence to direct their expenditure—I would rather *not* myself have anything to do with *that* department—not being a good accomptant—but in superintending all or any thing—*not* relative to the pecuniary detail—I am at their commandment.—Mr. Blaquiere's report in the papers is not quite the same with that in his private letters to Col. Napier—but he may be in the right to conceal partly the extent of the Greek divisions—especially as Mavrocordato was still in power when Mr. B. left the Morea.—I hope that his statement will be of some utility.—

8bre. 27th.

I was interrupted by a visitor on the 25th. and yesterday was Sunday.—With reference to what you say of the purchase of the Schooner—I can only answer that he is not likely to buy it—and *if* he buys—perhaps as little likely to pay the price—but you are—or *were* of a contrary opinion.—I shall be happy to confess your superior discernment. I hope you will give a careful look at my travelling carriage which I wish to have kept in good order.—The Prints also and some of my books (a life of Marceau the French General sent me by his Sister—) and some volumes inscribed tracts &c. which I believe I mentioned in a recent letter I wish to have reserved in case of disposal of the furniture &c.———It is not very probable that I should return before Spring—if even then—but it were idle to anticipate what must so much depend upon circumstances.—Here is a long epistle for you—will you tell the Hon[oura]ble Douglas Kinnaird that I have written to him to approve and sanction his proposal on a matter of business with reference to a Manor of mine—he will understand what is meant—I add this—in case he should not have received my reply to his letter—of the 14th. August—which I only got not very long ago.———My respects to Messrs Webb and B[arker?] I have received all their letters to which I presume the previous part of this will serve for answer without troubling them with a postage—Remember me to Mr. Sterling and all acquaintances—

Ever yrs. and truly
N B

8bre. 29th. 1823

P.S.—You surely care little (on my account) or should do for newspaper tattle or gossip of any kind—if any fact is falsely stated which appears to be of consequence—you have it in your power to contradict it—for you know as much nearly of my affairs public or private as I do myself.—I have recently seen something of a zealous Dr. Kennedy—a very good Calvinist—who has a taste for controversy and conversion —and thinks me so nearly a tolerable Christian that he is trying to make me a whole one.—I have found indeed one indisputable text in St. Paul's epistle to the Romans (Chapter 10th. I believe) which disposes me much to credit all the rest of the dicta of that powerful Apostle—— It is this (see the Chapter) "*For there is no difference between a* JEW *and a* GREEK"[3]—tell Messrs Webb and B[arker?] that I intend to preach from this text to Carridi and Corgialegno.—What think you? I hope that it is not a sin to say so.

[TO COUNTESS TERESA GUICCIOLI] *8bre. 29th. 1823*

My dearest T.—Enclosed is a letter from Pietro written upon a scurvy scrap of paper—but containing, I believe, all that is to the purpose relative to our present situation.—We are tolerably well and so forth—but the weather is cool—and mi-me ne &c. &c. &c.—Capite Eccelenza?[1]——I received yr. letter of the date of 7bre. and we have written by every opportunity.——Under Costa's[2] tuition—I presume that you have made a great progress in Metaphysics;—I have written nothing but letters or dispatches lately.—A Connection of mine—Lord Sydney Osborne came from Corfu yesterday to see me—and Pietro and I dine this afternoon with the English Resident to meet him. —I hope that your philosophical studies will furnish you with a little patience—and all will go well by and bye.—You may be sure that the moment I can join you again will be as welcome to me as at any period

[3] *Romans*, 10: 12.

[1] Origo says: "The nearest equivalent to this sentence is the French 'je m'en f . . . s'" (*The Last Attachment*, p. 366n.).

[2] Professor Paolo Costa, a friend of the Gambas, was forbidden to teach at the University of Bologna because of his liberal opinions and therefore tutored private pupils.

of our recollection.—There is nothing very attractive here to divide my attention—but I must attend to the Greek Cause both from honour and inclination.—

Messrs. Browne and Trelawney are in the Morea—where they have [been] very well received—and both of them write in good spirits and hopes. I am anxious to hear how the Spanish Cause will be arranged—as I think that it may have an influence on the Greek Contest.——I wish that both were fairly and favourably settled—that I might return quietly to Italy—and talk over with you *our*—or rather *Pietro's* adventures—some of which are very amusing—as also some of the incidents of our voyages and travels.—But I reserve them in the hope that we may laugh over them together at no very remote period.—We must get on horseback to ride over to Argostoli.—

Ever my dearest T. il tuo A. A. in E. +++
N B

[TO DOUGLAS KINNAIRD] *Cephalonia. 8bre. 29th. 1823*

My dear Douglas—I have received another letter from you to the same purpose—but had already answered in the *affirmative* to your proposition about Rochdale—and that more than once—hoping that you will make the best of the business for me that you can.—I have also added that I think the produce had better be laid out for the present in Exchequer bills—as bearing a moderate interest and little liable to loss besides being an easily reconvertible (into cash) security.—I trust also that you are getting in the Kirkby Mallory arrears due to us—and are trying (while the funds are high) to have some part of my funded property invested on a safe mortgage—this has been my wish for years as you know well.——

I have sent to Hobhouse various documents and dispatches from which he can furnish the proper information to the Committee—the Greek Gov[ernmen]t have invited me to Napoli di Romania—and I expect to proceed there in Novr.—You had better address to me by Genoa (to Messrs Webb and Barry) my letters reach me sooner through that Channel—as vessels sail frequently.—I shall take your advice about the reverend care of my purse and person—as far as is consistent with propriety;—the former has not yet suffered much—having only been lightened of about a thousand dollars—partly in aid of the Suliotes—and partly to some of the refugees—and also some expences for sending boats with dispatches &c.——and the latter is for the present in tolerable plight.—You, Gentlemen of the Committee, must exert yourselves—and I will second you as well as I can—but your newspaper accounts are highly exaggerated for neither Turks nor Greeks have done much this year.—I shall continue to state things to you all exactly as they are—or appear to me—and the best way *not* to despond is perhaps to commence with not being over-sanguine.—The Cause is good—and I think eventually *safe* (if the Holy Alliance leave the Greeks to themselves) and I am inclined to believe that the Committee may be of essential service—in forwarding supplies or monies—and obtaining a loan for the Independents—but there is still a good deal to be done and more than is imagined in your part of the World—for proofs—(or at least assertions) of which I refer you to high Authorities amongst the Greeks themselves— transmitted by me to Hobhouse.—

Ld. Sydney Osborne—came over yesterday [from] Corfu to meet me—and I dine with [the] Gov[ernmen]t Resident Col. Napier to-day to meet him;—he came up (i.e. Ld. S.) to Metaxata where I now am yesterday—and we had a luncheon and some talk together—I then rode back with him towards Argostoli.—He is in good preservation—and as Clever and insouciant as ever.—He tells me that Alvanley is at length "rectus in curia" with his creditors—and in possession of his long expected Uncle's property.——Tell him that I have discovered a text in St. Paul's epistle to the Romans Chapter 10th. of such unimpeachable veracity—that I have been converted into a firm believer of all the rest.—It is this (vide Chapter 10th.) "*For there is no difference between the* JEW *and the* GREEK" these are the literal words—and what is more to the purpose the literal truth.—Some of their Bankers tried to make me pay interest for my *own monies* in my *own possession* which I came to spend for their Cause too! and this I think equals or beats the tribes of Israel—unless perhaps the *ten* who are still supposed to exist in the heart of Asia.——But I "sorted them I trow"[1] having the Staff for the present in my own hand.—believe me

truly yr. affect[ionat]e

N B

[TO DOUGLAS KINNAIRD] *Cephalonia, November 10th. 1823*

[Part quoted in catalogue]

[1] Probably from Scott, *Guy Mannering*, Chap. 33: "bid them bring up the prisoner—I trow I'll sort him."

This will be forwarded to you by the Greek Deputies,[1] to whom I request your good offices. At the request of their Government I have agreed to advance the sum of four thousand pounds sterling, by way of loan, (as they apparently decline it as a gift) which is to be repaid in the event of their obtaining a subsidy in England. This sum is essential at this moment for the succour of Missolonghi and, whether it be repaid or not, I hope it may be of service to the cause. . . .

[TO LORD ERSKINE][1] *Cephalonia—9bre. 10th. 1823*

My dear Lord—The Greek Deputies have requested an introduction to your Lordship, and I willingly comply with their wishes.—I received your letter on the Greek Cause (which I propose to have translated into Romaic) some time ago—your usual Eloquence was never more nobly exerted.——Your efforts on this occasion will not form the least illustrious portion of a life so dear to Fame and Freedom. ——That it may be prolonged for the sake of your friends and country is the wish of all in common with

your most respectful and very affectionate friend and Servt.

NOEL BYRON

[TO LORD HOLLAND] *Cephalonia. 9bre. 10th. 1823*

My dear Lord—I take the liberty of recommending the Greek Deputies to your acquaintance and to that of Lady Holland to whom I desire my respects.—I think it probable that their acquaintance may be interesting to you—and am very sure that *Yours* will be useful to them and to their Country.—They will inform you of all that is worth knowing here—and (what is little worth knowing—unless you should

[1] On October 15 the Legislative Body had voted to ask for a loan of £800,000 from the Greek Committee in London and sent as deputies Jean Orlando and André Luriottis. They were also authorized to ask Byron for a temporary loan of £4,000, the agreement for which was signed on November 13th before the deputies left for England.

[1] Thomas, first Baron Erskine (1750–1823), was an enthusiastic Philhellene and one of the founders of the London Greek Committee. The pamphlet which he sent to Byron was *A Letter to the Earl of Liverpool on the Subject of the Greeks* (1822). It was a plea to the British Government to take action in support of the Greeks following the news of the massacres by the Turks on the island of Chios. It should be mentioned in passing that Hobhouse was put in Newgate in 1819 for writing a pamphlet attacking Erskine for his defence of the Whigs against the Reformers.

enquire after a former acquaintance) of the "*whereabouts*" and *what*abouts of

yrs. ever and truly
NOEL BYRON

[TO JOHN CAM HOBHOUSE] *Cephalonia. 9bre. 10th. 1823*

My dear H.—Herewith I recommend to you the Greek Deputies—whom Heaven prosper. I have bought a "Gross of Green Spectacles"—i.e. I have advanced four thousand pounds to the Greek Gov[ernmen]t to succour Messolonghi—and "the old Gentleman—his man Abraham and my horse Blackberry all trotted off apparently very well pleased with one another." But never mind—and pray "do not forget the importance of Monogamy—maintaining it against the Deuterogamists of the age."[1]

yrs. ever
N B

[BYRON'S LOAN AGREEMENT WITH THE GREEK DEPUTIES]
Cefalonia li 1/13 Novembre 1823

[Italian text in an unknown hand—signed by Byron and the Deputies—copy of original]

Dai recenti del Magistrato alla Sanità di Argostoli

Avendo richiesto il Governo provv[isori]o della Grecia un'imprestito di Tallare trenta mila da Sua Signoria il Lord Byron all' unico oggetto di offrire un pronto soccorso ai bisogni della Grecia occidentale, come risulta dai differenti Uff[i]zi delle competenti Autorità sedute al prelodato Lord, li sottoscritti Deputati per l'imprestito da Londra, che espressamente passati in Cefalonia ad ultimare anche questa urgente negoziazione, come più estesamente risulta dall'uff[ici]o del corpo Legislativo diretto al detto Lord in data 13 Ott[obr]e del N403.1803 [1823?]. si sono convenuti, come seg[uent]e——Il Nobile Lord s'impegna di corrispondere solamente quattro mila Lire Sterline d'Inghilterra in Cambiale sopra Londra per essere negoziata dai Mercanti Grant, e C. di Malta——

Questa Cambiale sarà estesa a nome del Sig[nor]e Giovanni Orlando d'Silva, uno dei sottoscritti Deputati, e da questo girata a nome del quì presente Sig[nor]e H. Brawne [Browne]——

1 Goldsmith, *The Vicar of Wakefield*, Chaps. 12 and 20.

Il Sig[nor]e Brawne [Browne] dovrà passare nel più sollecito modo in Malta, rescuotere [sic] questo denaro, ed indi recarsi in Cefalonia——— Sig[nor]e Brawne [Browne] al suo ritorno in Cefalonia dovrà in unione agli altri due soggetti———cioè———Destinati da Sua Signoria il Lord Byron, e dai Signori Deputati impiegare il suddetto denaro, giusta la volontà spiegata dal Gov[ern]o prov[visori]o della Grecia pei differenti preaccen[na]ti uffizi———

Rassegnano li sottoscritti Deputati Signori Orlando, e Luriotti per parte, e nome del provv[isori]o Governo di restituire la detta somma Lire quattro mila Sterline al Nobile Lord entro mesi sei, che sarà verificato l'imprestito di Londra. Se entro questo periodo non venissero pagati per la non realizzazione di detto prestito, si obbligano pure per parte, e nome del Governo loro di essergli pagato l'interesse del quattro per cento all'anno dal giorno d'oggi fino alla sua totale estinzione, che sarà ad ogni sua richiesta———

NOEL BYRON Pair d'Angleterre
GIO[VAN]NI ORLANDO
AND[REAS] LURIOTTIS

[TRANSLATION] *Cephalonia 1/13 November 1823*[1]

From the precincts of the Magistrate of Health of Argostoli

The provisional Government of Greece, having requested a loan of thirty thousand dollars from his Lordship, Lord Byron, for the sole purpose of providing prompt assistance for the needs of western Greece, as a result of the different offices [functions] of the qualified authorities meeting with the afore-mentioned praiseworthy Lord, the undersigned Deputies for the loan from London, who have come to Cephalonia expressly to conclude this urgent negotiation, as the most extensive result of the office of the Legislative Body directed to the said Lord 13 October of N. 403.1803 [1823?]. have agreed as follows.——— The Noble Lord pledges himself to pay only four thousand pounds English Sterling in a bill of exchange on London to be negotiated by the Merchants Grant and Co. of Malta.———

This bill of exchange will be made out in the name of Sig[nor]e Giovanni Orlando d'Silva, one of the undersigned Deputies, and endorsed by him to the name of the here present Mr. H[amilton]

[1] The date was twelve days earlier by the Old Style or Julian Calendar which the Greeks still used.

Browne———Mr. Browne will go in the quickest way possible to Malta, to receive the money, and from thence to return to Cephalonia. ———Mr. Browne upon his return in conjunction with the other two subjects will be obliged, as assigned by his Lordship, Lord Byron, and by the Deputies to use the aforementioned money in compliance with the wishes explained by the provisional government of Greece for the various aforementioned offices.———

The undersigned Orlando and Luriotti pledge on behalf of, and in the name of the provisional government, to repay the said sum of four thousand pounds Sterling to the Noble Lord within six months of the loan from London having taken place. If within this period the sum has not been paid because the said loan has not been realized, they are obliged just the same on behalf of, and in the name of their government to pay him the interest of four per cent a year from today until the loan has been paid off, which will be at his request.[2]

NOEL BYRON, Peer of England
GIOVANNI ORLANDO
ANDREAS LURIOTTIS

[TO DAVID GRANT] *Cephalonia. 9bre. 13th. 1823*

Sir,—I have answered your obliging letter of the 12th. of August by Capt. Symonds—and have now to avail myself of the advantage of your correspondence.—I yesterday drew bills for four thousand pounds sterling on my bankers in London Messrs Ransom and Co Pall Mall East—in favour of the Greek Provisional Government to enable part of their fleet to succour Messolonghi now in a state of blockade.—My letter of credit on Messrs Ransom and the bills will be presented to your house by Mr. Hamilton Browne—who is authorized to receive the amount in dollars and to carry them to this Island—the Greek Deputies paying the insurance and other expences incidental to business.—I have to request that you will have the goodness to remit the sum as soon as possible,—the bills are thirty days after sight—and I believe that Messrs Webb can—or have assured you of the goodness of the house on which they are drawn.—I do not know what the present exchange is at Malta—but I should prefer infinitely—nego-

2 Transcribed and translated by Ricki B. Herzfeld.

ciating with your house to transacting any business with other merchants of the Ionian Islands.[1]——I have the honour to be

your obliged and very obedt. humble Servt.

NOEL BYRON

[TO GERONIMO CORGIALEGNO] *9bre. 24, 1823*

[In Byron's hand]

Si pagarà al' proveditore tre tallari al' giorno compreso *il vino* ed altro come specificate secondo al' contratto—se egli non ha mandato il vino—questo deve essere ritenuto dal' conto.——La somma che il proveditore dunque ha da ricevere per trenti cinque giorni è cento e cinque tallari—meno il vino ed altro cibo notato da Lega—non spedito.——

La famiglia Moriote non riceverà da *questo* giorno più di sei tallari per mese per mantenere l'inferma madre—le ragazze se sono oneste—(ed *io* almeno non so nulla al' contrario) possano vivere in' onesto servizio—essendo giovani ed abili—quella famiglia ha gia ricevuta in soccorsi da me—(compresa cinquanta tallari pagati per loro debiti in Itaca) più di *cento e venti tallari* in tre mesi.

Gli sei tallari specificati per la madre pel' tempo a venire—debbono bastare—essendo due tallari di più di ciò che si paga al' meglio a un Soldato abile—e che forne anche la famiglia—la famiglia più numerosa della loro.—

N B

[TRANSLATION] *November 24, 1823*

Pay the supplier three dollars per day including *the wine* and anything else as specified according to the contract. If he has not sent the wine, this must be deducted from the bill. The sum that the supplier therefore is to receive for thirty-five days is one hundred and five dollars—minus the wine and other food noted by Lega as not having been sent.

The Morea family[1] will not receive from *this* day, more than six

[1] Byron in the end found means to negotiate the bills in Cephalonia and Zante through Hancock and Barff, for at least a part of the money. Browne did not return to Cephalonia from Malta with the dollars but continued his journey to England with the Deputies.

[1] The Chalandritsanos family.

dollars per month for supporting their invalid mother. The girls, if they are honest (and *I* at least do not know anything to the contrary) can live by honest work [service]—being young and able. That family has already received in assistance from me (including fifty dollars paid for their debts in Ithaca) more than *one hundred and twenty dollars* in three months.

The six dollars specified for the mother for the time to come, will have to do, being two dollars more than that which is paid at best to an able soldier who must also provide for a family—a family larger than theirs.[2]

N B

[TO COL. LEICESTER STANHOPE][1] *9bre. 25 o 1823*

Dear Colonel Stanhope—As far as my approval can be of any consequence I approve of ye letters—and regret that I missed you this morning.—I reinclose them—and also a subscription list which I have read over.—As I have no advices on that score from you or Colonel Napier and know nothing whatever of Mr. or Mrs. Flack or Slack—nor can ascertain who or what they were or are except that Mr Flack was an Auctioneer of Corfu—and that Mrs. Slack is *not* the most deserving of her sex—I can say no more on the subject till I see you or Col. N.—I acknowledge the receipt of the documents and also of the pamphlet with many thanks.—Believe me

very truly yrs in all sincerity and amity
NOEL BYRON

[TO JOHN BOWRING] *9bre. 29 o 1823*

Dear Sir—This letter will be presented to you by Mr. Hamilton Browne who precedes or accompanies the Greek Deputies.—He is both capable and desirous of rendering every service to the cause and information to the Committee.—He has been already of considerable advantage to both to my own knowledge.—Lord Archibald Hamilton[1]

[2] Transcribed and translated by Ricki B. Herzfeld.

[1] Stanhope arrived in Cephalonia on November 22, as an agent of the London Greek Committee to act with Byron. He left early in December for Missolonghi. See Biographical Sketch in Appendix IV.

[1] Lord Archibald Hamilton (1770–1827), M.P. for Lanarkshire from 1802 to 1827, perhaps pleased Byron because he had once moved a vote of censure on Castlereagh as president of the Board of Control (1809).

to whom he is related will add a weightier recommendation than mine. Corinth is taken[2]—and a Turkish Squadron said to be beaten in the Archipelago—the public progress of the Greeks is considerable—but their internal dissentions still continue.—On arriving at the Seat of Government—I shall endeavour to mitigate or extinguish them—though neither is an easy task.—I have remained here till now—partly in expectation of the Squadron in relief of Messolonghi—partly of Mr. Parry's detachment—and partly to receive from Malta or Zante the sum of four thousand pounds sterling—which at the desire of the Greek Government I have advanced for the payment of the expected Squadron.———The Bills are negociating and will be cashed in a short time—as they would have been immediately in any other mart—but the miserable Ionian merchants have little money and no great credit—and are besides *politically shy* on this occasion—for although I had the letters of Messrs Webb—(one of the strongest houses of the Mediterranean)—and also of Messrs Ransom———there is no business to be done on *fair* terms—except through *English* merchants—these however have proved both able and willing and upright as usual.[3]—

Col. Stanhope has arrived and will proceed immediately—he shall have my cooperation in all his endeavours—but from every thing that I can learn the formation of a brigade at present—will be extremely difficult to say the least of it.—With regard to the reception of foreigners—at least foreign officers—I refer you to a passage in Prince Mavrocordato's recent letter—a copy of which is enclosed in my packet sent by the Deputies.———It is my intention to proceed by sea to Nauplia di Romania[4]—as soon as I have arranged this business for the Greeks themselves. I mean the advance of two hundred thousand piastres for their fleet.———My time here has not been entirely lost—indeed you will perceive by some former documents—that any advantage from my *then* proceeding to the Morea—was doubtful.—We have at last moved the Deputies—and I have written a strong remonstrance on their divisions to Mavrocordato—which I understand—was forwarded to the Legislative by the Prince. ———With a loan they *may* do much—which is all—that for particular reasons *I* can say on that subject.———I regret to hear from Col. Stan-

[2] The fortress of Corinth was taken by the Greeks early in the year 1822, but was recaptured by the Turks in July of that year. It was again taken by the Greeks on Sept. 16, 1823.

[3] The banker-merchants Barff and Hancock of Zante and Cephalonia cashed Byron's bills of exchange from this time forward.

[4] Byron changed his plans soon after, when Mavrocordatos arrived in Missolonghi and urged him to come there.

hope that the Committee have exhausted their funds—is it supposed that a brigade can be formed without them? or that three thousand pounds would be sufficient? it is true Money will go further in Greece than in most countries but the regular force must be rendered a *national concern*—and paid from a *national fund*—and neither individuals nor Committees at least with the *usual* means of such as now exist—will find the achievement practicable.—I beg once more to recommend my friend Mr. Hamilton Browne—to whom I have also personal obligations for his exertions in the common cause—and have the honour to be

yrs. very truly
NOEL BYRON

[TO COUNTESS TERESA GUICCIOLI] *9bre. 29 o 1823*

[added to letter of Pietro Gamba to Teresa]

My dearest T.—What Pietro says is very reasonable—but we are at present so busy—that I have little time to write much in addition to his letter.———Here are arrived—English—Germans—Greeks—all kinds of people in short—proceeding to or coming from Greece—and all with something to say to me—so that every day—I have to receive them here or visit them in Argostoli.—The Greek affairs go on better —they have taken Corinth—and their fleet has had a victory near the Islands—but not in *these* waters.———I still hope to see you in Spring— and in the mean time entreat you to quiet your apprehensions and believe me ever

yr. a. a. in e. + + +
N B

P.S.—I regret to see in the English papers that Colonel Fitz Gibbon brother to my particular friend *Lord Clare* has eloped from Ireland with the wife of a friend; the affair makes much noise.—The woman had four children and carried two with her.

[TO THE GENERAL GOVERNMENT OF GREECE]

Cephalonia 30 9bre. 1823

[In scribe's hand—signed by Byron]

Il Colonello Stanhope &c. &c. venuto da Londra con commissioni dal Comitato Greco per agire in mia compagnia a favore della liberazione di Grecia si reca presso la sede del Governo per offrirvi i suoi servizi che potrebbero esservi di gran giovamento,—e per farvi gradire alcuni suoi progetti a vostro benefizio. Egli è membro di una delle più antiche e nobili famiglie dell'Impero Britannico, ed uno dei più esperti uffiziali della nostra armata. Confido che sarà accolto con quella cortesía con la quale furono tutti gli altri stranieri da me raccomandati —di che vi riferisco molte e sincere grazie.

Il Sig[no]re Anarghiro vostro inviato, tornando dee aver presentato la mia lettera al Governo—dalla quale comprenderete che io ho fatto ogni mio potere per sodisfare alla dimanda che il Governo mi ha fatta per mezzo de' suoi Inviati, Sig[no]ri Orlando e Luriotti. Un negoziante Inglese di Zante si è incaricato di realizzare le mie cambiali in favore del Governo Greco a giusto cambio. Alcuni negozianti Ionici ossia Greci sia per odio del Governo Greco o per intrighi privati, o per viltà politica ricusarono di realizzarle senza un'usura vergognosa, nonostante varie lettere di credito dalle prime case d'Italia o di Londra. Il Sig[no]re Corialegno [sic] si è tenuto offeso perchè il prelodato Governo non ha voluto eleggere il suo fratello a deputato per l'imprestito a Londra. Io raccomando al Governo di non nominare alcuno di quella famiglia ne' de' suoi amici a tale incarico poichè abbiam ragioni persuadenti che essi hanno delle viste particolari, ed in caso di una tal nomina io me stimerei in obbligo di far avvertire gl'Imprestanti Inglesi di tenersi in guardia con quelli co'quali trattano. Non dico ciò per alcun mio dispiacere che da lui mi fosse fatto, giacchè il Sig[no]re Corialegno, si è mostrato cortese a mio riguardo, dicendo che "come Banchieri daranno a me tutto che voglio, ma al Governo Greco, nulla." Ecco le precise loro parole.

L'affare dell'Imprestito, l'aspettation [sic] si lungamente sospirata della flotta, ed il non cessato pericolo di Missolonghi mi hanno ritenuto qui finora, e mi riterranno finchè alcune di queste cause siano tolte via. Quando il denaro destinato alla flotta sarà sborsato, io partirò, quantunque non vegga a che possa giovare la mia presenza in Morea nel presente stato delle cose. Quì sono arrivati contrari rumori di nuove dissenssioni nel governo Greco, anzì del principio d'una guerra civile. Desidero con tutto il mio cuore che siano falsi o almeno esaggerati, giacchè non saprei imaginare alcuna calamità che fosse più da temere per voi che quella. Devvo confessarvi francamente che se un qualunque ordine ed unione non si conferma, tutte le speranze di un imprestito torneranno vuote,—ogni soccorso che potesse la Grecia aspettare dagli Esteri, che certo non sarebbero ne pochi ne spreggevoli veranno sospesi, e forse affatto impediti,—e quel che è peggio le grandi Potenze d'Europa delle quali nessuna era nemica alla Grecia, e che parevano inclinare favorevoli d'accordo allo stabilmento di uno stato indipendente in Grecia si persuaderanno che i Greci non sono atti a governarsi per se stessi, e concerteranno qualche mezzo per far fine a' vostri disordini, che troncherà tutte le vostre più belle speranze, e tutte quelle de' vostri amici.

Permettete che vi aggiunga una volta per sempre:—Io desidero il bene della Grecia, e non altro: farò ogni mio potere per assicurarlo: ma non consento ne consentirò mai che il Pubblico ne' i privati Inglesi siano delusi sopra il vero stato delle cose Greche. Il resto dipende da voi, Signori, voi avete combattuto gloriosamente, conducetevi anche onoratamente coi vostri compatrioti e col mondo, ed allora non si potrà più dire come si è ripetuto per due milla anni collo storico Romano, che Filopemene fù l'ultimo dei Greci.—Non vogliate permettere che nemeno la Calunnia (e chi può evitarla specialmente in una lotta sì difficile!) possa paragonare il Pacha Turco al Patriotta Greco in pace, dopo che l'anno sterminato in guerra.

Vi prego di accettare quest &c. &c. &c.
N B Pari d'Inghilterra

[TRANSLATION] *November 30, 1823*[1]

Colonel Stanhope &c. &c. who has come from London with orders from the Greek Committee to work along with me for the liberation of Greece, approaches the seat of Government in order to offer you his services which might be of great advantage to you,—and to have you accept some of his projects for your benefit. He is a member of one of the oldest and most noble families of the British Empire, and one of the most skilful officers of our armed forces. I trust that he will be received with the same courtesy as have all the foreigners recommended by me—for which I give you many and sincere thanks.

Your envoy Sig[no]re Anarghiro having returned, must have presented my letter to the Government—from which you will understand that I have done everything in my power to satisfy the request that the Government has made of me by means of its envoys, Sig[no]re Orlando

[1] There are three copies of this letter in Italian in various hands, two in the National Library, Athens, and one in the Pforzheimer Library. One of the National Library copies has the signature in Byron's hand: "N. B. Pari d'Inghilterra". This copy is in a legible scribe's hand and is perhaps the copy actually sent. It is the one reproduced here. Moore has printed a translation of part of the letter (II, 690–691) and this was used by Prothero.

and Sig[no]re Luriotti. An English merchant of Zante has been entrusted with the cashing of my bills of exchange in favour of the Greek Government at a fair exchange. Several Ionic, or rather Greek, merchants, whether for hatred of the Greek Government, or for private conspiracies, or from political cowardice, refused to make the exchange without a shameful interest, notwithstanding several letters of credit from the first houses of Italy and London. Sig[no]re Corialegno [sic] is offended because the before mentioned worthy Government did not want to appoint his brother a Deputy to London for the loan. I implore the Government not to nominate any member of that family nor any of their friends for such a commission since we are convinced of their having some particular [i.e. self-interested] views, and in case of such a nomination I would deem it my obligation to warn the English lenders to be on guard with those with whom they were dealing. I do not say this for any displeasure that he has caused me, since Sig[no]re Corialegno has shown himself to be courteous in dealing with me, saying that "as Bankers they will give me all that I want, but nothing to the Greek Government." These are their precise words.

The affair of the Loan, the waiting for so long for the much desired fleet, and the ever-present danger to Missolonghi have kept me here until now, and will hold me here until some of these obstacles have been removed. When the money assigned for the fleet has been paid out, I will depart, although I cannot see how my presence in the Morea might be of benefit in the present state of affairs. Unfavourable rumours of new dissensions in the Greek Government, or rather of the start of a civil war, have reached here. I hope with all my heart that they are false or at least exaggerated, since I could not imagine any calamity that is more to be feared for you than this. I must admit to you frankly that if some kind of order and union is not confirmed, all hopes for a loan will be lost,—any assistance that Greece might expect from abroad, which certainly would not be inconsiderable nor contemptible, will be suspended, and maybe even stopped, and what is worse is that the great Powers of Europe, of which none was an enemy of Greece, and which seemed favourably inclined to agree with the establishment of an independent Greek state, will be persuaded that the Greeks are not capable of governing themselves and will arrange some means for putting an end to your disorder which will cut short all your most noble hopes, and all those of your friends.

Allow me to add this once more and for always: I want what is good for Greece and nothing else: I will do everything in my power to insure this: But I do not consent, nor will I ever consent to permit the

Public or private English citizens ever to be deluded about the true state of things in Greece. The rest depends on you, Gentlemen. You have fought gloriously, if you also conduct yourselves honourably with your compatriots and with the world, it will no longer be possible to echo those words of the Roman historian, which have been repeated for two thousand years—that Philopomene[2] was the last of the Greeks. You do not even want to permit that Calumny (and who can avoid her especially in so difficult a fight!) might compare the Turkish Pasha to the Greek Patriot in peace, after they have exterminated him in war.

I beg you to accept this &c. &c. &c.[3]

N B Peer of England

[TO PRINCE ALEXANDER MAVROCORDATOS]

Cefalonia 2 Decembre 1823

[In Pietro Gamba's hand—signed by Byron]

Eccelentissimo Principe—Il Colonello Stanhope figlio del Maggior-Generale Harrington ec. ec. ec. presentarà all' Altezza Vostra questa mia lettera. Egli è venuto da Londra in *50* giorni dopo aver visitato tutti i Comitati Greci di Germania—incaricato del nostro Comitato di operare in mia compagnia alla liberazione della Grecia. Credo che il suo nome, o la sua missione lo raccomanderanno abbastanza all' Altezza Vostra—senza che si abbisognino le raccomandazioni di uno straniero, quantunque sia un tale che rispetta ed ammira insieme coll' Europa intera—il coraggio, i talenti e sopra tutto la Probità del Principe Mavrocordato——

Mi duole oltremodo in [di] udire che durano sempre le interne dissenzioni della Grecia—e in un momento in cui ella potrebbe trionfare da ogni parte, come ha trionfato in alcune.

La Grecia ora è posta fra questi tre partiti—o conquistare la sua libertà—o diventare una dipendenza dei sovrani Europei o una Provincia Turca——ora può scegliere fra i tre.—Ma la guerra civile non può esser strada che agli ultimi due.—Se invidia la sorte della Valachia e della Crimea potrà ottenerla domani—se quella dell' Italia—posdomani—Ma se vorrà divenir la Grecia per sempre libera, vera e Indipen-

[2] Plutarch devotes a *Life* to Philopoemen, one of the great men of Greece's declining years in the third and second centuries B.C. He distinguished himself in the battle of Sellasia (221 B.C.) and in 208 B.C. was elected general of the Achaean League and in that year slew in battle Machinidas, tyrant of Lacedaemon.

[3] Transcribed and translated by Ricki B. Herzfeld.

dente conviene che si determini ora o non avrà più tempo—mai più—
Credetemi con piena stima e rispetto

N B
P[ari] d'In[ghilterr]a

P.S.—Vostra Altezza saprà già che io ho cercato di contentare il vostro Governo, quanto ho potuto, nelle sue richieste. Vorrei che questa flotta aspettata sì lungamente in vano fosse [?] arrivata—e soppratutto che l'Altezza vostra o nella flotta con publica [*sic*] missione o in qualunque modo si fosse accostata, e si accosti a queste parti. Mi creda di nuovo

Suo Dev[otissi]mo Servo
N B P[ari] d'In[ghilterr]a

[TRANSLATION] *Cephalonia December 2, 1823*

Most Excellent Prince—Colonel Stanhope, the son of Major-General Harrington, etc. etc. etc., will present this letter of mine to Your Highness. He has come from London in 50 days after having visited all of the Greek committees in Germany—charged by our committee to work together with me for the liberation of Greece. I believe that his name, or his mission, will be enough to recommend him to Your Highness, without the need of any other recommendation from a foreigner, even though he may be someone who respects and admires —together with all of Europe—the courage, the talents, and above all, the probity of Prince Mavrocordato——

It pains me exceedingly to hear that the internal dissensions of Greece still continue—and at a time when she could triumph everywhere, as she has triumphed in some places.

Greece now faces these three courses—to win her liberty, to become a Colony of the sovereigns of Europe, or to become a Turkish province.——Now she can choose one of the three—but civil war cannot lead to anything but the last two. If she envies the fate of Wallachia or of the Crimea she can obtain it tomorrow; if that of Italy, the day after tomorrow. But if Greece wants to become forever free, true, and Independent she had better decide now, or never again will she have the chance, never again. Believe me with the utmost esteem and respect.

N B P[eer] of E[ngland]

P.S.—Your highness already knows that I have tried to satisfy the requests of your Government as much as I could. I wish that this fleet, which we have waited for so long in vain, had arrived—and above all that Your Highness, either on board the fleet on a public mission, or in any other way, had come or would now come to these parts. Believe me again[1]

Your devoted Servant
N B P[eer] of E[ngland]

[TO JOHN BOWRING] *10bre. 7 o 1823*

Dear Sir—I confirm the above.—It is certainly my opinion that Mr. Millingen[1] is entitled to the same salary with Mr. Tindall[2]— and his service is likely to be harder.——I have written to you (or to Mr. Hobhouse *for* your perusal) by various opportunities—mostly private—also by the Deputies and by Mr. Hamilton Browne.——The Public success of the Greeks has been considerable—Corinth taken—Missolonghi nearly safe—and some ships in the Archipelago taken from the Turks.—But there is not only dissention in the Morea but *civil war*[3]—by the latest accounts, to what extent we do not yet know—but hope trifling.—For six weeks I have been expecting the fleet—*which has not arrived*—though I have at the request of the G[ree]k G[overnmen]t

[1] Transcribed and translated by Ricki B. Herzfeld.

[1] Julius Millingen was sent out by the London Greek Committee to offer his services as a doctor to the Greeks. He arrived in Cephalonia carly in November, 1823, and left for Missolonghi the middle of December. Millingen, while in Cephalonia, asked Byron to support his plea for more money from the Committee. Byron enclosed this letter to Bowring with Millingen's letter, to which he added some notes. Millingen had said that "the retreat of the Turks from before Missolonghi had rendered unnecessary the appearance of the Greek fleet." Byron added: "By the special providence of the Deity, the Mussulmans were seized with a panic, and fled; but no thanks to the fleet, which ought to have been here months ago, and has no excuse to the contrary, lately—at least since I had the money ready to pay." On Millingen's complaint that his hope of pay from the Greeks "turned out perfectly chimerical", Byron remarked: "and *will* do so, till they obtain a loan. They have not a rap, nor credit (in the islands) to raise one. A medical man may succeed better than others; but all these penniless officers had better have staid at home. Much money may not be required, but some must." (*LJ*, VI, 280–281n.) For more details about Millingen's association with Byron see Biographical Sketch, Appendix IV.

[2] Tindall helped Millingen establish a dispensary in Missolonghi and later left for Athens.

[3] The civil war was between the military party controlled by Kolokotrones, who had established the seat of the Executive in Nauplia, and the Senate or Legislative body in Argos. When Kolokotrones sent troops to arrest the members of the Senate, they fled to Kranidi and appointed a new Executive with Kondouriottes of Hydra as President. The best short account of the conflict and the personalities involved is in *LJ*, VI, Appendix V.

advanced (that is have prepared & have in hand) two hundred thousand piastres (deducting the commissions and bankers charges) of my own monies—to forward their projects.—The Suliotes now in Acarnania and elsewhere are very anxious that I should take them under my direction—and go over and *put things to rights* in the Morea —which without a force—seems impracticable—and really—though very reluctant (as my letters will have shown you) to take such a measure—there seems hardly any milder remedy.—However I will not do anything rashly,—and have only continued here so long in the hope of seeing things reconciled—and have done all in my power therefor.—Had I *gone sooner they would have forced me into one party or the other*—and I doubt as much now.—But we will do our best.

yrs. ever
N B

[TO JOHN BOWRING] *10bre. 10th. 1823*

Dear Sir,—Colonel Napier will present to you this letter.—Of his military character it were superfluous to speak.—Of his personal I can say from my own knowledge as well as from all public rumour or private report that it is as excellent as his military.—In short a better or a braver man is not easily to be found.—*He* is *our* Man to lead a regular force, or organize a national one for the Greeks.——Ask the Army—ask any body.——He is besides a personal friend of both P[rince] Mavrocordato—Col. Stanhope—and myself and in such concord with all three—that we should all pull together—an indispensable as well as a rare point—especially in Greece at present.—To enable a regular force to be properly organized—it will be requisite for the Loan holders to set apart at least £50-000 Sterling—for that particular purpose—perhaps more,—but by so doing they will guarantee their own monies—and "make assurance doubly sure".[1]—They can appoint Commissioners to see that part properly expended—and I recommend a similar precaution for the whole.—

I hope that the Deputies have arrived as well as some of my various dispatches (chiefly addrest to Mr. Hobhouse) for the Committee.—Col. Napier will tell you the recent special interposition of the Gods in behalf of the Greeks—who seem to have no enemies in heaven or [on] earth to be dreaded but their own tendencies to discord amongst themselves.——But these too it is to be hoped will be mitigated—and then

[1] *Macbeth*, Act IV, scene 1.

we can take the field in force on the offensive—instead of being reduced to the "petite Guerre" of defending the same fortresses year after year and taking a few ships—and starving out a castle, and making more fuss about them—than Alexander in his cups—or Buonaparte in a bulletin.—Our friends here have done something in the way of the *Spartans*—(though not one tenth of what is told) but have not yet inherited *their* style.—Believe me

yrs. ever & truly
N B

[TO DOUGLAS KINNAIRD] *10bre. 10 o 1823*

Dear Douglas—This will be delivered by Col. Napier—whom I request you to present to the Committee.—He is too well known to require me to say more than I have already said in my letter to Mr. Bowring—which See.——I have had only *two* letters from you—both (I think) of August—one however is without date—I have often written to acknowledge both—and to sanction or approve your acceptance of the Rochdale proposition.—I have been expending monies on the Greek Cause.—I shall probably have to *expend more*—and therefore require *more* to *expend*.—As I hope that you have gotten together the Kirkby Mallory dues—also arrears—also mine own especial fees and funds;—the Rochdale produce—and my income for the ensuing year—(and I have still of the present year something in hand—including my Genoese credit) ought to make a pretty sufficient sort of sum to take the field withal—and I like to do so with all I can muster—in case of anything requiring the same.—I shall be as saving of my purse and person as you recommend—but you know that it is as well to be in readiness with one or both in the event of either being required.—

yrs. ever and faithfully.
N B

P.S.—Col. Napier will tell you the recent news.

10bre. 11th. 1823

P.S.—I presume that you have also come to some agreement with Mr. M[urray] about "Werner".—The year is more than out since he published it.—Although the copyright should only be worth two or three hundred pounds—I will tell you what can be done with them—for three hundred pounds I can maintain in Greece at more than the *fullest pay* of the Provisional Gov[ernmen]t *rations* included—one hundred armed men *for three months*!—It is not that I am in any pressing need of monies—especially of this kind—but it is better to have all financial matters arranged of whatever description—rents—funds—purchase-monies—or printer's products—I presume that there is or will be something from "the Island" also—and from the sale of the other writings—but I do not reckon much on anything of that kind. H[unt] ought to have collected the works by this time—as before directed—and published the whole eleven new D[on] J[uan]s.——I am particular on this point only—because a sum of trifling amount even for a Gentleman's *personal* expences in *London* or *Paris*—in Greece can arm and maintain hundreds of men—you may judge of this when I tell you that the four thousand pounds advanced by me is likely to set a fleet and an army in motion for some months.—I request you to avoid all unnecessary disbursements (excepting for the Insurances) in England—whatever remains to be paid to lawyers and creditors (and you yourself say that it is but a sum not exceeding much my *whole* (Kirkby Mallory included) *half* year's income[)] can be settled after the Greek war—or the Greek Kalends;—for the dogs—especially the lawyers—have already had more than ever was justly owing to them. —But they shall have fair play—and I too I hope and trust—but prithee look to these recommended affairs.

[TO CHARLES F. BARRY] *10bre. 11 o 1823*

Dear Barry—As I have written to you lately—I shall not now trouble you at length.—The Greek external affairs go on well—the internal so so.——I expect Mavrocordato daily—I hear that I am joined in commission with him by the Gov[ernmen]t—and we are to proceed either against Prevesa or Patras.——But this is merely rumour—for I have no information of the report.—I have advanced four thousand pounds drawn directly on London—to the Greek Govt. to set their Squadron in motion.——The Deputies are gone to England to get the loan.—I have been detained here till now—(and am so *still*—) partly by expecting the approach of their fleet—and partly to negociate their monies—which has been done (or is doing rather) by Messrs Barff and Hancock—and in a handsome manner.—I have not yet received the dollars from Signor Corgialegno—but he has them ready he says—on demand. In my recent letter I abused the said Corgialegno to you pretty handsomely I believe—but rather more than he deserved—I guess—as one always does in a passion.—But I was exceeding wroth with him for behaving not very well to the Greeks.—But let it pass.—

You had better sell off all the things left in Genoa or Albaro—excepting my best travelling carriage—and some few books—presents from the authors—Sylla by Jouy[1]—the life of Gen[era]l Marceau—presented by his sister—a print of the same &c.—you will know the books by the authors' names being written by them on the blank leaves or title pages.—Also reserve a copy of "the Calyph Vathek[",][2]—and "Rome Naples and Florence in 1817"[3]—and the two prints of my daughter Ada;—but those of me—and the other furniture may be disposed of.—I pray you state to Mr. K[innair]d that I have written to approve of his acceptance of the offer for the Rochdale Manor—and wish to hear how he has arranged the business.——You may also tell him that I expect (through the channel of your house as most convenient for myself) further credits at the beginning of the year—not that I have any *personal* or pressing occasion—but I expect them—because it is likely the expences of part of the war will fall on me chiefly (that is as an *individual*) till the deputies obtain a *national* loan.—As I have embarked in the Cause I won't quit it,—but "in for a penny in for a pound"—I will do what I can—and all I can—in any way that seems most serviceable.—All this however renders my return rather prolonged and problematical—for who can govern circumstances?—I pray you to be of good cheer and believe me

yrs. ever
N B

[TO JOHN BOWRING] *10bre. 13bre* [sic] *1823*

Dear Sir—Since I wrote to you on the 10th Inst. the long-desired Squadron has arrived in ye waters of Messolonghi—and intercepted two Turkish Corvettes—ditto transports—destroying or taking all four,—except some of the crews escaped on shore in Ithaca—and an unarmed vessel with passengers chased into a port on the opposite side of Cephalonia.—The Greeks had fourteen Sail—the Turks *four*—but the odds don't matter—the Victory will make a very good *puff*—and be of some advantage besides.——I expect momentarily advices from

[1] See July 7, 1823, to Coulmann, note 1. (Vol. 10, p. 207.)
[2] Byron apparently had several copies of Beckford's *Vathek*. One was found with his books at Missolonghi.
[3] See May 29, 1823, to Henri Beyle. (Vol. 10, p. 189.)

Prince Mavrocordato—who is on board—and has (I understand) dispatches from the Legislative to me—in consequence of which after paying the Squadron (for which I have prepared and am preparing) I shall probably join him at Sea or on Shore. I add the above communication to my letter by Col. Napier—who will inform the Committee of every thing in detail much better than I can do.—

The Mathematical—Medical—and Musical preparations of the Committee have arrived and in good condition—abating some damage from wet—and some ditto from a portion of the letter-press being spilt in landing—(I ought not to have omitted the Press—but forgot it a moment—excuse the same) they are [pronounced?] excellent of their kind—but till we have an Engineer—and a Trumpeter—(we have Chirurgeons already) mere "pearls to Swine"—as the Greeks are ignorant of Mathematics—and have a bad ear for *our* Music;—the Maps &c.—I will put into use for them—and take care that *all* (with proper caution) are turned to the intended uses of the Committee—but I refer you to Colonel Napier—who will tell you that much of your really valuable Supplies should be removed till proper persons arrive to adapt them to actual service.—Believe me to be my dear Sir

yrs. ever

N B

P.S.—*Private.* I have written to our friend Douglas Kinnaird on my own matters—desiring him to send me out all the further credits I can command—(and I have a year's Income—and the sale of a Manor besides (he tells me) before me) for till the Greeks get *their* Loan—it is probable that I shall have to stand partly Paymaster—as far as I am "good upon *Change*"[1]—that is to say.—I pray you to repeat as much to *him*—and say that I must in the interim draw on Messrs Ransom most formidably.—To say the Truth I do not grudge it—now the fellows have begun to fight *again*—and still more welcome shall they be—if they will go on.——But they have had or *are* to have some four thousand pounds (besides some private Extraordinaries—for widows—orphans—refugees—and rascals of all descriptions) of mine at one "swoop"—and it is to be expected the next will be at least as much more and how can I refuse if they *will* fight?—and especially if I should happen ever [to] be in their company?—I therefore request and require that you should apprize my trusty and trustworthy trustee and banker and Crown and Sheet Anchor Douglas Kinnaird the Honourable—that he prepare all monies of mine—including the pur-

[1] Unidentified.

chase money of Rochdale Manor and mine income for the ensuing year A.D. 1824—to answer and anticipate any orders or drafts of mine for the Good Cause in good and lawful money of Great Britain &c. &c. &c. —May you live a thousand years!—which is 999 longer than the Spanish Cortes Constitution.

[TO COUNTESS TERESA GUICCIOLI] [*Dec. 14, 1823*]

[Added to a letter of Pietro Gamba to Teresa]

Carissima Pettegola[1]—But I forget that I must write to you in English by your own request,—well!—here we are still—but how long we may be so I cannot say.—The Greek affairs go on rather better—but I won't bore you with politics. Perhaps in the Spring—we shall be able to invite you to Zante to stay with the Grossetti's[2] and then I could come over and see you from the Morea or elsewhere. Or Pietro or I could run down to Ancona to convoy you hither—so you see—we think of your Excellency—and of your sentimental projects. The Climate up to this day—has been quite beautiful. Tuscany is Lapland in comparison—but to-day we have a high wind—and rain—but it is still as *warm* as your Prima vera.——

Pietro and I are occupied all day and every day with Greek business—and our correspondence already amounts to more volumes than even that of Santa Chiara—even when your Excellenza was in the course of your education. Pietro is full of magnificent projects—and the Greeks also—most of which *commence* and will I presume *end* (those of the Greeks I mean for Pietro is more sparing than I of our Soldi) in asking me for some money.——There is a rumour that the Legislative Govt. of the Morea—have named me jointly with Mavrocordato in some commission or other—but *which* or *what* I do not yet know—and perhaps it is only a rumour.——For my part—"me—me ne &c. &c." and leave them to project as they please—being neither ambitious nor enthusiastic on such points as you know—but always very much dearest T.

yrs. a. a. in E. +
N B

P.S.—Saluta l'Olimpia quando e *quanto* puoi della parte mia, ed anche la Giulia e la Laurina, non dimenticando Papa ed i due fratelli

1 "Dearest Gossip". Teresa tried to erase the word "Pettegola".
2 Gaetano Grassetti, a doctor friend of the Gambas, exiled from the Romagna in 1815 for having sided with the French.

&c. I Miei rispetti a Costa, e mille complimenti a sua *Siora.* Jeri fui preso dalla pioggio e "*mi duole* &c." ma non è che una cosa[passaggiera?] Pietro è stato ammalato—(lascio a *lui* dirvi di *qual' malatta*) ma Grazia alle cure dall' Dottoretto Bruno (chi è stato battezzato Brunetto *Latini* essendo piuttosto pedantico) è ora tornato in istato di salute.

[TRANSLATION OF POSTSCRIPT] *[Dec. 14, 1823]*

P.S.—Greet Olimpia from me as much and when you can and also Giulia and Laurina,[3] not forgetting Papa and your two brothers. My respects to Costa[4] and a thousand compliments to his good lady [*siora*, in Venetian dialect].

Yesterday I was caught in the rain and "*I ache* &c."[5] But it is only temporary. Pietro has been ill (I will let *him* tell you of *what ailment*) but thanks to the attentions of our little doctor Bruno, who has been christened Brunetto Latini, being rather pedantic, he is quite well again.

[TO THE GREEK COMMITTEE] *10bre. 15th. 1823*

I recommend this report strongly to the Consideration of the Committee—as I believe that it is agreed by Col. Napier and other men of experience—that it is on the whole faithful—intelligent and scientific. —Mr. Hastings[1] to the above qualities unites those of great courage and coolness as well as enterprise.

NOEL BYRON

[3] Sisters of Teresa.

[4] Professor Paolo Costa, a friend of the Gambas.

[5] Unidentified.

[1] Frank Abney Hastings (1794–1828) British naval Commander, joined the Greeks in 1822, but soon discovered that they were not very eager to welcome foreign officers or foreign advice. He wrote two long letters to Byron in the autumn of 1823. He reported that the merchant captains and sailors would rather "fail after their own manner than succeed by taking the advice of a franc." And he warned Byron that the Greeks were averse to using artillery or anything but their own muskets, and fought best as irregulars under their own leaders. In this letter, which Byron sent on to the London Committee with his own recommendation, he urged them to send out an armoured steamboat to help the Greeks obtain mastery of the seas. Despite the inaction of the Committee and the lack of encouragement from the Greeks, Hastings fitted up a steamboat, the *Karteria*, and had some spectacular successes against the Turks before he died of wounds in an attack on Anatolikon. Today there is a statue in his memory in the Garden of Heroes of the Revolution at Missolonghi.

[TO DOUGLAS KINNAIRD] *10bre. 23d. 1823*

Dear Douglas—A quarter of a year has elapsed since I have heard from you—but I have written through various channels to approve of yr. *Rochdale proposition* which I hope has gone on *well*. A Greek Vessel has arrived from the Squadron to convey me to Messolonghi—where Mavrocordato now is and has assumed the command—so that I expect to embark immediately.——Address however to Cephalonia—(through Messrs Webb and Barry of Genoa as usual) and get together all the means and credit of mine we can—to face the war establishment —for it is "in for a penny in for a pound" and I want to do all that I can for the Ancients. I have advanced them four thousand pounds—which got the Squadron to sea—and I made them forward the Deputies for the Loan—who ought to be soon in England—having sailed some weeks ago.—I have already transmitted to you a copy of their agreement &c. and to Hobhouse and Bowring various dispatches with copies or originals of correspondence more or less important. I am labouring too to reconcile their parties—and there is some hope *now* of succeeding.—Their *public* affairs go on well—the Turks have retreated from Acarnania without a battle—after a few fruitless attempts on Anatolikó,—and Corinth is taken—and the Greeks have gained a battle in the Archipelago—and the Squadron *here* too has taken a Turkish Corvette with some money and a Cargo—in short—if they can obtain a loan—I am of opinion that matters will assume & preserve a steady and favourable aspect for their independence.—

In the mean time I stand paymaster and what not—and lucky it is—that from the nature of the warfare and of the country—the resources even of an individual can be of partial and temporary service.—Col. Stanhope is at Messolonghi—probably we shall attempt Patras next—the Suliotes—who are friends of mine—seem anxious to have me with them—and so is Mavrocordato—if I can but succeed in reconciling the two parties—(and I have left no stone unturned there*for*—) it will be something—and if not—why we must go over to the Morea with the Western Greeks—who are the bravest—and at present the strongest —now that they have beaten back the Turks—and try the effect of a little *physical* advice—should they persist in rejecting *moral* persuasion. I suppose you know the state and names of the parties from my letters to Hobhouse and Bowring.——Once more (as usual) recommending to you my affairs—and more especially the reinforcement of my strongbox and credits from all lawful sources and *re*sources of mine—to their practicable extent—(and after all it is better playing at Nations than gaming at Almacks or Newmarket or in piecing or dinnering) and also requesting your Honour to write now and then one of those pithy epistles "touching the needful" so agreeable to the distant traveller. I remain

ever yrs.
N B

P.S.—Please to transmit any further credits through Messrs Webb and Barry who have been very civil and useful, all throughout.

[TO CHARLES F. BARRY] *10bre. 23d. 1823*

Dear Barry—I have received yr. three letters but can only reply briefly—as I expect to embark immediately for Messolonghi—where P[rince] Mavrocordato now is—a Greek Vessell has arrived from the Squadron to convey me there &c. I leave the enclosed letter to Mr. K[innaird] *open*, that you may read the news therein—you can put in a wafer and forward it immediately. I regret Ld. Blessington's behaviour about the bill[;] you know that he *insisted* on buying the Schooner—and had the bargain at his own price——if his bill is not paid—I must make it public—and bring the business—moreover—to a personal discussion—he shan't treat me like a tradesman *that* I promise him ——the whole purchase was of his own sueing and doing—and if *he* don't pay in one way—I must try another method of accompting.—

With regard to the things in Genoa—I really do not know what estimate to set upon them—the books and Snuff boxes would perhaps find [line cut out of manuscript] at least as except the Napoleon-box—they are of English manufacture (the Snuff-boxes i.e.) probably the Custom house would have slender claims on them—but this you will know better than I.——I have no intention of an immediate return—and circumstances do not seem to render it probable—I must see this Greek business out (or *it me*) and you might have surmised as much from the time I have already been in the vicinity.—I have sent back three of my servants the *two* included to whose families I passed an allowance which you will of course withdraw on their return. I mean Gaetano and Vincenzo—the other was a man of Count P. Gamba's—whose name I forget——Tita remains—very warlike and with his beard has acquired great consideration among the whiskered natives of the Islands.—

yrs. ever and truly
N B

P.S.—The advance you allude to in your postscript will of course be continued in the same proportion—and quarterly until I [order?] the contrary.

10bre. 24th. 1823

P.S.—Dear B—I can say nothing of Mr. Tindal's affairs, nor can enter into them further than that I advanced to him 100 dollars (to be repaid when he gets his expences from the Committee—) but will tell him what you say.—Remember me to Dr. Alexander—and tell him that Bruno is an excellent little fellow—and has done himself great honour with the sick here—and is in favour with the English—so is Gamba also.———[You] had better write to Countess Guic[ciol]i—to state that [her] brother and I are going (or gone) to Messolonghi—[and] that every thing is *quite pacific*—as well as the *business* we are upon.—This perhaps is not the exact or entire truth but it is as much as need to be stated to one who will naturally be anxious about her brother &c. &c. &c.———There will be something to be done yet—but if the Greeks get the loan—and will but keep the peace with one another—I think that they will win.—At any rate I shall "cast in my lot with the puir Hill Folk"[1] "for it shall never be said that I engaged to aid a Gentleman in a little affair of Honour and neither helped him off with it or on with it."[2] Till now—I could have been of little or no use—but the coming up of Mavrocordato—who has not only talents but integrity, makes a difference. The things left at Genoa may be disposed of (saving the travelling carriage and some books reserved) there are wines &c. and a table service rarely used and neat enough though plain—in the upper rooms—and—but—I suppose you know the whole already. In writing to Mr. Kinnaird—you may tell him that I may perhaps have to include the Rochdale purchase money (if received) among my credits—but as the sum is considerable enough—to render the interest an object—it can be invested in Exchequer bills and re-converted into Cash when I draw and *as* I draw. I suppose that is fair.

[TO JOHN BOWRING] *10bre. 26th. 1823*

Dear Sir—Little need be added to the enclosed Which have arrived this day except that I embark tomorrow for Messolonghi.—The intended operations are detailed in the annexed documents.———I have

[1] Scott's *Waverley*, Chap. 36.
[2] Unidentified.

only to request that the Committee will use every exertion to forward our views—by all it's influence and credit.—I have also to request you *personally* from myself to urge my friend and trustee Douglas Kinnaird (from whom I have not heard these four months nearly) to forward to me all the resources of my *own* we can muster for the ensuing year since it is no time to menager *purse*—or perhaps—*person*—I *have* advanced—and am advancing all that I have in hand—but I shall require all that can be got together—and (if Douglas has completed the sale of Rochdale—*that* and my years income for next year ought to form a good round sum) as you may perceive that there will be little cash of their own amongst the Greeks—(unless they get the loan) it is the more necessary that those of their friends who have any should risk it.——

The Supplies of the Committee are some useful—and all excellent in their kind—but occasionally hardly *practical* enough—in the present state of Greece—for instance the Mathematical instruments are thrown away—none of the Greeks know a problem from a poker—we must conquer first—and plan afterwards.—The use of the trumpets too may be doubted—unless Constantinople were Jericho—for the Hellenists have no ear for Bugles—and you must send us somebody to listen to them.—We will do our best—and I pray you to stir your English hearts at home to more *general* exertion—for my part—I will stick by the cause while a plank remains which can be honourably clung to—if I quit it—it will be by the Greek's conduct—and not the holy Allies or the holier Mussulmans—but let us hope better things.

ever yrs.
N B

P.S.—As much of this letter as you please is for the Committee—the rest may be "entre nous".——

P.S.[1]—I am happy to say that Colonel Leicester Stanhope and myself are acting in perfect harmony together—he is likely to be of great service both to the cause and to the Committee, and is publicly as well as personally a very valuable acquisition to our party on every account. He came up (as they all do who have not been in the country before) with some high-flown notions of the sixth form at Harrow or Eton, &c.; but Col. Napier and I set him to rights on those points, which is absolutely necessary to prevent disgust, or perhaps return; but now we can set our shoulders *soberly* to the *wheel*, without quarrelling with the mud which may clog it occasionally.

[1] This postscript is not with the manuscript, but is given in Moore, II, 699–700.

I can assure you that Col. Napier and myself are as decided for the cause as any German student of them all; but like men who have seen the country and human life, there and elsewhere, we must be permitted to view it in its truth, with its defects as well as beauties,—more especially as success will remove the former *gradually*.

N B

[TO DR. JAMES KENNEDY][1] *Dec. 26, 1823*

Dear Sir—I am too much employed to write.—Neither of these reports are true, and I presume that it is neither unjust nor ungracious to request that you will do me the favour of contradicting the words to which you allude[.][2] You will excuse the trouble I give you,—the imputation is of no great importance.——

yours ever
BYRON

[TO THOMAS MOORE] *Cephalonia, December 27th, 1823*

I received a letter from you some time ago. I have been too much employed latterly to write as I could wish, and even now must write in haste.

I embark for Missolonghi to join Mavrocordato in four-and-twenty hours. The state of parties (but it were a long story) has kept me here till *now*; but now that Mavrocordato (their Washington, or their Kosciusko) is employed again, I can act with a *safe conscience*. I carry money to pay the squadron, &c., and I have influence with the Suliotes, *supposed* sufficient to keep them in harmony with some of the dissentients;—for there are plenty of differences, but trifling.

It is imagined that we shall attempt either Patras, or the castles on the Straits; and it seems, by most accounts, that the Greeks,—at any rate, the Suliotes, who are in affinity with me of "bread and salt,"—expect that I should march with them, and—be it even so! If any thing in the way of fever, fatigue, famine, or otherwise, should cut short the middle age of a brother warbler,—like Garcilasso de la Vega,[1] Kleist,[2]

1 See Biographical Sketch in Appendix IV.

2 There is no clue to the nature of the rumours which Byron asked Kennedy to contradict.

1 Byron lists some poet-soldiers who died in battle. Garcilaso de la Vega, the "Prince of Spanish poets", born at Toledo in 1503, died from a wound while leading his men against a fortress near Frejus in 1536.

2 Ewald Christian von Kleist (born 1715) lost a leg and later died from the wound in fighting against the Russians at Kunnersdorff in 1759.

Korner,[3] Kutoffski[4] (a Russian nightingale—see Bowring's Anthology),[5] or Thersander,[6] or,—or somebody else—but never mind—I pray you to remember me in your "smiles and wine."[7]

I have hopes that the cause will triumph; but, whether it does or no, still "Honour must be minded as strictly as a milk diet."[8] I trust to observe both.

Ever, &c.

[TO JOHN CAM HOBHOUSE] *27th. 10bre. 1823*

Dear Hobhouse—I embark for Messolonghi. Douglas K[innair]d and Bowring can tell you the rest—I particularly require and entreat you to desire Douglas K[innair]d to send me soon Credits to the uttermost—that I may get the Greeks to keep the field—never mind *me*—so that the Cause goes on—if that is well—all is well.——Douglas must send me *my money* (Rochdale Manor included—if the sale is completed and the purchase money paid) the Committee must furnish *their* money—and the monied people *theirs*—with these we will soon have men enough—and all that.——

yrs. ever
N B

P.S.—Mavrocordato's letter says that my presence will "*electrify* the troops" so I am going over to "electrify" the Suliotes—as George Primrose went to Holland "to teach the Dutch English—who were fond of it to distraction."[1]

[TO DOUGLAS KINNAIRD] *10bre. 27th. 1823*

Dear Douglas—I am embarking for Missolonghi—Bowring can tell you the rest, for yr. despatches will go together.—I am passing

[3] Karl Theodor Körner (1791–1813) was killed in a skirmish with the French near Schwerin. He wrote his *Schwert-lied* a few hours before his death.

[4] Vasili Andreevitch Zhukovsky (1783–1851) wrote his *Minstrel in the Russian Camp* just before the battle on the Tarutino.

[5] Bowring had translated the *Minstrel* of Zhukovsky for his *Specimens of the Russian Poets*.

[6] Thersander was with Agamemnon on the expedition against Troy and was killed by Telephus.

[7] A phrase from one of Moore's *Irish Melodies*, "The Legacy".

[8] Unidentified.

[1] *Vicar of Wakefield*, Chap. 20.

"the Rubicon"—recollect that for God's sake—and the sake of Greece. —You must let me have all the means and credit of mine that we can *muster* or *master*—and that immediately—and I must do my best to the shirt—and to the skin if necessary.—Stretch my credit and anticipate my means to their fullest extent—if Rochdale sale has been completed I can keep an army *here*, aye, and perhaps command it.

Send me forthwith all the credits you can, and tell the Committee that they should "enact a man and put money in their purse."[1] Why, man! if we had but 100,000 *l* sterling in hand, we should now be half-way to the city of Constantine. But the Gods give us joy! "En avant", or as the Suliotes shout in their war cry—"Derrah! Derrah!" which being interpreted, means "On—On—On!"

Yours ever
N B

[TO COLONEL THE HON. LEICESTER STANHOPE]
Scrofer (or some such name), on board a Cephaloniote Mistico,[1]
Dec. 31st, 1823

My Dear Stanhope,—We are just arrived here, that is, part of my people and I, with some things, &c. and which it may be as well not to specify in a letter (which has a risk of being intercepted, perhaps);—but Gamba, and my horses, negro, steward, and the press, and all the Committee things, also some eight thousand dollars of mine (but never mind, we have more left, do you understand?) are taken by the Turkish frigates, and my party and myself, in another boat, have had a narrow escape last night (being close under their stern and hailed, but we would not answer, and bore away), as well as this morning. Here we are, with the sun and clearing weather, within a pretty little port enough; but whether our Turkish friends may not send in their boats and take us out (for we have no arms except two carbines and some

1 Perhaps a mixing of two phrases, from *Richard III*, Act V, scene 4, line 2, and *Othello*, Act I, scene 3, line 347.

1 Byron and his party left Argostoli the evening of Dec. 29, 1823, and arrived at Zante the next morning. They were travelling in two boats. Byron was in one called a "mistico", a long fast-sailing boat drawing little water. He had with him Dr. Bruno, his servant Fletcher, his Newfoundland dog Lyon, and the Moreote boy Lukas Chalandritsanos. Count Gamba was in the "bombard", a larger vessel, with most of the supplies and the servants. They left Zante in the evening and toward morning were intercepted by some Turkish warships. The mistico was able to escape and landed near the Scrofe rocks in a sheltered cove. The bombard was captured by the Turks.

pistols, and, I suspect, not more than four fighting people on board) is another question, especially if we remain long here, since we are blocked out of Messolonghi by the direct entrance.

You had better send my friend George Drake (Draco), and a body of Suliotes, to escort us by land or by the canals, with all convenient speed. Gamba and our Bombard are taken into Patras, I suppose;[2] and we must take a turn at the Turks to get them out: but where the devil is the fleet gone?—the Greek, I mean; leaving us to get in without the least intimation to take heed that the Moslems were out again.

Make my respects to Mavrocordato, and say, that I am here at his disposal. I am uneasy at being here; not so much on my own account as on that of a Greek boy[3] with me, for you know what his fate would be; and I would sooner cut him in pieces and myself too than have him taken out by those barbarians. We are all very well.

N B

The Bombard was twelve miles out when taken; at least, so it appeared to us (if taken she actually be, for it is not certain); and we had to escape from another vessel that stood right between us and the port.

[TO HENRY MUIR][1] *Dragomestri. J[anua]ry 2d. 1823 [1824]*

My dear Muir—I wish you many returns of the season—and happiness therewithal.—Gamba and the Bombarda (there is strong reason to believe) are carried into Patras by a Turkish frigate—which we saw chase them at dawn on the 31st.—We had been down under the stern in the night believing her a Greek till within pistol shot—and only escaped by a miracle of all the Saints (our Captain says) and truly I am of his opinion—for we should never have got away of ourselves.—They were signalizing their Consort with lights—and had illuminated the ship between decks—and were shouting like a Mob—but then why did they not fire? perhaps they took us for a Greek brulotte—and were

[2] Gamba was taken into Patras, but treated very well because the Captain of the bombard was known by the Turkish commander, and after a few days was released with all his cargo and arrived in Missolonghi before Byron.

[3] Lukas Chalandritsanos. See Biographical Sketch in Appendix IV.

[1] Dr. Henry Muir was Health Officer at Argostoli. It was at his house that Dr. Kennedy, a Methodist, expounded his doctrines of Christianity and tried to convert Byron and the officers of the garrison. Muir shared Byron's skeptical views and was one of his most intimate friends during his stay in Argostoli. His recollections of Byron were published in *Notes and Queries*, 6th series, Vol. IX, p. 81, 1884.

afraid of *kindling* us—they had no colours flying even at dawn nor after.—At daybreak my boat was on the coast—but the wind unfavourable for *the port*—a large vessel with the wind in her favour standing between us and the Gulph—and another in chace of the Bombard—about 12 miles off or so.—Soon after they stood (i.e. the Bombard and frigate—) apparently towards Patras and a Zantiote boat making signals to us from the shore to get away—away we went before the wind—and ran into a Creek called Scrofes (I believe) where I landed Luke and another (as Luke's life was in most danger) with some money for themselves and a letter for Stanhope and sent them up the country to Messolonghi, where they would be in safety,—as the place where we were could be assailed by armed boats in a moment—and Gamba had all our arms except two carbines—a fowling piece—and some pistols.—In less than an hour—the vessel in chace neared us—and we dashed out again—and showing our stern (our boat sails very well) got in before night to Dragomestre[2]—where we now are.—But where is the Greek fleet? I don't know—do *you*? I told our Master of the boat that I was inclined to think the two large vessels (there were none else in sight) Greeks—but he answered "they are too large—why don't they show their colours?[''] and his account was confirmed be it true or false—by several boats which we met or passed. As we could not at any rate have got in with that wind—without beating about for a long time—and as there was much property and some lives to risk (the boy's especially) without any means of defence—it was necessary to let our boatmen have their own way.——I dispatched yesterday another messenger to Messolonghi—for an escort—but we have yet no answer. We are here (those of my boat) for the fifth day—without taking our cloathes off—and sleeping on deck in all weathers—but are all very well and in good spirits.—It is to be supposed that the Govt. will send for their own sakes an escort as I have 16000 dollars on board—the greater part for their service.——I had (besides personal property to the amount of about 5000 more) 8000 dollars in specie of my own—without reckoning the Committee's stores—so that the Turks will have a good thing of it—if the prize be good.—I regret the detention of Gamba &c.—but the rest we can make up again—so tell Hancock to set my bills into cash—as soon as possible—and Corgialegno to prepare the remainder of my credit with Messrs Webb to be turned into monies.—I shall remain here (unless something extraordinary occurs) till Mavrocordato sends—and then go on—and act according to circumstances.—My respects to the two

[2] Modern Astakos on the coast above Missolonghi.

Colonels—and remembrances to all friends—tell "*Ultima Analise*"[3] that his friend Raidi[4] [sic] did not make his appearance with the brig—though I think that he might as well have spoken with us *in* or *off* Zante—to give us a gentle hint of what we had to expect.

yrs. ever affectly.

N B

P.S.—Excuse my scrawl on account of the pen and the frosty morning at daybreak—I write in haste a boat starting for Kalamo.[5]—I do not know whether the detention of the Bombard (*if* she be detained for I cannot swear to it and can only judge from appearances—and what all these fellows say) be an affair of the Govt. and Neutrality and &c.—but she *was stopped* at least 12 distant miles from any port—and had all her papers regular from *Zante* for *Kalamo* and *we also*.—I did not land at Zante being anxious to lose as little time as possible—but Sir F[rederick] S[toven][6] came off to invite me &c. and every body was as kind as could be—even in Cephalonia.—

[On cover] Lord Byron presents his respects to the Commandant of Kalamo and will feel particularly obliged if that Gentleman will forward this letter to Argostoli. [Request]ing his pardon for the trouble.

[TO CHARLES HANCOCK[1]] [*January 2, 1824*]

Dear Sr. "*Ancock*"[2]—Here we are—the Bombard taken or at least missing—with all the Committee stores—my friend Gamba—the horses—negro—bulldog—Steward—and domestics—with all our implements of peace and war—also 8000 dollars;—but whether they will be lawful prize or no—is for the decision of the Governo of the Seven Islands.—I have written to Dr. Muir by way of Kalamo with all particulars.—We are in good condition and what with wind and weather and being hunted or so a little—sleeping on deck &c. are in

[3] "Count Delladecima, to whom he gave this name, in consequence of a habit which that gentleman had of using the phrase 'in ultima analise', frequently in conversation." (Moore, II, 708.) See Oct. 25, 1823, to Barry, note 2.

[4] It should be Praidi, who was secretary to Prince Mavrocordatos.

[5] Kalamos was one of the smaller Ionian Islands near the mainland.

[6] British Resident at Zante.

[1] A British merchant at Argostoli, who with his partner Samuel Barff on Zante handled Byron's bills of exchange. See Biographical Sketch in Appendix IV.

[2] This letter is a postscript to one in Italian from Dr. Bruno who wrote at Byron's request to give details of their predicament. Dr. Bruno had begun: "Pregiatissimo Sig[no]r Ancock".

tolerable seasoning for the country and circumstances.—But I foresee that we shall have occasion for all the cash I can muster at Zante and elsewhere—Mr. Barff[3] gave us 8000 and odd dollars—so there is still a balance in my favour.—We are not quite certain that the vessels were Turkish which chaced—but there is strong presumption that they were —and no news to the contrary.—At Zante every body from the Resident downwards—were as kind as could be—especially your worthy and courteous partner.—Tell our friends to keep up their spirits—and we may yet do very well——I [disembarked] the boy[4] and another Greek who were in most per[il]—the boy at least *from* the *Morea*—which put them in safety on shore near Anatoliko I believe—and [as for me and mine we] must stick by our Goods—

yrs. ever

N B

I hope that Gamba's detention will be only temporary, as for the effects and monies—if we have them well!—if otherwise—patience. [I wish you a happy new year and all our friends the same.][5] P.S. Remember me to Muir and every body else.—I have still the 16000 dollars with me—the rest were on board the Bombarda.—

[TO LORD SYDNEY OSBORNE] *Messolonghi. Jy. 7th. 1824*

My dear Sydney—Enclosed is a *private* communication from Prince Mavrocordato to Sir Thomas Maitland—which you will oblige me much by delivering.—Sir Thomas can take as much or as little notice of it—as he pleases—but I hope—and believe that it is rather calculated to conciliate—than to irritate on the subject of the late events near Ithaca and Santa Maura[1]—which there is every disposition on the part of the Govt. here to disavow—and they are also disposed to give any satisfaction in their power.—You must all be aware how difficult it is under existing circumstances for the Greeks to keep up discipline —however well they may be disposed to do so.—I am doing all I can to convince them of the necessity of the strictest observance of the regulations of the Islands—and I trust with some effect.—

I arrived here a few days ago—after all sorts of adventures—one of my boats taken by the Turks—(but since released) the other chaced from Creek to Creek—as far as Dragomestri—and twice driven on the

[3] See Biographical Sketch in Appendix IV.
[4] Lukas Chalandritsanos.
[5] Sentence in brackets from *LJ*, VI, 303; missing in MS.
[1] See Cephalonia Journal, Dec. 17, 1823, p. 33.

rocks on the passage near Scrophes—by stress of weather—and narrowly escaping complete shipwreck.—I gave up the hole below decks to one of the people who was ill—but notwithstanding all kinds of weather—and sleeping constantly on deck—I never was better. So much so—that being somewhat *obscured* by five days and nights without ablution or change of cloathes—I thought the shortest way to kill the fleas—was to strip and take a swim—which I did on the evening of the third (I think) contrary to the remonstrance of crew—passengers —and physician—who prognosticated Cramp or fever—but idly enough —for my cold bath set all to rights—and I have been the better for it ever since.—

I was received here with every possible public and private mark of respect &c. &c. I came opportunely enough to pay their Squadron— &c.—and I have engaged to maintain a certain number of troops— with whom it is probable that I shall have to march—when an expedition now projecting takes place.[2]——If you write to any of our friends—you can say that I am in good health and spirits—and that I shall stick by the cause as long as a man of honour can—without sparing purse—or (I hope—if need be) person.——With regard to what may occur to myself—I take it a man is as liable to danger in one place as in another upon the whole—but whether it be so or not—in circumstances of this kind—such should be a secondary consideration with his friends as well as himself.

Yrs. ever dear Sydney
N B

[TO CHARLES HANCOCK] *Messolonghi. Jy. 13th. 1824*

Dear Sr. H.—Many thanks for yrs. of ye 5th. ditto to Muir for his. —You will have heard that Gamba and my vessel got out of the hands of the Turks safe and intact—nobody knows well how or why—for there is a mystery in the story somewhat melodramatic—Captain Valsamachi[1]—has I take it spun a long yarn by this time in Argostoli; —I attribute their release entirely to Saint Dionysius of Zante—and

[2] This was the proposed attack on the fortress of Lepanto (Navpactos), on the north side of the Gulf of Corinth. Byron counted much on leading his Suliote soldiers to the siege, but the assault was postponed and never took place, for the Suliotes were unruly and thought of nothing but extorting money from their foreign leader and refused to "fight against stone walls".

[1] Captain of the Greek "bombard" when it was captured by the Turkish vessel and taken into harbour at Patras. The fact that he had once saved the life of the Captain of the Turkish ship accounted for the good treatment of Gamba and his eventual release with all his cargo.

the Madonna of the Rock near Cephalonia.—The adventures of my separate bark were also not finished at Dragomestre.—We were conveyed out by some Greek Gunboats—and found the Leonidas brig of war at Sea to look after us.—But blowing weather coming on we were driven on the rocks—*twice*—in the passage of the Scrophes—and the dollars had another narrow escape.—Two thirds of the Crew got ashore over the bowsprit—the rocks were rugged enough—but water very deep close in shore—so that she was after much swearing and some exertion got off again—and away we went with a third of our crew leaving the rest on a desolate island—where they might have been now—had not one of the Gunboats taken them off—for we were in no condition to take them off again.—Tell Muir that Dr. Bruno did not show much fight on the occasion—for besides stripping to the flannel waistcoat—and running about like a rat in an emergency—when I was talking to a Greek boy[2] (the brother of the G[ree]k Girls in Argostoli) and telling him the fact that there was no danger for the passengers whatever there might be for the vessel—and assuring him that I could save both him and myself—without difficulty (though he can't swim) as the water though deep was not very rough—the wind *not* blowing *right* on shore—(it was a blunder of the Greeks who missed stays) the Doctor exclaimed—"Save *him* indeed—by G–d—save *me* rather—I'll be first if I can" a piece of Egotism which he pronounced with such emphatic simplicity—as to set all who had leisure to hear him laughing—and in a minute after—the vessel drove off again after striking twice—she sprung a small leak—but nothing further happened except that the Captain was very nervous afterwards.—To be brief—we had bad weather almost always—though not contrary—slept on deck in the wet generally—for seven or eight nights—but never was in better health (I speak personally) so much so that I actually bathed for a quarter of an hour on the evening of the fourth inst. in the sea—(to kill the fleas and others) and was all the better for it.——We were received at Messolonghi with all kinds of kindness and honours—and the sight of the fleet saluting &c. and the crowds and different costumes was really picturesque.—We think of undertaking an expedition soon—and I expect to be ordered with the Suliotes to join the army—all well at present—we found Gamba already arrived—and every thing in good condition.—Remembrance to all friends—

yrs. ever

N B

[2] Lukas Chalandritsanos, who had been sent to Missolonghi by land but apparently returned with a Greek boat which came to escort Byron into port.

P.S.—You will I hope use every exertion to realize the Assetts—for besides what I have already advanced—I have undertaken to maintain the Suliotes for a year—([and] accompany them either as a Chief or [word torn out with seal] whichever is most agreeable to the Government) besides sundries.—I do not quite understand Browne's "*letter of Credit*"—I neither gave nor ordered a letter of Credit that I know of—(and though of course if you have done it—I will be responsible) I was not aware of any thing—except that I would have backed his bills—which you said was unnecessary.—As to *orders*—I ordered nothing but some *red* cloth—and oil cloth—both of which I am ready to receive—but if Gamba has exceeded my commission the other things must be sent back *for I cannot permit anything of the kind nor will.* —The Servants' journey will of course be paid for—though *that* is exorbitant.—As for Browne's letter—I do not know anything more than I have said—and I really cannot defray the charges of half Greece and the Frank adventurers besides.———Mr. Barff must send us some dollars soon—for the expences fall on me for the present.——

P.S. 2d.—Jy. 14th. 1824 Will you tell Saint (Jew) Geronimo Corgialegno—that I mean to draw for the balance of my credit with Messrs Webb & Co;—I shall draw for two thousand dollars—(that being about the amount more or less—)but to facilitate the business I shall make the draft payable also at Messrs Ransom and Co's Pall Mall East London.—I believe I already showed you my letters (but if not I have them to show) by which besides the Credits now realizing—you will have perceived that I am not limited to any particular amount of credit with my bankers—The Honourable Douglas my friend and trustee is a principal partner in that house—and having the direction of my affairs—is aware to what extent my present resources may go—and the letters in question were from him.—I can merely say that within *the current* year, 1824, besides the money already advanced to the Greek Govt. and the credits now in your hands and yr. partner—(Mr. Barff) which are all from the income of 1823 (I have anticipated nothing from that of the present year hitherto) I shall—or ought to have at my disposition upwards of an hundred thousand dollars—(including my income—and the purchase money of a manor recently sold) and perhaps more—without impinging on my income for 1825—and not including the remaining balance of 1823.—

yrs. ever
N B

P.S.—Many thanks to Colonel Wright and Muir for their exertions about the vessell.—

[TO CHARLES HANCOCK] *Messolonghi. Jy. 17th. 1824*

Dear Sir—I have answered at some length yr. obliging letter—and trust that you have received my reply by means of Mr. Tindal.[1]—I will also thank you to remind Mr. Tindal that I would thank him to furnish you on my account with *an order on the Committee* for one hundred dollars which I advanced to him on their account through Signor *Corgialegno's* agency at Zante on his arrival in Oct[obe]r— as it is but fair that the said Committee should pay their own expences.—An order will be sufficient—as the money might be inconvenient for Mr. T[indal] at present to disburse.——I have also advanced to Mr. Blackett[2] the sum of fifty dollars which I will thank Mr. Stevens to pay to you on my account from monies of Mr. Blackett now in his hands—I have Mr. B[lackett]'s acknowledgement in writing.—As the wants of the State here are still pressing—and there seems very little Specie stirring—except mine—I still stand paymaster—and must again request you and Mr. Barff to forward by a *safe* channel (if possible) all the dollars you can collect on the bills now negociating—I have also written to Corgialegno for two thousand dollars—being about the balance of my separate letters from Messrs Webb & co. making the bills also payable at Ransom's in London.—Things are going on better—if not well—there is some order—and considerable preparation—I expect to accompany the troops on an expedition shortly[3]—which makes me particularly anxious for the remaining remittance as "money is the Sinew of War" and of Peace too—as far as I can see—for I am sure there would be no peace here without it.—However—a little *does* go a good way which is a comfort. The Govt. of the Morea—and of Candia[4]—have written to me for a further advance from my own peculium of 20- or 30-000 dollars to which I demur for the present—(having undertaken to pay the Suliotes as a free gift and other things already,[5] besides the loan which I have already advanced) till I receive letters from England which I have reason to expect.—When the expected Credits arrive I hope you will bear a hand—otherwise I must have recourse to Malta—which will be losing time—and taking trouble—but I do not wish you to do more than is perfectly agreeable to Mr. Barff and to yourself.—I am very well—and have no

1 See Dec. 7, 1823, to Bowring, note 2.

2 Blackett was an English artisan who was ill. He returned to Cephalonia.

3 To Lepanto. See Jan. 7, 1824, to Lord Sydney Osborne, note 2.

4 Crete.

5 When Byron arrived in Missolonghi he agreed to take under his command 600 Suliote soldiers. He undertook to pay for 500 and expected the Government to support 100, but the whole burden soon fell on him.

reason to be dissatisfied with personal treatment—or with the posture of public affairs,—others must speak for themselves.

yrs. ever & truly
NOEL BYRON

P.S.—Respects to Col's Wright and Duffie and the Officers civil and military—also to my friends Muir and Stevens particularly and to Della Decima.

[TO CHARLES HANCOCK] *Messolonghi Jy. 19th. 1824*

Dear Sir—Since I wrote on ye 17th. I have received a letter from Mr. Stevens enclosing an account from Corfu—which is so exaggerated in price—and quantity— that I am at a loss whether most to admire Gamba's folly—or the merchant's knavery.——All that *I* requested Gamba to order was red cloth enough to make a *jacket*—and some oil skin for trunks &c.—the latter has *not* been sent—the *whole* could not have amounted to 50 dollars.—The account is 645!!!—I will guarantee Mr. Stevens against any loss—of course—but I am not disposed to take the articles (which I never ordered) nor to pay the amount.—I will take 100 dollars worth—the rest may be sent back—and I will make the merchant an allowance of so much per Cent—or if that is not to be done—we must sell the whole by auction at what price the things may fetch—for I would rather incur the dead loss of *part*—than be incumbered with a quantity of things to me at present superfluous or useless.——Why!—I could have maintained 300 men for a month for the sum in Western Greece! When the dogs and the dollars and the Negro and the horses fell into the hands of the Turks—I acquiesced with patience (as you may have perceived) because it was the work of the Elements—of War—or of Providence—but this is a piece of mere human knavery or folly—or both—and I neither can nor will submit to it.—I have occasion for every dollar I can muster—to keep the Greeks together—and I do not grudge any expence for the Cause—but to throw away as much as would equip—or at least maintain a corps of excellent ragamuffins with arms in their hands to furnish Gamba and the Doctor with "blank books" (see list) broad Cloth—Hessian boots and horse-whips (the *latter* I own they have richly earned) is rather beyond my endurance—though a pacific person—as all the world knows—or at least my acquaintances.——

I pray you to try to help me out of this damnable commercial speculation of Gamba's—for it is one of those pieces of imprudence or folly—

which I don't forgive him in a hurry.—I will of course see Stevens free of expence out of the transaction—by the way the Greek of a Corfiote —has thought proper to draw a bill and get it *discounted* at 24 dollars— if I had been there—it should have been *protested* also.—Mr. Blackett is here ill—and will soon set out for Cephalonia.—He came to me for some pills—and I gave him some reserved for particular friends—and which I never knew any body recover from under several months— but he is no better—and (what is odd—) no worse—and as the Doctors have had no better success with him—than I—he goes to Argostoli—sick of the Greeks and of a Constipation. I must reiterate my request for *Specie*—and that speedily—otherwise public affairs will be at a standstill here.——I have undertaken to pay the Suliotes for a year—to advance in March 3000 dollars besides to the Govt. for a balance due to the troops—and some other smaller matters for the Germans and the Press—&c. &c. &c. so what with these and the expences of my own suite which though not extravagant is expensive (with Gamba's d----d nonsense) I shall have occasion for all the monies I can muster—and I have credits wherewithal to face the undertakings if realized—and expect to have more soon—believe me

ever and truly yrs.

N B

[TO G. STEVENS[1]] *Messolonghi Jy. 19th. 1824*

My dear Sir/—I have just received yr. very kind letter—you will have heard long ago—that Gamba got away without damage—and that after some escapes of my own boat (twice pretty narrowly from Shipwreck, as our boatmen ran us on the rocks) and some fatigue and hard weather—we all got in to Messolonghi.—For further particulars —I refer you (if it interests you) to Gamba's epistle and mine to Mr. Hancock and to Muir.—With regard to the order—and bills &c. of Gamba—and all these bales of Cloth—which are a perfect mystery to me (as I never heard of them till this moment) Gamba must explain himself with you—for I know nothing of the matter—nor will have anything to do with it except to see that *you* sustain no loss—of course; —if he and Master Browne[2] have managed this between them, I can only say that they are fitter to manage their own concerns than mine— and that I am—(as I have always been) a damned fool to permit them to interfere in any business of my own.—However—no possible blame

[1] Customs officer in Argostoli.

[2] Byron's translation of Dr. Bruno's name.

can attach to you—and as I said before "coute qui coute"—you shall sustain no loss whatever.—

I have little news to add to what are contained in my letters to Hancock and Muir—we are discussing and preparing for active operations—and (as I have told Hancock—) I must muster all the means in my compass as I am paymaster "pro tempore" and Heaven knows what besides——willing to do what I can—in any post in which they may be pleased to place me—and having no choice—being about as fit for one as another—and tr[uly] not ambitious of a very high one—which is more than can be said of some of our adventurers.——Blackett returns to Cephalonia—very unwell—and (like all the rest hitherto) thoroughly tired of the Greeks and of their cause into the bargain.—He owes me fifty dollars—which I will trouble you to remit from his monies to Hancock on account—I have Blackett's acknowledgement. This accursed Cloth merchandizing of Gamba—seems likely to cost more than five hundred men—for a month nearly;—for it is certain that *here*—few five hundred men have received so much for almost a year.—But this comes of letting boys play the man—all his patriotism diminishes into the desire of a sky blue uniform and be d——d to him—for a coxcomb.—Best remembrances to all friends military and civic—and to Delladecima[.]

ever yrs. faithfully
N B

P.S.—I fear the only remedy (and that is a bad one) is to have the things sold by auction for what they will fetch and to abide by the loss on the sale—I shall at any rate save something by this—and pay rather less for Gamba's imprudence—and my own folly; I can not in the present circumstances of the Greeks afford to throw away a sixpence except upon *their* nonsense—and Gamba's must stand over till another time.—You will therefore have the goodness to dispose of them as you best can—as for me—I mean to stick by the Greeks to the last rag of canvas or shirt—and not to go snivelling back like all the rest of them up till now nearly—if it can be avoided, that is to say.——I must also say that the prices are said to be very exorbitant (of the cloth account) but of this I am no judge—except that I have to pay for it.——

[TO YUSUFF PASHA] *Missolonghi, Jy. 23d. 1824*

[Draft in Byron's own hand]

Altezza—Un bastimento con alcuni miei amici e domestici è stato portato sotto i Castelli da una frigata Turca. E stato il quel [nave?] rilasciato per ordine di A[ltezza] V[ostro]. Io lo ringrazio non per aver' rilasciato il bastimento—poiche quello ebbe bandiera neutrale e protezione Inglese—dunque nessun aveva diritto di ritenerlo—ma par aver' trattato i miei amici con somma cortesia—finchè [erano?] sotto la di lei disposizione.——Nella speranza di fare una cosa non dispiace [all'?] V[ostro] A[ltezza] io ho pregato il Governo Greco qui—di mettere [all' mio?] disposizione quattro prigionieri mussulmani—ciò che Ella ha gentilmente accordata.——Li mando dunque in libertà a V. A. per contracambiare di ciò che ho potuto alla di Lei cortesia.——Sono mandati senza condizione—ma se la cosa può meritare un luogo nella vostra memoria—pregherò solamente V. A. di trattare con humanità [sic] qualche Grecho [sic] che può essere [costi?] o che accadere nelle mani dei Mussulmani—giacchè li orrori della Guerra sono sufficienti in loro stesse senza aggiungere nè da una parte e dell' altra della durezza a sangue freddo.—

Ho l'onore di essere &c. &c. &c.

[At the top of a copy (corrected) of this letter in the hand of Pietro Gamba, Byron has written:]

Fy. 29th. 1824. This is the Copy of a letter sent to Jussuff Pacha with four Turkish prisoners released at my request—the other four and twenty were sent by me to Prevesa with a letter for the English Consul General.

N Bn

[TRANSLATION] *J[anuar]y 23d. 1824*

Highness—A ship with some of my friends and servants on board was brought under the turrets of a Turkish frigate. It was then released on the order of Your Highness. I thank you, not for having released the ship—since it had a neutral flag and was under English protection, so that no one had the right to detain it—but for having treated my friends with the utmost courtesy—while they were at your disposition. ——In the hope of performing an action not displeasing to Your Highness I have asked the Greek Government here to place four Mussulman prisoners in my hands.—I now release them to Your Highness in recompense, as far as is possible, for your Courtesy.—They are sent without conditions—but if the circumstances could win a place in your memory I would only beg Your Highness to treat with humanity any Greek who may be [captured?] or fall into the hands of the Mussulmans—Since the horrors of war are sufficient in themselves without adding cold-blooded ruthlessness on either side.—

I have the honour to be etc. etc. etc.[1]

[TO MESSRS BARFF AND HANCOCK] *Messolonghi.—Jy. 24th. 1824*

Gentlemen—I have the honour to advise you that I have this day drawn on your house for the sum of thirteen hundred dollars in two drafts one of one thousand—and the other of three hundred dollars. ——It is probable that in a day or two I may draw for one thousand more in the same manner.——You can place these sums to my account —deducting them from the balance (at present in your hands) of and for

yr. very obedt. Servt. and obliged friend
NOEL BYRON

P.S.—All well *here* as *yet*. I will write soon more in detail.—My respects to all friends.—I sent letters to Argostoli this day by another boat.

[TO GREEK CAPTAINS OF PRIVATEERS] *G[ennaï]o 27 1824*

[In Byron's own hand]

Lord Byron risponde ai sottoscritti Signori—che certamente Egli si è interessato per la liberazione della mantenata barca Ionia—ma ciò solamente per il' vantaggio del' Governo Greco e dei Greci istessi—i quali altramente vanno precipitarsi in una lite Summossima col' Governo Ionio—ed Inglese—della quale non si vede ancora che il principio.—Sopra la decisione dei tribunali Lord Byron non ha e non pretende la minima influenza;—I Giudici e la legge decideranno secondo la codice;—Lord Byron si contenta di far il *suo* proprio dovere —e quel' dovere era in questo momento—di rappresentare al' Governo Greco—la consequenza inevitabile delle loro procedure—in riguardo alla bandiera Ionia——Lord Byron non ha e non può avere nessun' interessa personale—nè per una parte—nè per l'altra.—

[TRANSLATION] *Jan. 27, 1824*

Lord Byron replies to the subscribers of the petition, that doubtless

[1] Translated by Antony Peattie.

he feels himself interested in the restoration of the Ionian boat, [the *Don Giovanni*]; but that he is so solely for the sake of the Greek government, and of the Greeks themselves, who, unless they comply, will rush headlong into a most dangerous controversy with the Ionian and with the English Governments,[1] of which the beginning alone can as yet be seen. Over the decision of the tribunals, Lord Byron has not, nor pretends to have, the slightest influence. The judges and the law must decide according to the code. Lord Byron has confined himself to doing that which is *his* own duty, which in this case was to represent to the Greek government the inevitable consequences of their proceedings with respect to the Ionian flag. Lord Byron neither has, nor can have, any personal interest for one side or the other.[2]

[TO SAMUEL BARFF] *Messolonghi*, [*Jan. 27, 1824*]

[Written at end of letter of Pietro Gamba to Barff]

Dear Sir—The Turkish Fleet is on the look out—so that I request you to take care *how* you send me *specie*—though we are in great want of it at present—for the Govt.—If a *safe* conveyance occurs—let us see some—

yrs. ever
N BN

P.S.—I write in great haste.—The Hon[oura]ble Captain Yorke[1] of the Vessel now here on remonstrance with the Greeks—will carry to Zante all the public news probably——will you present my respects to Col. Stoven[2]—and Mr. [Banier?][3]—and my remembrances to Dr. Thomas[4] if you see them.—I hope that things here will go on well—some time or other. I will stick by the Cause as long as a Cause exists first or second.——

[1] The Greeks had captured an Ionian caïque and confiscated merchandise worth about 400 dollars. Byron believed it was in the interest of the Greeks to keep on good terms with the European powers, especially the English in the Ionian Islands, who, though they (representing the British Government) were ostensibly neutral, had already been of great service to them.

[2] Translation (modified) from Gamba, p. 136.

[1] Captain Yorke of the English gun-brig *Alacrity* had come to Missolonghi to ask restitution of the privateers. Byron supported his claim, which was for half the value of the cargo seized. When the Greeks refused to pay, Byron supplied the money himself as if it were from the Government, in order to avoid trouble and embarrassment to them.

[2] Sir Frederick Stoven was the British Resident at Zante.

[3] Unidentified.

[4] English physician at Zante.

[TO COUNTESS TERESA GUICCIOLI] *Missolonghi*, [*Jan. 27, 1824*]

[Added to letter of Pietro Gamba to Teresa]

My dearest Teresa—We have been here since 10bre. 31 o—or rather since G[ennai]o 8 o[1] for that was the day on which we arrived.—You will have heard of our adventures from other quarters.—We are well and all here is well—I will write soon at greater length—in the interim Love me—and be assured—that you are the most Beloved of yrs. + + +

N Bn

[TO CAPTAIN YORKE] *Messolonghi. Jy. 27th. 1824*

Ld. Byron presents his Compliments to Capt. Yorke. The Stock such as was attainable in this place and the neighbourhood—is sent—and Ld. B. has only to regret that it is not more worth sending—it is however the best that could be extracted from this Marsh. There has been no account sent in—and the price must be in itself so very trifling—that Ld. B. begs Capt. Yorke will not think a moment on the subject—as on some future occasion Ld. B. hopes to indemnify himself with interest from the Navy stores and more particularly those of Captain Yorke.——[1]

[TO JOHN BOWRING] *Messolonghi J*[*anuar*]*y 28, 1824*

Dear Sir/—As Colonel Stanhope will probably have written frequently to inform the Committee of the state of public affairs here and throughout Greece—I have little to say on that subject—and as to my private concerns they can have no attraction for anybody—further than as connected with the emancipation of this country.——I hope that the Hon[oura]ble Douglas Kinnaird has received my various letters written in Cephalonia—because (as far as my own resources go) they bear a reference to public matters here—and to say the truth—till either the Public or the Capitalists come forward—and that *speedily*—I shall probably have more demands upon me—than an individual how-

[1] The "mistico" with Byron on board actually landed at Missolonghi on Jan. 4, and he went ashore the following morning.

[1] A note with the manuscript, now in the British Library, says that Capt. Yorke having left port in the *Alacrity*, the letter was never delivered and remained among Lega Zambelli's papers.

ever well disposed—or even provided—can—or could—easily supply. ——If the Committee in lieu of stores could furnish pecuniary succours to the Greeks—I am inclined to think that the service rendered would be more considerable.——

We are blockaded here by the Turkish Squadron sixteen sail in all—frigates—Corvettes—and Craft included.—An English Brig of War has been here to reclaim some boats taken,—the affair of Ithaca has spoilt—or retrograded all our relations with the Islands for the present;—and I cannot but condemn the want of discipline and authority which has led to the acts of *piracy* in question (for they are no better) and to the measures in consequence of the English Govt.;—I must speak freely here as well as elsewhere—and as I never flattered Power—neither will I sanction License;—The Greeks are acting in my opinion neither wisely nor well in permitting for a moment the predatory detention of the Ionian vessels;—if they choose to commence buccaneering—be it so—but let it be without pretension to any better excuse than that of necessity.—

On my way here—my boats had some narrow escapes—one vessel (A Bombard) was taken by the Turks into Patras—and afterwards released—the other (on board of which I was) was pursued but got away and afterwards ran twice on the rocks between this and Dragomestre—but after 8 days—we got back again and in to Messolonghi—where we were very well received—and—by most accounts—arrived at a proper time to be of some—at least *temporary* utility.

An expedition of about two thousand men is planned for an attack on Lepanto—and for reasons of policy with regard to the native Capitani—who would rather be (nominally at least) under the command of a foreigner—than of one of their own body—the direction it is said—is to be assigned to me—there is also another reason—which is—that if a Capitulation should take place—the Mussulmans might perhaps rather have *Christian* faith with a Franc than with a Greek—and so be inclined to concede a point or two;—these appear to be the most obvious motives for such an appointment—as far as I or any body else can conjecture—unless there be *one* reason more—*viz*—that under present circumstances—no one else—(not even Mavrocordato himself) seems disposed to accept such a nomination—and though my desires are as few as my deserts upon this occasion—I do not decline it—being willing to do as I am bidden—and as I pay a considerable portion of the Clans—I may as well see what they are likely to do for their money—besides I am tired of hearing nothing but talk—and Constitutions—and Sunday Schools—and what not &c.—all excellent things in their time and place—and *here also*—whenever they have means—money—leisure—and freedom to try the experiment.—If anything particular occurs—I will state it—or if I cannot—Col. S[tanhope] will keep the Committee duly apprized—

I am ever and truly yrs.
N B

P.S.—Parry is not arrived yet—I presume from this retardment that he is the same Parry who attempted the *North* pole—and is (it may be supposed) now essaying the *South*.

[TO ANDREAS LONDOS] *Messolonghi—30/18 Gennaio 1824*

[In Pietro Gamba's hand—signed by Byron]

Stimattissimo Signore ed Amico—Mi è stato gratissimo il vedere i vostri caratteri[.] La Grecia è sempre stata per me come è per tutti gli uomini di una qualche educazione e sentimente la terra promessa del valore delle arti e della libertà in tutti i secoli—ed i viaggi che feci nella mia Gioventù fra le sue rovine certamente non avevano diminuito il mio Amore per la Patria degli Eroi ma oltre ciò io ho verso di voi dei doveri di Amicizia e di riconoscenza per la vostra Ospitalità durante il mio soggiorno nel Paese, dal quale siete divenuto uno dei difensori ed Ornamenti. Il rivedervi, e servire la vostra Patria al vostro fianco, e sotto ai vostri occhi—sara per me uno dei momenti più felice della mia vita [.] Intanto vi prego di comandarmi e credermi adesso come per sempre stato

Vostro [devotissimo?] A[mico] e Servo.
NOEL BYRON. Pari d'Inghilterra

[TRANSLATION] *Missolonghi—30/18 January—1824*

Most esteemed Sir and friend—The sight of your handwriting gave me the greatest pleasure. Greece has ever been for me, as it must be for all men of any feeling or education, the promised land of valour, of the arts, and of liberty throughout all the ages; and the journeys I made in my youth amongst her ruins certainly had not diminished my love for the heroes' native land. In addition to this, I am bound to yourself by ties of friendship and gratitude for the hospitality which I experienced from you during my stay in that country,[1] of which you are now become one of the defenders and ornaments. Seeing you again and serving your country at your side and under your eyes, will be one of the happiest moments of my life. In the mean time, I beg you to command me and believe me now as always

your [most devoted] Friend and Servant
NOEL BYRON, Peer of England[2]

[TO EDWARD BLAQUIERE] *Feb. 1, 1824*

[Note added to the letter of Mavrocordatos in French]

. . . Certainly *not,* unless P. Mavrocordato wishes to risk his influence, and the hopes of Greece for the present.[1] . . . I have hardly a moment to write for the boat is going—things look well—d——n the Chevaliers d'Industrie de Malte.[2] Keep up your spirits and we will see what is to be done.

[TO PRINCE ALEXANDER MAVROCORDATOS]

Missolonghi li 5 febbraio 1824

[In an unknown hand—signed by Byron and Stanhope]

Principe—Abbiamo l'onore di informarvi che il Comitato Greco di Inghilterra ha mandato in Grecia un' elaboratorio completo coi necessarii artefici, che si stabilisce ora in Missolonghi. Il Comitato con questa sua misura, come in tutte le altre, brama di avvanzare le cognizioni, e del pari la Libertà della Grecia.

Quest' elaboratorio è capace di preparare, e formare tutti i materiali dei guerra tanto pel servizio marittimo, che di terra. Può costrurre bastimenti di qualunque specie, fondere cannoni, mortai, palle, e bombe

[1] Byron and Hobhouse had in 1809 stayed for several days with the young Londos at Vostitza (modern Aigion) on the south shore of the Gulf of Corinth. Although Londos was then a Cogia Basha, or governor of the district under the Turks, he manifested strong patriotic feelings at the mention of the name of Rhiga, founder of the Hetairia, a society that fostered nationalistic sentiments. Rhiga was executed by the Turks in 1798 for his political activities.

[2] This translation is a modification of that given in Moore, II, 729.

[1] Mavrocordatos had declined Blaquiere's invitation to come to England.

[2] There was a rumour that the Resurrection Knights of Malta, under the influence of France, had offered to assist the Greeks with a loan in exchange for the island of Rhodes and other eastern islands belonging to Greece. (See Stanhope, p. 108.) This was another argument for hastening the English loan.

di Schreipnel; costrurre carri d'ogni forma, fare polvere, razzi alla Congreve, ed ogni sorta di fuochi incendiari.

Il Direttore, o mastro di fuoco può dare insegnamenti per la pratica dell'artiglieria, per gettare de bombe, i razzi, e per tutta l'arte di fabbricare ogni materiale di guerra. Questo elaboratorio puossi considerare non solo qual' utile sorgente di tutti i bignos [bisogni] della guerra, ma pure qual modello, e scuola.

Avendo fatto uno schizzo del carattere di questa parte; desideriamo di informarvi che esso tutto è solo per la pubblica utilità, perciò vi preghiamo di additarci immantinente in qual modo volete servirvi di questo stabilimento. Bramiamo pure di sapere quali sono gli oggetti che giudicate necessari da prepararsi per l'espedizione che è sul punto di intraprendersi. E nell' aspettativa di una pronta risposta, passiamo con distinta stima a dirci

di V[ostro] Ecc[elenza] divotissimi Servi

NOEL BYRON

LEICESTER STANHOPE

[TRANSLATION] *Missolonghi, February 5, 1824*

Prince,—We have the honour of informing you that the Greek Committee of England has sent a complete laboratory to Greece, with all the necessary craftsmen, which is now being established in Missolonghi.[1] The Committee by this measure, as in all others, hopes to advance the knowledge, and thereby the liberty, of Greece.

This laboratory is capable of preparing and manufacturing all war materials for land as well as for maritime service. It can construct ships of every type, cast cannons, mortars, bullets, and Shrapnel bombs, construct [artillery] carriers of every sort, make powder, Congreve rockets, and every sort of incendiary fire.

The Director, or fire master, can give instructions for the use of artillery, for throwing bombs and rockets, and for the whole craft of producing every material of war. This laboratory can be considered not only a useful source for all the needs of war, but also a model and a school.

Having made a sketch of the character of this equipment, we wish to inform you that all of this is only for the public benefit. Therefore we

[1] Early in February William Parry, the fire-master sent out by the London Greek Committee, arrived with the store ship *Ann* and a number of mechanics and craftsmen for the construction of war materials for the Greeks. For details of Parry see Biographical Sketch in the Appendix IV.

beg you to point out to us at once, in what way this factory might be of service to you. We also would like to know which articles you consider necessary to prepare for the expedition that is about to take place. And in awaiting your prompt reply, we declare ourselves with the utmost esteem, Your Excellency's

Most devoted Servants[2]
NOEL BYRON
LEICESTER STANHOPE

[TO CHARLES HANCOCK] *Messolonghi. F[ebbrai]o 5 o 1824*

Dear Sir—Dr. Muir's letter and yrs. of the 23d. reached me some days ago,—tell Muir that I am glad of the promotion for his sake—and of his remaining near us for all our sakes,—though I cannot but regret Dr. Kennedy's departure—which accounts for the previous earthquakes and the present English weather in this climate.—With all respect to my medical pastor—I have to announce to him that amongst other firebrands, our firemaster Parry (just landed) has disembarked an elect blacksmith—entrusted with three hundred and twenty two Greek testaments,——I have given him all facilities in my power for his works spiritual and temporal—and if he can settle matters as easily with the Greek Archbishop and hierarchy I trust that neither the heretic nor the supposed Sceptic will be accused of intolerance.——

By the way—I met with the said Archbishop at Anatoliko[1] (where I went by invitation of the Primates a few days ago—and was received with a heavier cannonade than the Turks probably) for the second time—(I had known him here before) and he and P[rince] Mavrocordato—and the Chiefs and Primates & I all dined together—and I thought the Metropolitan the merriest of the party—and a very good Christian for all that.——But Gamba (we got wet through on our way back) has been ill with a fever and Cholic—and Luke (not the Evangelist—but a disciple of mine) has been out of sorts too—and so have some others of the people—and I have been very well—except that I caught cold yesterday with swearing too much in the rain at the Greeks —who would not bear a hand in landing the Committee stores and nearly spoiled our combustibles;—but I turned out in person and made

[2] Transcribed and translated by Ricki B. Herzfeld.

[1] Gamba (*Narrative*, p. 151 ff.) gives an account of the visit of Byron and Mavrocordatos and others to the village of Anatolico, a few miles up the coast from Missolonghi. The town had bravely defended itself from an attack from a much larger force of Turks. It received Byron as if he were a conquering hero.

such a row as set them in motion—blaspheming at them all from the Government downwards—till they actually did *some* part of what they ought to have done several days before—and this is esteemed as it deserves to be—a wonder.——

Tell Muir that notwithstanding his remonstrance—which I receive thankfully—it is perhaps best that I should advance with the troops for if we do not do something soon we shall have a third year of defensive operations—and another siege and all that—we hear that the Turks are coming down in force and sooner than usual—and as these fellows do mind me a little—it is the opinion that I should go,—firstly—because they will sooner listen to a foreigner than one of their own people—out of native jealousies—secondly, because the Turks will sooner treat or capitulate (if such occasions should happen) with a Frank than a Greek—and thirdly,—because nobody else seems disposed to take the responsibility—Mavrocordato being very busy here—the foreign military men too young—or not of authority enough to be obeyed by the natives—and the Chiefs—(as aforesaid—) disinclined to obey any one except or rather than one of their own body.——

As for me—I am willing to do what I am bidden and to follow my instructions—I neither seek nor shun that nor any thing else that they may wish me to attempt—and as for personal safety—besides that it ought not to be a consideration—I take it that a man is on the whole as safe in one place as another—and after all he had better end with a bullet than bark in his body;—if we are not taken off with the sword—we are like to march off with an ague in this mud-basket—and to conclude with a very bad pun—to the ear rather than to the eye—better—*mart*ially—than *marsh*-ally;—the Situation of Messolonghi is not unknown to you;—the Dykes of Holland when broken down are the Desarts of Arabia for dryness in comparison.——

And now for the sinews of War——I thank you and Mr. Barff for your ready answer which next to ready money is a pleasant thing.——Besides the Assets—and balance—and the relics of the Corgialegno correspondence with Leghorn and Genoa (I sold the dog's flour tell him but not at *his* price) I shall request and require from the beginning of March ensuing—about five thousand dollars every two months—i. e. about twenty five thousand within the current year—at regular intervals—independent of the sums now negociating. I can show you documents to prove that these are considerably *within* my supplies for the year in more ways than one—but I do not like to tell the Greeks *exactly—what*—I *could* or would advance on an emergency—because otherwise they will double and triple their demands (a disposition that they have already shown) and though I am willing to do all I can *when* necessary—yet I do not see why *they* should not help a little—for they are not quite so bare as they pretend to be by some accounts.——

Fy. 7th. 1824

I have been interrupted by the arrival of Parry and afterwards by the return of Hesketh[2] who has not brought an answer to my epistles which rather surprizes me.—You will write soon I suppose. Parry seems a fine rough subject—but will hardly be ready for the field these three weeks;—he and I will (I think) be able to draw together—at least *I* will not interfere with or contradict him in his own department, he complains grievously of the mercantile and en*thu*sy*mu*sy (as Braham pronounces enthusiasm) part of the Committee—but greatly praises Gordon[3] and Hume[4],—Gordon *would* have given three or four thousand pounds and come out himself—but Bowring or somebody else disgusted him—and thus they have spoiled part of their subscription and cramped their operations.——Parry says Blaquiere is a humbug;—to which I say nothing.—He sorely laments the printing and civilizing expences—and wishes that there was not a Sunday School in the world—or *any* school *here* at present save and except always an academy for Artilleryship.——He complained also of the Cold—a little to my surprize—firstly because there being no chimneys—I have used myself to do without other warmth than the animal heat and one's Cloak—in these parts—and secondly because I should as soon have expected to hear a Volcano sneeze—as a Fire-master (who is to burn a whole fleet—) exclaim against the atmosphere.—I fully expected that his very approach would have scorched the town like the burning glasses of Archimedes.—Well—it seems that I am to be Commander in Chief—and the post is by no means a sinecure—for we are not what Major Sturgeon calls "a Set of the most amicable officers" whether we shall have "a boxing bout between Captain Sheers and the Colonel"[5] I cannot tell—but between Suliote Chiefs—German Barons—English Volunteers—and adventurers of all Nations—we are likely to form as goodly an allied army—as ever quarrelled beneath the same banner.—

[2] Capt. Henry Hesketh was a young Englishman in the Greek service whom Byron sent with letters to Argostoli.

[3] Thomas Gordon, see p. 39, note 1.

[4] Joseph Hume M.P. was another wealthy Scot who was one of the active members of the London Greek Committee. For an account of the Committee and its members see William St. Clair, *That Greece Might Still Be Free*, p. 140 *passim*.

[5] Samuel Foote, *The Mayor of Garratt*, Act I, scene 1.

Fy. 8th. 1824

Interrupted again by business—yesterday—and it is time to conclude my letter.—I drew some time since on Mr. Barff for a thousand dollars—to complete some money wanted by the Govt.—The said Government got cash on that bill *here* and at a profit—but the very same fellow who paid it to them—after promising to give me money for other bills on Barff to the amount of thirteen hundred dollars either could not or thought better of it;—I had written to Barff advising him —but had afterwards to write to tell him of the fellow's having not come up to time.——You must really send me the balance soon—I have the Artillerists—and my Suliotes to pay and heaven knows what besides—and as every thing depends upon punctuality—all our operations will be at a stand still—unless you use dispatch.—I shall send to Mr. Barff or to you—further bills on England for three thousand pounds—to be negociated as speedily as you can——I have already stated here and formerly—the sums I can command at home—within the year—(without including my credits or the bills already negociated or negociating—or Corgialegno's balance of Messrs Webb's letter) and my letters from my friends (received by Mr. Parry's vessel) confirm what I already stated.—How much I may require in the course of the year I can't tell but I will take care that it shall not exceed the means to supply it.——

yrs. ever
N B

P.S.—I have had by desire of a Mr. *Gerostati*?[6]—to draw on Demetrius Delladecima (is it our friend "in Ultima Analise") to pay the Committee expences;— I really do not not [sic] understand what the Committee mean by some of their [proceedings?];——Parry and I get on very well *hitherto*—how long this may last Heaven knows—but I hope it will for a good deal for the Greek service depends upon it—but he has already had some *miffs* with Col. S[tanhope]—and I do all I can to keep the peace amongst them—however Parry is a fine fellow—extremely active—and of strong—sound—practical talent by all accounts.——Enclosed are bills for three thousand pounds—drawn in the mode directed (i.e. parcelled out in smaller bills—) a good opportunity occurring for Cephalonia—to send letters on I avail myself of it. —Remembrances to Stevens and all friends—also my Compliments and everything kind to the Colonels and officers.

P.S.—2d. or 3d. Fy. 9th. 1824. I have reason to expect a person

[6] Unidentified.

from England directed with papers (on business) for me to sign—somewhere in the Islands—by and bye;—if such should arrive would you forward him to me by a safe conveyance—as the papers regard a transaction with regard to the adjustment of a lawsuit—and a sum of several thousand pounds—which I or my bankers and trustees for me—may have to receive (in England) in consequence.—The time of the probable arrival—I cannot state—[but] the date of my letters is the 2d. Novr. and I suppose that he ought to arrive soon.—

[TO DOUGLAS KINNAIRD] *Messolonghi Fy. 9th. 1824*

My dear Douglas—I have received yrs. of the 2d. Novr.—The sooner the papers to be signed in the Rochdale business the better—and it is essential that the money should be paid—as I shall have occasion for it all—and more—to help on the Greeks—and fight it out. Hunt's Son went back sick from Malta—but I have received his letter which is very satisfactory—if all be true that be up-come.—Bid him go on and prosper.[1]—The Deputies should be arrived ere now.—Parry is here—and he and I agree very well—and all is going on hopefully for the present—considering circumstances.——I march (according to orders) against Lepanto shortly with two thousand men.——I have this day drawn on your house various bills to the amount of three thousand pounds *Sterling*—which you will debit or credit accordingly—and according to any funds received or in the course of being so—as Income—Noel estates due—Rochdale purchase—Copyrights &c. &c. &c. En attendant—with some impatience—further letters of credit—for which I have written by every opportunity—I pray you to consider this as essential and indispensable. Your Committee ought to stir a little more. We shall have work this year for the Turks are coming down in force—and as for me I must stand by the Cause.

yrs ever
N B

[TO SAMUEL BARFF] *Missolonghi [Feb. 11, 1824]*

[Added to letter of Pietro Gamba to Barff]

[1] John Hunt published Cantos VI to XVI of *Don Juan*. Cantos XII, XIII, and XIV had been published in December, 1823, but Cantos XV and XVI did not appear until March 26, 1824, a few days before Byron died. Hunt's son was on his way to join the Philhellenic cause when he was turned back by illness.

Dear Sir—The Bearers—Mr. Fawke [Fowke] and Mr. Hodges[1] are authorized to receive the balance to what amount may be ready from you or Mr. Hancock—I have also enclosed bills on England for a further sum of three thousand pounds in a letter to Mr. Hancock—

yrs. ever truly
N B

[TO COUNTESS TERESA GUICCIOLI] *Missolonghi [Feb. 11, 1824]*

[Added to letter of Pietro Gamba to Teresa]

My dearest T.—All well,—I will write shortly at greater length.—I have found a very pretty Turkish female infant of ten years old—whom I mean to send to you by and bye—she is beautiful as the Sun—and very lively—you can educate her—[1]

yrs. ever
N B

[NOTE ON SULIOTES] *Fe[bbrai]o 15 o 1824*

Having tried in vain at every expence—considerable trouble—and some danger to unite the Suliotes for the good of Greece—and their own—I have come to the following resolution.—

[1] Fowke was one of the English artisans who came with Parry. John M. Hodges was a laboratory assistant to Parry, who was later induced by Stanhope to found the *Greek Telegraph*. He had come out on the *Ann* and was well thought of by Parry. After Byron's death he continued in the Greek service and kept a journal, part of which was published in a private pamphlet by his great-grandson, Norman Tucker, in 1948. Unfortunately this published part of the diary starts in October, 1824, but the pamphlet contains some information about, and quotations from, the earlier diary covering the period of Byron's life and death in Missolonghi. This earlier diary went to another branch of the family and was sold at Puttick and Simpson's sale on June 17, 1904.

[1] This Turkish girl, Hatagée (nine years old, according to Millingen), and her mother, were refugees or rather slaves of the Greeks. Most of their male relatives had been massacred in the first days of the Revolution. Dr. Millingen had taken them into his household to protect them. Byron took an interest in the little girl and wanted to send her either to Teresa or to his sister, and even had the fleeting notion that she might be taken by Lady Byron as a playmate for his daughter Ada. In the end he asked Dr. Kennedy to care for her and her mother, who had learned that her husband was alive and with Yussuf Pasha. Byron had curiously anticipated the situation in *Don Juan* (Canto VIII) where the hero rescued a little Turkish girl in the battle of Ismael.

I will have nothing more to do with the Suliotes—they may go to the Turks or—the devil ⟨but if⟩ they may cut me into more pieces than they have dissensions among them, sooner than change my resolution—[1]

For the rest I hold my means and person at the disposal of the Greek Nation and Government the same as before.

[1] The Suliote soldiers had demanded that about 150 of the 300 or 400 hundred be raised above the rank of common soldier. The purpose was to increase their pay. Byron was angry and disillusioned. The Suliotes found that they had gone too far and agreed to form a new corps directly under Byron's control. He agreed reluctantly, but he was dispirited by the necessity of postponing the attack on Lepanto and by a more realistic view of the soldiers he had idealized as the bravest and best of the Greeks.

JOURNAL[1]

February 15th. 1824

Upon February 15th—(I write on the 17th. of the same month) I had a strong shock of a Convulsive description but whether Epileptic—Paralytic—or Apoplectic is not yet decided by the two medical men who attend me—or whether it be of some other nature (if such there be) it was very painful and had it lasted a moment longer must have extinguished my mortality—if I can judge by sensations.—I was speechless with the features much distorted—but *not* foaming at the mouth—they say—and my struggles so violent that several persons—two of whom—Mr. Parry the Engineer—and my Servant Tita the Chasseur are very strong men—could not hold me—it lasted about ten minutes—and came on immediately after drinking a tumbler of Cider mixed with cold water in Col. Stanhope's apartments.—This is the first attack that I have had of this kind to the best of my belief. I never heard that any of my family were liable to the same—though my mother was subject to *hysterical* affections. Yesterday (the 16th.) Leeches were applied to my temples. I had previously recovered a good deal—but with some feverish and variable symptoms;—I bled profusely—and as they went too near the temporal Artery—there was some difficulty in stopping the blood—even with the Lunar Caustic—this however after some hours was accomplished about eleven o'clock at night—and this day (the 17th.) though weakly I feel tolerably convalescent.———

With regard to the presumed cause of this attack—as far as I know there might be several—the state of the place and of the weather permits little exercise at present;—I have been violently agitated with more than one passion recently—and a good deal occupied politically as well as privately—and amidst conflicting parties—politics—and (as far as regards public matters) circumstances;—I have also been in an anxious state with regard to things which may be only interesting to my own private feelings—and perhaps not uniformly so temperate as I may generally affirm that I was wont to be—how far any or all of these may have acted on the mind or body of One who had already undergone many previous changes of place and passion during a life of

[1] This is the last entry in the journal which Byron began in Cephalonia.

thirty six years I cannot tell—nor——but I am interrupted by the arrival of a report from a party returned from reconnoitring a Turkish Brig of War just stranded on the Coast—and which is to be attacked the moment we can get some guns to bear upon her.—I shall hear what Parry says about it—here he comes.—

[GENERAL ORDERS TO THE SULIOTES][1]

Messolonghi. 17th. Feb[ruar]y 1824

The 1st. Reg[imen]t of Suliotes will parade for service this Morning & march under the orders of the Count Pietro Gamba to their place of destination.

The Artillery Company under the Command of Captain Parry will parade immediately for fatigue Duty & actual Service—

It is expected that every Officer, Non-Commissioned Officer, Soldier, & Civilian, will obey all orders given with promptitude & alacrity—

Generale

NOEL BYRON

Col. of the 1st Regt. of Suliotes

&

Com[mand]er in Chief of Western Greece[2]

[TO SAMUEL BARFF] *Missolonghi. [Feb. 19, 1824]*

[Note at end of letter in Italian in Lega Zambelli's hand]

Remember mc to Dr. Thomas with all kindness—and make my respects to the Resident and Mr. Baynes. I have to request your attention to the above as I wish to know if the men arrived at their destination safely.[1]

N B

[In margin opposite an illegible portion of Zambelli's letter]
I will do what I can in this matter and have a promise of his [like?] from the Prince M.

N B

[TO SAMUEL BARFF] *Fy. 21st. 1824*

Dear Sir—I am a good deal better though of course weakly—the

[1] Written by Parry with corrections in Byron's hand.

[2] A document, written by Prince Mavrocordatos in florid French, dated Jan. 24, 1824, commissioned Byron commander of all the forces that were to march against Lepanto. It was the kind of flattery to which Byron was not immune, and was intended to encourage him to devote his finances as well as his leadership to the cause. (See Gamba, pp. 133–134.)

[1] Lega, at Byron's request, had inquired about Blackett, who was ill and was sent with a companion to Zante for medical attention.

leeches took too much blood from my temples the day after and there was some difficulty in stopping it, but I have since been up daily—and out in boats or on horseback—today I have taken a warm bath and live as temperately as can well be without any liquid but water &c. and without animal food. Besides the four Turks sent to Patras [I] have obtained the release of four and twenty women and children—and sent them at my own expence to Prevesa—that the English Consul General may consign them to their relatives—I did this by their own desire.—

Your cases of dollars arrived safely (as Lega has stated) and were very opportune—I have received some letters from England—one from the Hon[oura]ble Douglas Kinnaird (my trustee and a partner of Messrs Ransom & Co.) states that he expected to receive within a week a sum of eleven thousand two hundred and fifty pounds Sterling on my account; his letter is dated the twenty third of November. I hope that you have forwarded to him my letter (it was enclosed in the packet for Cefalonia which I directed you to open) as it was of *advice* that I had drawn through your house for the three thousand pounds—the 2d. and 3d. bills for which—are now enclosed duly signed.—Matters here are a little embroiled with the Suliotes and foreigners &c. —but I still hope better things—and will stand by the cause as long as my health and circumstances will permit me to be supposed useful.—

yr. obliged & faith[fu]l Servt.

N B

[On cover] recommended with Ld. B's compliments to the ear of the Director of the Sanità.

[TO DOUGLAS KINNAIRD] *Messolonghi. Fy. 21st.* [*22d?*] *1824*

My dear Douglas—I received yr. letter of 9bre 23d and Hobhouse's of the 6th. 10bre.—with some others and all satisfactory; so far so good.—I have said and say again that I am willing to accept a mortgage and to lend my monies upon fair terms (—4 per cent if that is the best medium) and of course on those which others accept—but the Security ought to be *good*. I wish you could settle that matter—as I hope by this time that you have the Rochdale business;—I agree to your proposition of a *fee* of one hundred guineas *to* and to your eulogy also *of* Mr. Crabtree, and I wish these matters were well settled, while the funds are high. I have been here some time—after some very narrow escapes from the Turks—and also from being ship-wrecked (we were twice upon the rocks) but this you will have heard truly or falsely through other channels—and I *won't* bore you with a long story.—I have also been very seriously unwell—but am getting better—and can ride about again—so pray—quiet our friends on that Score.—For public affairs here I refer you to Stanhope's and Parry's reports;—we are making the best fight we can—and without being too sanguine—we still have good hopes of the Greeks and of their cause.—The Deputies will or *should* have arrived by this time.—I drew the other day on your house for three thousand pounds—to carry on the war—but my intention of taking the field in person—has been interrupted for the present by a smart illness—from which I am slowly convalescing.———

It is not true that I ever *did—will—would—could* or *should* write a *satire* against Gifford—or a hair of his head—and so tell Mr. Murray. ———I always considered Gifford as my *literary* father—and myself as his "*prodigal* Son"—and if I have allowed his "fatted calf" to grow to an Ox before he kills it on my return—it is only because I prefer beef to veal.———I shall be very glad to hear a good account of Hunt's—and of all other *accounts*—for we have expences here—I assure you—and I may require my Rochdale as well as Kirkby Mallory proceeds—not omitting my funded products—for aught I know—unless they get (the Greeks that is to say) their loan—and perhaps even then. I must do the thing properly and handsomely—and so far I have succeeded in supporting the Government of *Western* Greece for the present which would otherwise have been dissolved—but Stanhope and Parry can tell you the particulars.—If you have got the eleven thousand and odd pounds—(as you say you expected on 9bre. 23d. shortly to receive them) these—with what I had in hand—and my income for the current year—to say nothing of contingencies from H[un]t's proceeds—or others—will or might enable me to keep "the sinews of war"[1] properly strong.—If the Deputies are honest fellows—and obtain the loan—they will repay the £4000 (as agreed upon) advanced in 10bre.—and even then—I shall save little or indeed less than little—since I am maintaining the whole machine nearly (in *this* place at least) at our own cost.—But—let the Greeks but succeed—and I don't care for myself.—

yrs. ever
N Bn

P.S.—I have obtained from the Greeks the release of eight and twenty Turkish prisoners, men, women, and children, and sent them to Patras and Prevesa at my own expence.

[1] Bacon's essay "Of the True Greatness of Kingdoms".

[TO MR. MAYER][1] *[Feb. 21, 1824?] [Undated]*

Sir,—Coming to Greece, one of my principal objects was to alleviate as much as possible the miseries incident to a warfare so cruel as the present. When the dictates of humanity are in question, I know no difference between Turks and Greeks. It is enough that those who want assistance are men, in order to claim the pity and protection of the meanest pretender to humane feelings. I have found here twenty-four Turks, including women and children, who have long pined in distress, far from the means of support and the consolations of their home. The Government has consigned them to me: I transmit them to Prevesa, whither they desire to be sent. I hope you will not object to take care that they may be restored to a place of safety, and that the Governor of your town may accept of my present. The best recompense I can hope for would be to find that I had inspired the Ottoman commanders with the same sentiments towards those unhappy Greeks who may hereafter fall into their hands. I beg you to believe me, &c.

[N BYRON]

[TO SAMUEL BARFF (*a*)] *Messolonghi. Fy. 21st. [22.?] 1824*[1]

Dear Sir—Since my yesterday's letter—a Greek here wishes to advance seven hundred dollars on a draft on your house—and although what you have already sent rather exceeds (I believe) the bills hitherto negociated—yet as you have more in the course of negociation—I venture—(I hope without offence) to accept his proposal as a convenience to him—as well as to me—for I am obliged to support the Government here for the present.—My health seems improving—especially from riding—and the warm bath—but even if any thing occurred—you need not doubt that the bills will be duly paid—as my affairs are all properly arranged at home—and the Hon[oura]ble D. Kinnaird—is one of my executors as well as trustees and much of my property is personal—at least much more than sufficient to cover larger sums by a good deal than any that I am likely to spend here. Six Englishmen will be soon in Quarantine at Zante—they are artificers—and have had enough of Greece in fourteen days—if you could recommend them to a passage home I would thank you,—they are good men enough—but do not quite understand the little discrepancies in these

[1] The English Consul in Prevesa.

[1] Since Byron had written to Barff on Feb. 21 on money matters, it is likely that this letter is misdated and should be Feb. 22.

countries—and are not used to see shooting and slashing in a domestic quiet way or (as it forms here) a part of house-keeping.[2]—If they should want anything during their Quarantine—you can advance them *not more* than a dollar a day (amongst them) for that period—to purchase them some little extras—as comforts—(as they are quite out of their element) I cannot afford them more at present.—The Committee pays their passage.—As my Secretary and myself wrote yesterday—I will not now trouble you further than to subscribe myself

your obliged and faithful Servt.
N B

P.S.—I request you carefully to forward the enclosed letter.—

[TO SAMUEL BARFF (*b*)] *Messolonghi Fy. 22d. 1824*

Dear Sir—I write these two lines of advice to state that the Greek has advanced five hundred and twenty dollars as per draft instead of seven hundred—as he proposed originally—which you will notice conformably.—Last night at nine o'clock we had a pretty smart shock of an earthquake which I hope has done no damage in the Islands——most of our English here (the Artificers I mean) begin to think that they are in another world—between guns and swords—and earthquakes—and such matters as do not come within their usual business. —Believe me

yrs. ever
N BN

[TO MESSRS. BARFF AND HANCOCK]
Missolonghi 23d. Feb[ruar]y 1824

Sirs—Having understood that you had honoured Col. Stanhope's draft on J. Bowring Esqre for the amount of one hundred pounds Sterl[in]g and placed the same to the credit of my account with you as produce I have to request you will pay into the hands of Mr. J. M. Hodges the value of the same in dollars after deducting all charges appertaining to the transaction; you will likewise be pleased to deliver

[2] There had been a near riot in the town because of friction between the soldiers and the citizens, and on the 19th Lieutenant Sass of the artillery corps, on guard duty, was killed by a Suliote who sought entrance. The frightened mechanics, who had been there only two weeks, left in a body.

to the above gentleman in addition to that sum fifty Dol[lar]s an am[oun]t which I have since advanced to Col. Stanhope—I am Sirs

Yours truly &c.

Noel Byron

P.S.—You will have received two or three letters and a packet which I sent yesterday by another opportunity.—[1]

[TO AUGUSTA LEIGH] *Messolonghi. Fy. 23d. 1824*

My dearest Augusta—I received a few days ago your and Lady B[yron]'s report of Ada's health with other letters from England for which I ought to be and am (I hope) sufficiently thankful—as they were of great comfort and I wanted some—having been recently unwell—but am now much better—so that you need not be alarmed.——You will have heard of our journeys—and escapes—and so forth—perhaps with some exaggeration—but it is all very well now—and I have been some time in Greece which is in as good a state as could be expected considering circumstances—but I will not plague you with politics—wars—or *earthquakes*—though we had another very smart one three nights ago which produced a scene ridiculous enough as no damage was done except to those who stuck fast in the scuffle to get first out of the doors or windows—amongst whom some recent importations fresh from England—who had been used to quieter elements—were rather squeezed in the press for precedence.——I have been obtaining the release of about nine and twenty Turkish prisoners—men women and children—and have sent them at my own expence home to their friends—but one a pretty little girl of nine years of age—named Hato or Hatageé has expressed a strong wish to remain with me—or under my care—and I have nearly determined to adopt her—if I thought that Lady B[yron] would let her come to England as a Companion to Ada (they are about the same age) and we could easily provide for her—if not I can send her to Italy for education.—She is very lively and quick and with great black Oriental eyes—and Asiatic features—all her brothers were killed in the revolution—her mother wishes to return to her husband who is at Prevesa—but says that she would rather entrust the Child to me—in the present state of the Country——her extreme youth and sex have hitherto saved her life—but there is no saying—what might occur in the course of the *war* (and

[1] Only the signature and the postscript are in Byron's hand. The body of the letter is written by some unknown scribe.

of *such* a war) and I shall probably commit her to the charge of some English lady in the Islands for the present.—The Child herself has the same wish—and seems to have a decided character for her age;—you can mention this matter if you think it worth while—I merely wish her to be respectably educated and treated—and if my years and all things be considered—I presume it would be difficult to conceive me to have any other views.——

With regard to Ada's health—I am glad to hear that it is so much better—but I think it right that Lady B[yron] should be informed and guard against it accordingly—that her description of much of her disposition and tendencies very nearly resembles that of my *own* at a similar age—except that I was much more impetuous.—Her preference of *prose* (strange as it may now seem) *was* and indeed *is* mine—(for I hate *reading* verse—and always did) and I never invented anything but "*boats—ships*" and generally something relative to the Ocean—I showed the report to Colonel Stanhope—who was struck with the resemblance of *parts* of it to the *paternal* line—even *now*.—But it is also fit—though unpleasant—that I should mention—that my recent attack and a very severe one—had a strong appearance of *Epilepsy*—*why*—I know not—for it is late in life—it's first appearance at thirty-six—and as far as *I know*—it is *not hereditary*—and it is that it may not *become* so—that you should tell Lady B[yron] to take some precautions in the case of Ada;—my attack has not returned—and I am fighting it off with abstinence and exercise and thus far with success—if merely casual it is all very well.

[No signature in MS.]

[TO COUNTESS TERESA GUICCIOLI] *F[ebbrai]o 24 o 1824*

[At end of Pietro Gamba's letter to Teresa]

My dearest T.—Pietro will have told you all the news—but I have not read the whole of his letter. We are all very well *now*—and every thing appears to wear a hopeful aspect.—Of course you may suppose that a country like this is not exactly the place to pass the Carnival in; but it is nevertheless better than could be expected all things considered.——I am going out on horseback—and Pietro has hardly left me room enough on this paper to add more at present—but I hope to see you this Spring and to talk over these and all other matters,—so be of good cheer and love

ever yrs. most a a in e + + +
N Bn

[TO ANDREAS LONDOS]

Γενναιότατε Στρατηγέ καί Καλέ Φίλε!

Σᾶς εἶμαι κατά πολλά ὑπόχρεος διά τήν εὐάρεστον μνήμην τήν ὁποίαν διαφυλάττετε δι' ἐμέ, καί διά νά ἀκολουθήσω τό παράδειγμα Σας εὐαρεστοῦμαι νά ἀφήσω κατά μέρος τά κομπλιμέντα νά φερθῶ φιλικῶς καί νά ἀναφέρω ἀμέσως περί τῶν τῆς Ἑλλάδος ὑποθέσεων.

Ἐξ αἰτίας ἀσθενείας ἥτις ἐξαίφνης μέ συνέβη, ἀπό τήν ὁποίαν δέ χάριτι θεία ἤδη ἀνέλαβα, καί περισσότερον ἐξ αἰτίας τινῶν διχονοιῶν συμβάντων ἐδῶ μεταξύ τῶν Σουλιωτῶν, οἱ ὁποῖοι ἔμελλον νά σχηματίσουν τό νεῦρον τῶν κατά τῆς Ναυπάκτου δυνάμεων μας, καί δι' ἄλλας τινάς περιστάσεις ὁμοίως ἀνελπίστους, ὑποχρεώθην ἄν ὄχι νά παραιτήσω τουλάχιστον νά ἀναβάλλω τήν κατά τῆς Ναυπάκτου ἐκστρατείαν μας. Δέν θέλομεν δέ τήν ἀμελήσει, καί μήτε ἡ Γενναιότης Σας πρέπει νά παραιτηθῆτε ἀπο τοῦ νά στενοχωρήσητε τό κατά δύναμιν τά φρούρια Πάτρων καί Καστέλι τοῦ Μωρέως.

Θέλω Σᾶς στειλειτά δύο Κανόνια τοῦ Κάμπου μέ τά ἀνήκοντα ἐφόδια ἀλλ' ἐπιθυμοῦμεν νά διευθύνατε πρός τά ἐδῶ 12 Ἀνθρώπους Σας μέ δύο ἀξιοματικούς διά νά γυμνασθῶσι εἰς τά ἀναγκαίας ἐπί τούτῳ ἀπό τόν Διρετόρον τῆς Ἀρτιλερίας, τά ὁποῖα δύνανται νά μάθουν εἰς διάστημα 10 ἡμερῶν. Δέν ἀμφιβάλλω ἀπό τήν διδομένην διά τῆς ἀνδρείας καί γνώσεων Σας πεῖραν ὅτι θέλετε τά μεταχειρισθεῖ κατά τόν καλοίτερον τρόπον.

Ἐπιθυμῶν νά Σᾶς εἴδω ὅσον τάχιστα, Σᾶς παρακαλῶ νά μέ ἔχητε εἰς τόν ἀριθμόν τῶν εὐνοϊκῶν Σας φίλων.

(signed)

Μεσολόγγιον 24 Φεβρουαρίου 1824.

NOEL BYRON
Pair d'Angleterre

Πρός τόν Γενναιότατον Στρατηγόν Κύριον Ἀνδρέα Λόντον εἰς Βοστίτζαν.

[Translation]
(Original MS in neat Greek script signed by Byron.

Missolonghi, 24 February 1824.

Most Brave General and Good Friend!—I am most grateful to you for the pleasant memory you have kept of me; and to follow your example, I am pleased to leave the compliments aside, to behave as a friend, and to mention the affairs of Greece immediately.

On account of a sudden illness, from which I have recovered with divine grace, and mostly on account of some discord that has arisen here among the Souliots, who were meant to form the core of our force that would attack Nafpaktos [Lepanto], and on account of other similarly unforeseen circumstances, I was obliged if not to abandon, at least to postpone our campaign against Nafpaktos. We will not neglect it, neither must your Braveness give up harrassing the fortresses of Patras and Casteli in the Morea as much as possible.

I will send you the two field guns with their munitions, but we would like you to direct here 12 of your men with two officers, to be trained by the Artillery Director in whatever is necessary, which can be learned in a ten-day period. I have no doubt that, because of your bravery and experience, you will use them in the best possible way.

Wishing to see you as soon as possible, I ask you to consider me among the number of your best friends.

NOEL BYRON
Peer of England[1]

[TO JOHN MURRAY] *Messolonghi.—Fy. 25th. 1824*

I have heard from Mr. Douglas K[innair]d that you state "a report of a satire on Mr. Gifford having arrived from Italy—*said* to be written by *me*!—but that *you* do not believe it."—I dare say you do not nor any body else I should think—whoever asserts that I am the author or abettor of anything of the kind on Gifford—lies in his throat.—I always regarded him as my literary father—and myself as his prodigal son; if any such composition exists it is none of mine——*you* know as well as any body upon *whom* I have or have not written—and *you* also know whether they *do* or did not deserve that same——and so much for such matters.—You will perhaps be anxious to hear some news from this part of Greece—(which is the most liable to invasion) but you will hear enough through public and private channels on that head.—I will however give you the events of a week—mingling my own private peculiar with the public for we are here jumbled a little together at present. On Sunday (the 15th. I believe) I had a strong and sudden convulsive attack which left me speechless though not motionless—for some strong men could not hold me—but whether it was epilepsy—catalepsy—cachexy—apoplexy—or what other *exy*—or *opsy*—the Doctors have not decided—or whether it was spasmodic or nervous

[1] Transcription and translation by Professor M. Byron Baizis.

&c.—but it was very unpleasant—and nearly carried me off—and all that—on Monday—they put leeches to my temples—no difficult matter—but the blood could not be stopped till eleven at night (they had gone too near the temporal Artery for my temporal safety) and neither Styptic nor Caustic would cauterize the orifice till after a hundred attempts.—

On Tuesday a Turkish brig of war ran on shore—on Wednesday—great preparations being made to attack her though protected by her Consorts—the Turks burned her and retired to Patras—on thursday a quarrel ensued between the Suliotes and the Frank Guard at the Arsenal——a Swedish Officer was killed—and a Suliote severely wounded—and a general fight expected—and with some difficulty prevented—on Friday the Officer buried—and Capt. Parry's English Artificers mutinied under pretence that their lives were in danger and are for quitting the country——they may.—On Saturday we had the smartest shock of an earthquake which I remember (and I have felt thirty slight or smart at different periods—they are common in the Mediterranean) and the whole army discharged their arms—upon the same principle that savages beat drums or howl during an eclipse of the Moon—it was a rare Scene altogether—if you had but seen the English Johnnies who had never been out of a Cockney workshop before! or will again if they can help it—and on Sunday we heard that the Vizir is come down to Larissa with one hundred and odd thousand men.——

In coming here I had two escapes one from the Turks (one of my vessels was taken—but afterwards released) and the other from shipwreck—we drove twice on the rocks near the Scrophes—(Islands near the Coast). I have obtained from the Greeks the release of eight and twenty Turkish prisoners—men women and children—and sent them to Patras and Prevesa—at my own charges—one little Girl of nine years old—who prefers remaining with me—I shall (if I live) send with her mother probably to Italy or to England—and adopt her.—Her name is Hato—or Hatagée—she is a very pretty lively child—all her brothers were killed by the Greeks—and she herself and her mother merely spared by special favour—and owing to her extreme youth—she was then but five or six years old. My health is now better and [I] ride about again—My office here is no sinecure—so many parties—and difficulties of every kind—but I will do what I can—Prince Mavrocordato is an excellent person and does all in his power—but his situation is perplexing in the extreme—still we have great hopes of the success of the contest.—You will hear however more of public news from plenty of quarters—for I have little time to write—believe me

yrs. &c. &c.

N Bn

[TO THOMAS MOORE] *Messolonghi. Western Greece. March 4th. 1824*

My dear Moore/—Your reproach is unfounded. I have received two letters from you and answered both previous to leaving Cephalonia.—I have not been "quiet" in an Ionian Island but much occupied with business—as the G[ree]k Deputies (if arrived) can tell you.—Neither have I continued "Don Juan"—nor any other poem—you go as usual—I presume by some newspaper report or other.[1]——When the proper moment to be of some use—arrived—I came here—and am told that my arrival (with some other circumstances—) *has* been of at least temporary advantage to the Cause.—I had a narrow escape from the Turks—and another from Shipwreck on my passage.—On the 15th. (or 16th.) Fy.—I had an attack of Apoplexy or Epilepsy—the physicians have not exactly decided *which*—but the Alternative is agreeable. ——My Constitution therefore remains between the two opinions—like Mahomet's sarcophagus between the Magnets.[2]——All that I can say is—that they nearly bled me to death—by placing the leeches too near the temporal Artery—so that the blood could with difficulty be stopped even with Caustic. I am supposed to be getting better, slowly however—but my homilies will, I presume, for the future—be like the Archbishop of Granada's.—In this case "I order you a hundred ducats from my treasurer and wish you a little more taste."[3]—

For Public matters I refer you to Col. Stanhope's and Capt. Parry's reports—and to all other reports whatsoever.——There is plenty to do—war without—and tumult within—they "kill a man a week" like Bob Acres in the country.[4]—Parry's Artificers have gone away in alarm—on account of a dispute—in which some of the natives and foreigners were engaged—and a Swede was killed—and a Suliote wounded.—In the middle of their fright—there was a strong shock of an Earthquake—so between that and the sword—they boomed off in a

[1] Moore had written that he had heard that "instead of pursuing heroic and warlike adventures, he was residing in a delightful villa, continuing 'Don Juan'" (Gamba, *Narrative*, p. 48). Byron was irritated by this conception of his activities and was cooler than usual in his reply to Moore.

[2] It was common legend that Mahomet's tomb was suspended in air between two loadstones. It was referred to by Prior (*Alma*, II, 199, 200), and by Scott in *Quentin Durward* (Chapter 4).

[3] *Gil Blas*, Book IV, Chap. 4.

[4] *The Rivals*, Act IV, scene 1.

hurry—in despite of all dissuasions to the contrary.——A Turkish brig ran ashore the other day—and was burnt to prevent her from being taken.—I have obtained the release of about thirty Turkish prisoners—and have adopted one little girl of about nine years old—her name is Hato or Hatagée—her family were nearly all destroyed in the troubles.—If I live—she will be provided for respectably—as I mean to send her to my daughter.—I hope that she will turn out well.—You—I presume—are either publishing or meditating that same.—Let me hear from and of you—and believe me in all events

ever and truly[5] yrs.

N B

P.S.—Tell Mr. Murray that I wrote to him the other day—and hope that he has received or will receive the letter.

[TO JAMES KENNEDY] *Missolonghi, March 4, 1824*

My Dear Doctor,—I have to thank you for your two very kind letters, both received at the same time, and one long after its date. I am not unaware of the precarious state of my health, nor am, nor have been, deceived on that subject. But it is proper that I should remain in Greece; and it were better to die doing something than nothing. My presence here has been supposed so far useful as to have prevented confusion from becoming worse confounded, at least for the present. Should I become, or be deemed useless or superfluous, I am ready to retire; but in the interim I am not to consider personal consequences; the rest is in the hands of Providence,—as indeed are all things. I shall, however, observe your instructions, and indeed did so, as far as regards abstinence, for some time past.

Besides the tracts, &c. which you have sent for distribution, one of the English artificers (hight Brownbill a tinman) left to my charge a number of Greek Testaments, which I will endeavour to distribute properly. The Greeks complain that the translation is not correct, nor in *good* Romaic: Bambas[1] can decide on that point. I am trying to recon-

[5] When he printed this letter, Moore, who could not bear to have the public think that Byron was less cordial than usual in his last letter to him, changed this to "Ever and affectionately yours".

[1] Neophytos Vambas (Bambas), whom Finlay describes as a pedant and a visionary, was a Chiot who had attached himself to Demetrius Hypsilantes, one of the rival leaders of the early days of the revolution. But Vambas was unfit for a political counsellor and had become a teacher on Cephalonia where he was respected for his learning. (See Finlay, VI, 173.)

cile the clergy to the distribution, which (without due regard to their hierarchy) they might contrive to impede or neutralize in the effect, from their power over their people. Mr. Brownbill has gone to the Islands, having some apprehension for his life (not from the priests, however), and apparently preferring rather to be a saint than a martyr, although his apprehensions of becoming the latter were probably unfounded. All the English artificers accompanied him, thinking themselves in danger, on account of some troubles here, which have apparently subsided.

I have been interrupted by a visit from Prince Mavrocordato and others since I began this letter, and must close it hastily, for the boat is announced as ready to sail. Your future convert, Hato, or Hatageé, appears to me lively, and intelligent, and promising, and possesses an interesting countenance. With regard to her disposition I can say little, but Millingen, who has the mother (who is a middle-aged woman of good character) in his house as a domestic (although their family was in good worldly circumstances previous to the Revolution), speaks well of both, and he is to be relied on. As far as I know, I have only seen the child a few times with her mother, and what I have seen is favourable, or I should not take so much interest in her behalf. If she turns out well, my idea would be to send her to my daughter in England (if not to respectable persons in Italy), and so to provide for her as to enable her to live with reputation either singly or in marriage, if she arrive at maturity. I will make proper arrangements about her expenses through Messrs. Barff and Hancock, and the rest I leave to your discretion and to Mrs. K.'s, with a great sense of obligation for your kindness in undertaking her temporary superintendence.

Of public matters here, I have little to add to what you will already have heard. We are going on as well as we can, and with the hope and the endeavour to do better. Believe me,

Ever and truly, &c.,

[TO THE LONDON GREEK COMMITTEE] *Missolonghi 4th. March 1824*

Gentlemen,—I am desirous to introduce to your notice the bearer of this Baron Adam Friedel[1] who appears (from his well authenticated

[1] Friedel, who carried a lithographic press on his back, was an artist, and a charming adventurer, who had claimed to be a Danish Baron, but was nothing of the sort. When he was exposed among the foreign volunteers at Corinth, he burst into tears but carried his pretensions elsewhere in Greece. He had joined Byron's brigade in Missolonghi. What he intended to propose to the Committee in London

papers & the knowledge he possesses of the present state of the affairs in Greece having lately returned from the Morea) to be an individual who may be usefully consulted by your Honourable Committee. I have at his particular request furnished him with this letter to avail himself herewith for that purpose—& I am Gentlemen

yours most sincerely &c.

NOEL BYRON[2]

[TO SAMUEL BARFF] *Missolonghi, March 5th, 1824*

Dear Sir,—If Sisseni[1] is sincere, he will be treated with, and *well* treated; if he is not, the sin and the shame may lie at his own door. One great object is to heal those internal dissensions for the *future*, without exacting too rigorous an account of the past. The Prince Mavrocordato is of the same opinion, and whoever is disposed to act fairly will be fairly dealt with.

I *have heard* a *good deal* of Sisseni, but not a *deal* of *good*: however, I never judge from report, particularly in a revolution.

Personally, I am rather obliged to him, for he has been very hospitable to all friends of mine who have passed through his district. You may therefore assure him that any overtures for the advantage of Greece and its internal pacification will be readily and sincerely met *here*. I hardly think that he would have ventured a deceitful proposition to me through *you*, because he must be sure that in such a case it would eventually be exposed. At any rate, the healing of these dissensions is so important a point, that something must be risked to obtain it. I hope that you received my letters sent on a former occasion by a Zanteote. Mr. Hodges (Mr. Parry's Commissary) says that you did a day after

we do not know, but in later years he set himself up as an engraver in London and married the sister of John Hodges. (See Feb. 11, 1824 to Barff.) He produced a series of striking romantic portraits of heroes of the Greek Revolution, including one of Byron in his Hellenic helmet. See St. Clair, *That Greece Might Still Be Free*, pp. 89, 376.

2 This letter is written in a neat scribe's hand and signed by Byron.

1 Georgio Sessini, an apothecary at Gastouni on the west coast of the Pelopon nesus, was descended from a Venetian provveditore. When the Revolution broke out he headed a band that drove out the Turks. Then he proceeded to rule the district and acquired a fortune, maintaining his independence from the other Greek leaders and the provisional Government. Now he proposed to join forces with the others and asked for supplies and support.

his arrival, but as you do not allude to them I should be glad to have this confirmed by yourself.

Believe me, yours ever and truly,
NOEL BYRON

[TO SIR FREDERICK STOVEN][1] *Messolonghi, March 8th. 1824*

. . . Some Greeks have applied to me to endeavour to interest your feelings in behalf of their relatives who were taken in an Ionian boat and carried to Patras. The circumstances of their being taken in an *Ionian* boat is that on which their hope is chiefly grounded. It would be an Act of humanity if the release of these poor people could be obtained or at least their lives spared, and I think that the request might be made with some hope of success—as I lately sent back to Prevesa and Patras eight and twenty Turkish prisoners whom the Greeks gave up at my instance. . . .

It would also be very much for the benefit of both sides if they could be induced to conduct themselves with some regard to the laws of War—or any laws whatsoever.

[TO JOHN BOWRING] *Messolonghi 9th. March 1824*

[In flourishing scribe's hand][1]

Sir—Herewith enclosed you'll receive Bills drawn by Prince A. Mavrocordato for the Sum of Five hundred and fifty Pounds, which Sum I Have paid into the Hands of the Prince, and have accepted Bills to that Amount, made payable at your House; The Hon[oura]ble Douglas Kinnaird will present the Bills, and I trust that funds are placed in your Hands sufficient to Honor them. I am Sir

Yours truely [sic]
NOEL BYRON

P.S.—The Prince informs me that Mr. Luriotti has funds in his Hands to Answer the Amount & which will be at your disposal.
[In Byron's hand] P.S. Excuse my writing by proxy—but we are full of business.—

yrs. ever
NOEL BYRON

[1] British Resident (head of government) at Zante.
[1] The scribe's hand is that of William Parry, the fire-master.

There is another letter of advice (besides the Italian ones[)]—from Mavrocordato—enclosing one to Mr. Luriotti.

[TO SAMUEL BARFF] *Messolonghi 9th. March 1824*

[In Parry's hand]

Sir—Having accepted Bills of Prince A. Mavrocordato to the amount of Five hundred and fifty pounds *St[erlin]g* you [wi]ll therefore Honor a Draft of Prince A. Mavrocordato to that Amount (deducting every mercantile Expence) and placing the Bill to my Account, you [wi]ll oblige Sir

yours truely [sic]
NOEL BYRON

[In Byron's hand] I wrote lately have you received the letters? some were in answer to yrs. of a late date.—

P.S.—Dear Sir—As P[rince] Mavrocordato has applied to me for a loan of 550 £ St[erlin]g—I have thought it better (to save you the risk and bother of negociating *Greek* bills—) to take his draft in my favour and you will merely have to advance the amount from the balance of my recent bills—deducting expences and freight of course—as if in my own case—

yrs. ever
N BN

[TO SAMUEL BARFF] *Messolonghi March 10th. 1824*

Dear Sir—Enclosed is an answer to Sr. Parruca's letter[1] and I hope that you will assure him further from me that I have done—and am doing all I can to re-unite the Greeks with ye Greeks.——I have had to advance P[rince] Mavrocordato 550 pounds S[terlin]g (as per advice) for which he will draw upon you—from my balances in yr. hands—(on the recent bills) you will have ye goodness to remit him

[1] According to Gamba (*Narrative*, pp. 207–208) Parucca "had been engaged two months before by the partisans of Pietro Bey to set out for London, and there to thwart the negotiations of the deputies Orlando and Luriotti; but he never went. He now wrote to Lord Byron, praying him to come into the Peloponnesus, to assist in bringing about an union of all parties." Gordon (*History of the Greek Revolution*, Vol. II, p. 103) described Parucca as "a clever but exceedingly worthless person", who had supported the military faction against the Greek constitutionalists.

thc value in dollars—deducting the exchange—and expences—as in my own case on other remittances—and according to the rules of business.———With regard to the remaining proceeds—you will of course deduct all sums paid by you or by Mr. Hancock on my account—and you will also retain from one to two thousand dollars in hand to answer any further similar expences; the rest you can perhaps give or obtain an order for *here*—or at least of a portion——since the risk and freight would thus be avoided—but if *not*—you can send it to me in the usual way at your own convenience.———P[rince] Mavrocordato—has given me drafts on Messrs. Bowring and advice to Louriotti and Orlandi—for the sum he is to receive—but It is not quite clear whether they will be paid;—much—indeed—every thing will probably depend upon their affairs going on well—and their obtaining a loan.—Even in the event of a loss—it were not to be regretted—so that it does them any good in the mean time.

I have answered yr. letters—but yours (and I suppose mine too) arrive irregularly—and generally those of the latest date—a week or so before the others.—We hear (as you do) of the Moslem preparations—and must make the best fight that circumstances will permit.—I am extremely obliged by your offer of yr. Country house—(as for all other kindness) in case that my health should require my removal—but I cannot quit Greece while there is a Chance of my being of any (even *supposed*) utility—there is a Stake worth millions such as I am——and while I can stand at all—I must stand by the Cause.——When I say this—I am at the same time aware of the difficulties—and dissensions—and defects of the Greeks themselves—but allowances must be made for them by all reasonable people. Believe me

yrs. ever and truly obliged

N Bn

P.S.—I am not aware that I shall require further monies immediately but if I draw further on my Correspondents—for a couple of thousand pounds more or less by and bye—I wish to know previously—whether you would negociate the bills;—my chief—indeed *nine tenths* of my expences here are solely in advances to—or on behalf of the Greeks—and objects connected with their Independence.—

[TO JAMES KENNEDY] *Missolonghi, March 10, 1824*

Dear Sir,—You could not disapprove of the motto to the Telegraph more than I did,[1] and do; but this is the land of liberty, where most people do as they please, and few as they ought.

I have not written, nor am inclined to write, for that or for any other paper, but have suggested to them, over and over, a change of the motto and style. However, I do not think that it will turn out either an irreligious or a levelling publication, and they promise due respect to both churches and things, *i.e.* the editors do.

If Bambas[2] would write for the Greek Chronicle, he might have his own price for articles.

There is a slight demur about Hato's voyage, her mother wishing to go with her, which is quite natural, and I have not the heart to refuse it; for even Mahomet made a law, that in the division of captives, the child should never be separated from the mother. But this may make a difference in the arrangement, although the poor woman (who has lost half her family in the war) is, as I said, of good character, and of mature age, so as to render her respectability not liable to suspicion. She has heard, it seems, from Prevesa, that her husband is no longer there. I have consigned your Bibles to Dr. Meyer;[3] and I hope that the said Doctor may justify your confidence; nevertheless, I shall keep an eye upon him. You may depend upon my giving the society as fair play as Mr. Wilberforce[4] himself would; and any other commission for the good of Greece will meet with the same attention on my part.

I am trying, with some hope of eventual success, to reunite the Greeks, especially as the Turks are expected in force, and that shortly. We must meet them as we may, and fight it out as we can.

I rejoice to hear that your school prospers, and I assure you that your good wishes are reciprocal. The weather is so much finer, that I get a good deal of moderate exercise in boats and on horseback, and am willing to hope that my health is not worse than when you kindly

[1] The *Telegrafo Greco* was an Italian language paper fostered by Stanhope, who recommended the motto: "The world our country, and doing good our religion". When Hodges, who had been put in charge of the paper, arrived in Cephalonia with the prospectus, Dr. Kennedy was alarmed by its utilitarian view of religion and its radical slant, and he wrote to Byron about it.

[2] See March 4, 1824, to Kennedy, note 1.

[3] Dr. Jean Jacques Meyer, a doctrinaire Swiss, with Stanhope's approval started and edited the *Hellenica Chronica*, a Greek language paper that Byron feared would embroil Greeks and foreign readers alike. Gordon (*History of the Greek Revolution*, Vol. II, p. 109) called Meyer "a hot-headed Republican". See March 19, 1824, to Barff.

[4] William Wilberforce, the English Evangelical reformer, besides being an ardent anti-slavery advocate, helped found the Bible Society in 1803.

wrote to me. Dr. Bruno can tell you that I adhere to your regimen, and more, for I do not eat any meat, even fish.

Believe me ever, &c.

P.S.—The mechanics (six in number) were all pretty much of the same mind. Brownbill was but *one*. Perhaps they are less to blame than is imagined, since Colonel Stanhope is said to have told them, "*that he could not positively say their lives were safe.*" I should like to know *where* our life *is* safe, either here or any where else? With regard to a place of safety, at least such hermetically-sealed safety as these persons appeared to desiderate, it is not to be found in Greece, at any rate; but Missolonghi was supposed to be the place where they would be useful, and their risk was no greater than that of others.

[TO CHARLES HANCOCK] *Messolonghi 10th. March 1824*

[In Parry's hand]

Sir—I send by Mr. J. M. Hodges a Bill drawn on Sig[no]r C. Jerostetti[1] [sic] for Three hundred and Eighty six pounds on account of the Hon[oura]ble the Greek Committee, for carrying on the Service of this place—But Count Deladecima [sic] sent no more than Two hundred Dollars—until he should receive instructions from C. Jerostetti—therefore I am obliged to Advance that Sum to prevent a positive stop being put to the Laboratory Service at this place &c. &c.

I beg you'll mention this business to Count D. Deledecima [sic] who has the Draft and every account—and that Mr. Barff in conjunction with yourself will endeavour to arrange the money account, and when received forward the same immediately to Missolonghi.—

I am Sir yours very truely

[In Byron's hand] So far is written by Capt. Parry—but I see that I must continue ye letter myself.—I understand little or nothing of the business—saving and except that like most of the present affairs here —it will be at a stand still—if monies be not advanced—and there are few here so disposed—so that I must take the chance as usual.—

You will see what can be done with Delladecima—and Gerostati and remit this sum—that we [may] have some quiet—for the Committee have somehow embroiled their matters—or chosen Greek Correspondents more Grecian than ever the Greeks are wont to be.—

yrs. ever

N Bn

[1] Unidentified. Byron spelled the name Gerostati.

P.S.—A thousand thanks to Muir for his Cauliflower—the finest I ever saw or tasted—and I believe the largest that ever grew out of Paradise—or Scotland.——I have written to quiet Dr. Kennedy about the new Paper (with which I have nothing to do as a writer—please to recollect and say) I told the fools of Conductors—that their motto would play the devil—but like all mountebanks—they persisted.—Gamba—who is anything but *lucky*—had something to do with it—and as usual—the moment he had—matters went wrong.—It will be better—perhaps in time.—But I write in haste—and have only time to say before the boat sails that I am

ever yrs.
N Bn

P.S.—Mr. Finlay[2] is here—and has received his money.—

[TO SIGNOR DEMETRIUS PARUCCA] *Marzo 11. 1824*

[In Byron's own hand]

Illustrissimo Signore—Ho l'onore di rispondere alla di lei lettera,—Io non bramo altro—ne ho mai bramato—se non a vedere prima di tutto i Greci in pace fra loro. Io mi son reso qua per ordine del' Governo Greco, e fino che non ho un' invito dal' suddetto Governo 〈Greco〉 non me pare che debbo sortire della Rumelia per il Peloponneso—particolarmente come questa parte e più esposta al'inimico.—Per altro—se la mia presenza può giovare quantunque poco a riconciliare i due—o più partiti—son pronto di rendermi—o come mediatore—o se fosse necessario—come ostaggio.—In questi affari io non ho nè mirè personali ne odii particolari—ma il sincero desiderio di meritare il nome di amico di vostra patria e patrioti. Ho l'onore di essere.—

[TRANSLATION] *March 11, 1824*

Sir—I have the honour of answering your letter. I do not want nor have ever wanted anything other than to see first of all the Greeks at

[2] The young George Finlay, who later wrote a seven-volume history of Greece, had called on Byron at Metaxata in October. He had just come from his studies in Germany to join the Greek cause. In November he left for the Peloponnesus with the Government agent Anarghiros and joined Stanhope and Trelawny in Athens. Early in February he arrived in Missolonghi with letters from them to Byron and Mavrocordatos inviting them to a conference of Greek leaders at Salona (modern Amphissa).

peace with one another. I came here by invitation of the Greek Government, and until that Government has invited me, I do not think that I ought to leave Roumelia for the Peloponnesus; and the more so, as this part is exposed in a greater degree to the enemy. On the other hand, if my presence can really be of any help at all in reconciling two or more parties, I am ready to go any where, either as a mediator, or, if necessary, as a hostage. In these affairs I have neither personal aims nor private prejudices, but the sincere wish of deserving the name of a friend of your country, and of her patriots.

I have the honour etc.[1]

[TO DOUGLAS KINNAIRD] *Messolonghi March 12th. 1824*

Dear Douglas/—Enclosed is an account in dollars of the monies advanced by me to the Greeks since my engagement in their cause. By this you will perceive that I require reinforcements.—I have drawn in favour of Messrs Barff &c for three thousand pounds St[erlin]g therefore, in the expectation of further credits which I hope are on the way.

March 13th

I was interrupted yesterday—and must write to-day—without much certainty that the letter will reach you—for the Plague has broken out this morning in the town—and of course precautions will be taken in the Islands and elsewhere.—It has been supposed to be communicated from the Morea—be that as it may, a Man from thence has just died of it—as my Physician says—whom I have just seen—as well as the Prince Mavrocordato.———What the event may be cannot of course be foreseen.—To resume—It would be advantageous nay—even necessary for me—or for my heirs—that you should sell out of the 3 per Cent Consols now while they are so high—it might make a difference of ten thousand pounds in our favour on the original Sum invested. Surely Bland would consent to this—and wait for the occurrence of a Mortgage at four per Cent—or take one on fair security.—I wish much to impress this upon your mind.—I hope that you have arranged the Rochdale business—as well as you could and completely according to your wishes.—I hear that Hunt has been found libellous;—we must pay the expences and his fine—if he had consented to my coming over as I requested—this would not have fallen upon *him*—but to this he frequently objected—declaring that they would not prosecute the

[1] This translation is a modification of that in Gamba, *Narrative*, p. 209.

Author—but the publisher.—I shall be the more anxious to hear from you—as the Communication will probably be interrupted for some time to come—Whatever may [occur?] to me—believe me that I [am] and was—and will be—(as long as I am at all)

ever yrs. very faithfully and affectly.

NOEL BYRON

[TO DOUGLAS KINNAIRD] *Messolonghi. March 13th. 1824*

Dear Douglas—Since I sent off my letter this morning I perceive that I omitted to enclose the account mentioned of the sum I have advanced to or on behalf of the Greeks since my arrival in this Climate. —As I wrote so recently I have little to add except to report softly my strongest recommendation that you would sell out of the funds for me —while they are so very high—and favourable—and take a Mortgage —for the investment of the monies at four per Cent if requisite. 2dly.— to pay H[un]t's expences for his trial and fine—3dly.—to receive the Rochdale monies—and 4thly. to send me out Credits as I may possibly require all available sums for the assistance of the Cause here.

yrs. ever and truly

N BN

P.S.—The Plague has broken out here this morning—as I mentioned to you in my former letter of this day's date. There is of course some alarm, and precautions are taken—but to what purpose or with what effect remains to be seen.——

P.S.—2d. [Suppose?] you could [sell?] out—and if a mortgage be *got* [at four per cent reco]llect that the great gain in the [interest?] [would make up for?] the delay. It might be ten thousand pounds advantage. [Fragment on another sheet] . . . twice lately—but add two lines by another opportunity—merely to request you to sell out while the funds are high and to invest at four per Cent—if better terms on good security are not easily to be obtained.———For my observations upon other points of business—I refer you to my two former letters— which will I hope reach you in safety.

Ever yrs.

N BN

P.S.—Stanhope's and Parry's reports will apprize you of the state of public affairs here for the present.——

[TO COUNTESS TERESA GUICCIOLI] *March 17th, 1824*

[At end of letter from Pietro Gamba to Teresa]

My dearest T.—The Spring is come—I have seen a Swallow to-day—and it was time—for we have had but a wet winter hitherto—even in Greece.—We are all very well, which will I hope—keep up your hopes and Spirits. I do not write to you letters about politics—which would only be tiresome, and yet we have little else to write about—except some private anecdotes which I reserve for "viva voce" when we meet—to divert you at the expense of Pietro and some others.—The Carnival here is curious—though not quite so elegant as those of Italy.——

We are a good many foreigners here of all Nations—and a curious mixture they compose.——I write to you in English without apologies—as you say you have become a great proficient in that language of birds.——To the English and Greeks—I generally write in Italian—from a Spirit of contradiction, I suppose—and to show that I am Italianized by my long stay in your Climate.——Salute Costa and his lady—and Papa and Olimpia and Giulia and Laurina—and believe me—dearest T. t.A.A.—in E.

N Bn

[TO SAMUEL BARFF] *Missolonghi, March 17, 1824*

[Note at end of Italian letter of Lega Zambelli to Barff][1]

Dear Sir—I hope that you have received my various letters in reply to yours.

yours ever
NOEL BYRON

[TO COLONEL LEICESTER STANHOPE]

Messolonghi. March 19th. 1824

My dear Stanhope—P[rince] Mavrocordato and myself will go to Salona to meet Ulysses—and you may be very sure that P. M. will accept any proposition for the advantage of Greece.[1]—Parry is to

[1] Lega told Barff that the rumour of the plague having arrived at Missolonghi was a false alarm.

[1] Ulysses (or Odysseus) had won over both Trelawny and Stanhope, but Byron and Mavrocordatos mistrusted him. Yet at Stanhope's request they consented to meet him for a conference at Salona to try to unify Eastern and Western Greece.

answer for himself on his own articles—if I were to interfere with him—it would only stop the whole progress of his exertions—and he is really doing all that can be done without more aid from the Govt. which neither works nor pays.—What can be spared will be sent—but I refer you to Capt. Humphries'[2] report—and to C[ount] Gamba's letter for details upon all subjects.—In the hope of seeing you soon—and deferring much that [will be to?] be said till then—believe me

ever and truly yrs.

N Bn

P.S.—Your two letters (to me) are sent to Mr. Barff as you desire—pray Remember me particularly to Trelawny whom I shall be very much pleased to see again.

[TO SAMUEL BARFF] *Messolonghi. March 19th. 1824*

Dear Sir—As Count Mercati[1] is under some apprehensions of a *direct* answer to *him* personally on Greek Affairs—I reply—(as you authorized me) to you who will have the goodness to communicate to him the enclosed.—It is the joint answer of P[rince] M[avrocordat]o and of myself to S. G. S[essini]'s propositions.—You may also add both to him and to Parrucca—that *I* am perfectly sincere in desiring the most amicable termination of their internal dissensions—and that I believe P[rince] Mavrocordato to be so also—otherwise I would not act with him—or any other—whether Native or foreigner.——

If Lord Guilford[2] is at Zante—or if *he* is not—if Signor Trikupi[3] is there—you would oblige me by presenting my respects to one or both—and by telling them—that from the very first I foretold to Col. Stanhope and to P[rince] Mavrocordato that a Greek Newspaper (or indeed any other) in *the present state* of Greece—might—and probably *would* lead to much mischief and misconstruction—unless under *some* restric-

[2] William H. Humphreys had come out with Parry, but he left with Stanhope for Athens in February. He arrived again in Missolonghi on March 18 with letters from Trelawny and Stanhope and left once more on the 21st with replies.

[1] Unidentified. Probably another Greek from the Morea, like Sessini and Parucca, who wanted Byron to shift his influence and his money to that area.

[2] The English Hellenophile who founded the Greek university at Corfu.

[3] Spiridion Tricoupi, son of a Primate of Missolonghi, was, according to Gamba, "educated by the means furnished by Lord Guilford, and was acquainted with the French, English, and Italian languages". He had been selected as deputy to the General Government to represent Western Greece. He arrived in Missolonghi early in April and was present to deliver the funeral oration over Byron's body. He later played a prominent part in the political life of Greece.

tions—nor have I ever had anything to do with either—as a Writer—or otherwise, except as a pecuniary Contributor to their support on the outset which I could not refuse to the earnest request of the Projectors. Col. S[tanhope] and myself had considerable differences of opinion on this subject—and (what will appear laughable enough—) to such a degree that he charged me with *despotic* principles—and I *him* with Ultra-radicalism.——Dr. Meyer the Editor with his unrestrained freedom of the Press—takes the Freedom to exercise an unlimited discretion—not allowing any articles but his own and those like them to appear—and in declaiming against restrictions—cuts, carves, and restricts—(as they tell me) at his own will and pleasure.—He is the Author of an article against Monarchy[4]—of which he may have the advantage and fame—but they (the Editors) will get themselves into a Scrape—if they do not take care.——Of all petty tyrants he is one of the pettiest—as are most demogogues that ever I knew;——he is a Swiss by birth—and a Greek by assumption—having married a wife—and changed his religion.——I shall be very glad and extremely anxious for some favourable result to the recent pacific overtures of the contending parties in the Peloponnese.—

Ever yrs. very truly
N Bn

[TO JOHN BOWRING] *March 19th, 1824*

Dear Sir,—Preparations are making for the ensuing campaign. Col. S[tanhope] and Capt. Parry's reports will have instructed the Committee. Means and money will be required; men are in plenty, if we have the former. I shall endeavour to do my duty.

Yours,
N. B.

P.S.—Prince Mavrocordato and L[ord] B[yron] go to Salona. I (L.B.) request Mr. Bowring to urge the Hon. Douglas Kinnaird to send L. B. credits to the extent of L. B.'s resources. Here there are the greatest difficulties of every kind for the moment—but they have hope—and will fight it out.—N.B.

[TO SAMUEL BARFF] *March 22d. 1824*

Dear Sir—Mr. Dunn has received in the course of my stay in

[4] In the 20th number of the *Greek Chronicle* Meyer published a violent attack on the Austrian monarchy and Byron suppressed the number.

Tuscany and the Genoese territory some thousand dollars of mine—always paid without demur or delay—because I made it a rule to have no long accounts in Italy, however high the prices.—His *present* pretension to a much smaller sum is however of a different kind—being an affair (not very creditable to him nor to the persons whom he recommended) of the letting of a house[1]—the demand for which I told him when I saw him at Leghorn—I would certainly not comply with for some time to come at any rate—as I was neither satisfied with the *account* nor the *amount*.—At the same time I then and there paid him a much larger sum on other accounts—which I conceived to be fairer—as I had frequently done before.—I will not accept *this* bill—and I request that you will say as much—and restate what I have stated to you,—as before to *himself* repeatedly.——I will take care however that he shall be no sufferer eventually—but for the present he may wait—as he can well afford; the transaction was one in which he involved me—with a Scoundrel—whom he well knew to be so and whom he ought to have made known as such to me.——He never had to wait for any account of mine *before*—nor should he *now*—had he treated me well in the business,—as it is—he must have patience,—it will be a lesson to him—how he allows men who have used him fairly—and dealt with him considerably—(as I have) to be cheated through his intervention.——You will in consequence remark that I have requested you not to make any advance to him for the present on my accompt.——I appeal to himself—to say whether I have not always dealt with him honourably and readily—and I happen to have his book with me as a voucher.—You will have heard that the Alarm of the Plague has subsided here.——

If the Greek Deputies (as seems probable) have obtained the loan——the sums I have advanced may perhaps be repaid—but it would make no great difference—as I should still spend them in the Cause—and more to boot——though I should hope to better purpose than paying off arrears of fleets that sail away, and Soldiers that won't march, which, *they say*—what has hitherto been advanced—has been employed in.——But that was not my affair—but of those who had the disposal of affairs—and I could not decently say to them—you shall do so and so—because &c. &c. &c.——In a few days—P[rince] Mavrocordato and myself—with a considerable escort intend to pro-

[1] The Villa Dupuy at Montenero near Leghorn where Byron lived with the Gambas and Teresa from the middle of May until the first days of July, 1822. He quarrelled with the owner, Francesco Dupuy, and entered into a lawsuit which he lost.

ceed to Salona at the request of Ulysses and the Chiefs of Eastern Greece—to concert if possible a plan of Union between Western and Eastern Greece—and to take measures offensive and defensive for the ensuing Campaign.——M[avrocordato] is *almost* recalled by the *new* Govt. to the Morea—(to take the lead I rather think) and they have written to propose to me to go either to the Morea with him—or to take the general direction of affairs in this quarter—with General Londo, and any other I may choose to form a Council.—A[ndre]a Londo is my old friend and acquaintance since we were lads in Greece together.—It would be difficult to give a positive answer till the Salona meeting is over—but I am willing to serve them in any capacity they please—either commanding or commanded—it is much the same to me—as long as I can be of any presumed use to them.—Excuse haste.—It is late—and I have been several hours on horseback—in a country so miry after the rains—that every hundred yards brings you to a brook or a ditch—of whose depth—width—colour—and contents—both my horses and their riders have brought away many tokens.—

Yrs. Ever &c.
N BN

P.S.—I hope that you have received the answer for Sr. Perruca—and also a reply *through* you to Sr. C. Mercati.—I also wrote on some business of P[rince] Mavrocordato's—some bills of his that is to say—in England—on which I have advanced him an order on you from the balance in yr. hands—with some directions as to the rest—which you can remit here or order some one to pay for you in this place. Would you request my friend Dr. Thomas to obtain for me some good *English* Calcined Magnesia (I paying for it of course) and send it over.—B[elieve] me with many thanks to [words torn out with seal] over.——Tell Dr. Thomas I have not written to him—but that you can tell him all that I could.—When anything very particular [happens I] will send him a detail.

[TO SAMUEL BARFF] *Missolonghi, March 26th, 1824*

Dear Sir,—Since your intelligence with regard to the Greek loan,[1] P[rince] Mavrocordato has shown to me an extract from some correspondence of his, by which it would appear that three commissioners

[1] See March 30, 1824, to Bowring, note 2.

are to be named to see that the amount is placed in proper hands for the service of the country, and that my name is amongst the number. Of this, however, we have as yet only the report.

This commission is apparently named by the Committee or the contracting parties in England. I am of opinion that such a commission will be necessary; but the office will be both delicate and difficult. The Weather, which has lately been equinoctial, has flooded the country, and will probably retard our proceeding to Salona for some days, till the road becomes more practicable.

You were already apprized that P[rince] Mavrocordato and myself had been invited to a conference by Ulysses and the Chiefs of Eastern Greece. Cap. Parry will write to you himself on the subject of the artificers' wages, but with all due allowance for their situation, I cannot see a great deal to pity in their circumstances. They were well paid, housed and fed, expenses granted of every kind, and they marched off at the first alarm; were *they* more exposed than the rest? or *so much*? neither are they very much embarrassed, for Cap. Parry says that *he knows* all of them have money, and one in particular a considerable sum. He accuses them of having sold some things, and appropriated others, as also with mutiny, etc., etc., upon which charges, all and each, I pronounce nothing, but state them as stated to me by their master, so named by their employers the Committee.

I hear (and am indeed consulted on the subject) that in case the remittance of the first advance of the Loan should not arrive immediately the Greek General Government mean to try to raise some thousand dollars in the islands in the interim, to be repaid from the earliest instalments on their arrival. What prospects of success they may have, or on what conditions, you can tell better than I: I suppose, if the Loan be confirmed, something might be done by them, but subject of course to the usual terms. You can let them and me know your opinion. There is an imperious necessity for some national fund, and that speedily; otherwise what is to be done? The Auxiliary Corps of about two hundred men, paid by me, are, I believe, the sole regularly and properly furnished with the money, due to them weekly, and the officers monthly. It is true that the Greek Government give their rations; but we have had three mutinies, owing to the badness of the bread, which neither native nor stranger could masticate (nor dogs either), and there is still great difficulty in obtaining them even provisions of any kind.

There is a dissension among the Germans about the conduct of the agents of *their* Committee, and an examination amongst themselves instituted. What the result may be cannot be anticipated, except that it will end in a *row,* of course, as usual.

The English are all very amicable, as far as I know; we get on too with the Greeks very tolerably, always making allowance for circumstances; and *we* have no quarrels with the other foreigners.

March 28. I have had your order delivered to the Greeks with the Bill. You will please to recollect that I wish you to retain in hand from one to two thousand dollars to answer any expenses of mine in the Islands, and the rest of the balance can be remitted by Bills on this place or otherwise. I am not in any immediate want of cash tho' I have considerable expenses with the Brigade, etc.; besides the advance to Mavrocordato, the Town owes me three thousand dollars which *were to have been repaid* on the 1st inst. and I *wanted* them for the public service. I shall probably send you some more drafts on England soon to be negociated at leisure, and kept ready by you for me in case of any emergency.

My own personal expenditure does not form a fourth of what I have at present to lay out here. The account of the surrender of Lepanto *would* have been amusing had it been true .... but the Suliotes, instigated by Noti Botzari and Stornaris, had no mind to march against "stone walls" they said, and were impracticable besides from their private dissensions. They went towards Arta, but have hitherto done little that we hear of; but we expect better things by and bye.

Ever and truly yours,

N B

P.S.—I have received Signor Perrucca's second letter.—If my presence be *really* required in the Morea—by *both* parties as a step towards mediation between them—*why* do not Colocotroni's party invite me as well as the Govt of Cranidi? Were I to interfere without their sanction—it would be deemed officious and useless.—But you can see what *they really mean* from the Sr. M[ercat]i and Perr[ucc]a.——

[TO DOUGLAS KINNAIRD] *Messalonghi, March 30th, 1824*

My Dear Douglas,—Signor Zaimi,[1] the third Greek Deputy, will

[1] Finlay (*History of Greece,* Vol. VI, p. 334) wrote of Andreas Zaimes: "His disposition was generous, and his private conduct upright; but his position as a hereditary primate made him ambitious, while nature had made him neither energetic nor courageous. He thrust himself forward as a statesman and military chief, but he was too weak for a political leader, and utterly unfit for a soldier." Zaimes was associated with Andreas Londos in the so-called second civil war (November, 1824) whose object seemed to be to bring into their own sphere the proceeds of the English loan.

present this to you; and in his behalf I bespeak good hospitality and usual kindness. The other Deputies here can, could or should have presented an introductory epistle to you, as well as to others, on their arrival. The same letter enclosed also a copy of the paper signed by themselves and drawn up in their own way—on my advancing 4000 £ Sterling to the Greek Govt. which was (by their own express wish) to be repaid in the event of their obtaining a national loan in London, which it should seem that they have accomplished. I have also to apprize you that I have cashed for P[rince] Mavrocordato bills to the amount of 550 £ Sterling, which bills are drawn on Mr. Bowring and directed to you. P[rince] Mavrocordato says that SS. Orlando and Luriotti have assets to supply the needful to the said Mr. Bowring, a fact which you will duly ascertain, or otherwise the 550 £ Sterling, monies advanced by me on the specified bills[,] may be in some sort likely to hitch in their progress to payment.

The Greek Cause up to this present writing hath cost me of mine own monies about thirty thousand Spanish dollars *advanced*, without counting my own contingent expences of every kind. It is true, however, that every thing would have been at a stand still in Messalonghi if I had not done so. Part of this money, more particularly the 4000 £ advanced, and guaranteed by the Gk Deputies is, or ought to be, repaid. To this you will look, but I shall still spend it in the Cause, for I have some hundred men under my command, regularly paid and pretty men enough.

I have written to you repeatedly, imploring you to sell out of the Funds while they are high, and to take four per cent.—or any per cent. —on landed security for the monies.

I have also been, and am, anxious to hear how you have succeeded with Rochdale, the Kirkby Arrears, the new publications, the settling the lawsuits, etc., etc., etc., and always concluding by a request for all possible credits to the extent of my resources, for I must do the thing handsomely.

I have been very unwell, but am supposed to be better, and almost every body else has been ill too—Parry and all, tho' he is a sort of hardworking Hercules. We have had strange weather and strange incidents—natural, moral, physical, martial and political, all which you will hear of perhaps, truly or falsely, from other quarters—I can't gossip just now. I am called to a Congress at Salona with P. Mavrocordato to meet Ulysses and the Eastern Chiefs on State affairs, and on the opening Campaign. What the result is likely to be I cannot say. The General Govt. have assured me the direction of this province, or to join them in the Morea. I am willing to do anything that may be useful.

We were to have besieged Lepanto, but the Suliotes did not like the service "against Stone walls," and have had a row besides with some foreigners, in which blood was spilt on both sides, so that that scheme was postponed. Capt. Parry is doing all that circumstances will permit in his department, and indeed in many others, for he does *all* that is done here, without any aid except the Committee's and mine, for the Gk. local Govt. have not a *sou, they* say, and are in debt besides. I have two hundred and twenty five regulars and irregulars in my pay—and had five hundred of the latter, but when they quarrelled amongst themselves, and tried to heighten their pretensions besides, I boomed them off; and by dint of so doing, and turning restive when fair means would not do, the rest are reduced to very good order, and the *regulars* have all along behaved very well, upon the whole—as well as any other troops anywhere. Six Guns belong to this auxiliary Corps of Artillery, which, by the way, is the only *regularly paid* corps in Greece. The Govt. only give them rations—and those reluctantly: they have mutinied twice on account of bad bread, and really with cause, for it was quite unmasticable; but we have gotten a new Commissary, and a Baker, instead of the Bricklayer who furnished the former loaves, apparently,—and with not very good bricks neither. Yesterday there was a Court Martial on a man for stealing; the German Officers wanted to flog, but I positively prohibited anything of the kind: the culprit was dismissed the service—publicly, and conducted through the town to the Police Office to have him punished according to the Civil law. Same day, one amicable officer challenged two others; I had the parties put under arrest until the affair was accommodated: if there is any more challenging, I will call them all out and wafer one half of them.

Matters, however, go on very tolerably, and we expect them to mend still further now that the Greeks have got their loan, and may be organized. Believe me,

Ever your and truly,
N[OE]L B[YRO]N

[TO JOHN BOWRING] *Messolonghi. March 30th. 1824*

Dear Sir—Signor Zaimi the third Greek Deputy will deliver this letter of introduction—which he has requested—although I told him that it was superfluous as his name and nation were ample recommendation in themselves.—I have received yrs of the 4th. February in which you mention having received mine of the 10th and 12th 9bre. 1823.——As you merely allude to them—and do not state the receipt of several other communications—addrest either to yourself or to Mr. Hobhouse for your perusal—some of them containing documents of considerable importance relative to the Cause or information connected with it—I am to conclude that these have not arrived.——

Col. Stanhope's and Capt. Parry's reports will have informed the Committee of what is doing or has been done here—and Signor Zaimi will be able to communicate still further—what will render any detail of mine unnecessary.——I shall observe the Committee's directions with regard to the Officers and Medical men. Mr. Tyndale [sic][1] had stated to me—that he *had* a claim on the Committee for 35 £ Sterling—as passage money—and some others of the Officers foreign or native—have preferred in a slighter degree—similar pretensions.—To Mr. Tyndale I advanced 100 dollars—and to the Germans a smaller sum.——I am not stating this—as calling upon the Committee to *repay me*—sensible that such advances are at my own risk—but I do wish seriously to impress upon the Committee—either *not* to send out officers of any description—or to provide for their maintenance.——I am at this moment paying nearly *thirty Officers**, of whom five and twenty would not have bread to eat (in Greece that is) if I did not.——Even their rations are obtained with difficulty—and their actual pay comes from myself.——I am called to a meeting at Salona—with Ulysses and other Chiefs—on business in a few days—the weather and the flooding of the rivers has delayed P[rince] Mavrocordato and myself for some time—but appear to be now settling.——

The News of the Loan have [has] excited much expectation and pleasure amongst the Greeks[2]—the dissensions in the Morea still

* [Byron's marginal note] It is to be observed however that most of these are either German or other foreigners, but very few of the English are better provided—it is true that they do not claim actual pay from the Committee—but they state that hopes were held out to them which the Greek Govt have not realized.——

[1] Tindall helped Dr. Millingen establish a dispensary in Missolonghi in January and then left for Athens.

[2] The first loan to the Greeks was signed by the Deputies, Jean Orlando and Andreas Luriottis on February 21, 1824. It was in the name of the London Greek Committee, but it was actually negotiated by the bankers Loughnan, Son, and O'Brien, who acted as agents and took a large commission. The loan was ostensibly for £800,000, but it was discounted at 41 per cent, so that the purchasers paid only £59 for £100 of stock. It was guaranteed by the whole national wealth of Greece. Since two years' interest at 5 per cent was withheld, the Greek Government was to receive only about £300,000 after all deductions. Byron, Stanhope, and Col.

continue—and hamper them a good deal—but the Opening of the Campaign will probably re-unite the parties—at least—if that do not —nothing will.———P[rince] Mavrocordato will write to you by this opportunity—I cashed some bills for him (for 550 £ Sterling) lately-drawn by him on you—for which—he says that S.S. Orlando and Luriotti have assetts to answer the amount.—This you will know better than I can do.—I have the honour to be

yr. very obedt. and faithful Servt.
NOEL BYRON

P.S.—I shall continue to pursue my former plan of stating to the Committee things as they *really* are—I am an enemy to Cant of all kinds—but it will be seen in time—who are or are not the firmest friends of the Greek Cause—or who will stick by them longest—the Lempriere dictionary quotation Gentlemen—or those who neither dissemble their faults nor their virtues.—"I could mouthe"[3] as well as any of them if I liked it—but I reserved (when I was in the habit of writing) such things for verse—in business—plain prose is best—and simplest—and was so—I take it even amongst the antient Greeks themselves—if we may judge from their history. You surprize me by what you say of Baring[4]—I thought that he had been a wiser man.—It would have been a very good reason for not lending money to the offender—but I do not see what the Greeks had to do with the offence. ———They may say what they will of the work in question[5]—but it will stand—and as high as most others in time.———This latter observation is addrest to you—as an *author*—I have only recently received your translation[6]—from which I promise myself much pleasure—the Russians are greatly obliged to you—but I did not know that you so greatly admired their Czar—their poetry—at least in your version—will be [words torn off with seal] than [words torn off] princes. Remember me to any acquaintances or friends of the C[ommitt]ee and to the two Deputies.

Napier were named as commissioners. But when the first instalment arrived in Zante in May in the *Florida*, Byron was dead and it was held by Samuel Barff for some time before a new commissioner was appointed. In the meantime the *Florida* carried Byron's body back to England. For an account of the complicated speculations and peculations connected with the Loan both in England and in Greece, see St. Clair, *That Greece Might Still Be Free*, p. 209 ff.

[3] *Hamlet*, Act V, scene 1.

[4] Baring Brothers were international bankers. The particular reference here is not clear, but it must have had something to do with the Greek loan.

[5] *Don Juan?*

[6] Bowring had published *Specimens of the Russian Poets*, his own English translations of selected Russian authors.

[TO THE EARL OF CLARE] *Messolonghi March 31st. 1824*

My dearest Clare—This will be presented to you by a live Greek Deputy—for whom I desiderate and solicit your countenance and good will.—I hope that you do not forget that I always regard you as my dearest friend—and love you as when we were Harrow boys together—and if I do not repeat this as often as I ought—it is that I may not tire you with what you so well know.——I refer you to Signor Zaimi the Greek Deputy—for all news public and private.—He will do better than an epistle in this respect.——I was sorry to hear that Dick[1] had exported a married woman from Ireland not only on account of morals but monies—I trust that the Jury will be considerate. I thought that Richard looked sentimental when I saw him at Genoa—but little expected what he was to land in.—Pray who *is* the Lady? the papers merely inform us by dint of Asterisks that she is Somebody's wife—and has Children—and that Dick—(as usual) was "the intimate friend of the confiding husband["]. It is to be hoped that the Jury will be bachelors—pray take care of *yourself*—Clare—my dear—for in some of your letters I had a glimpse of a similar intrigue of yours—have a care of an Eclât—ye Irish Juries lay it on heavy—and then besides you would be fixed for life—with a *second-hand* Epouse—whereas I wish to see you lead a virgin Heiress from Saville Row to Mount-Shannon.—Let me hear from you at your best leisure—and believe me ever and truly my dearest Clare—

yrs.

NOEL BYRON

P.S.—The Turkish fleet are just bearing down to blockade this port—so how our Deputy is to get by—is a doubt—but the Island-boats frequently evade them.—The Sight is pretty—but much finer for a Limner than a Lodger.—It is the Squadron from the Gulph of Corinth—(Hodie—Gulph of Lepanto); they (the Greeks I mean) are all busy enough as you may suppose—as the Campaign is expected to commence next Month.—But as aforesaid I refer you for news to the Bearer.——

1 Clare's younger brother Richard Hobart Fitzgibbon succeeded him as the third and last Earl of Clare in 1851.

[TO THE COUNTESS OF JERSEY] *Messolonghi. March 31st. 1824*

My dear Lady Jersey—Allow me to request your benevolence and an occasional invitation or introduction in behalf of Signor Zaimi the third Greek Deputy who will make an excellent Lion on account of his name and nation—and is besides a young and a worthy man. I trust that both you and Lord Jersey occasionally recollect him who is always

very much yrs.
NOEL BYRON

[TO JOHN CAM HOBHOUSE] *Messolonghi. March 31st. 1824*

My dear Hobhouse—I have written a long letter to D[ouglas] K[innair]d which will save you the perusal of an epistle in detail from this now celebrated city.—Signor Zaimi who requests an introduction (for which this will serve) can give you all the gossip of Greece public and private—foreign and domestic. He is ye third Deputy on the loan business which we hear is concluded to a certain extent.—I recommend the bearer to your politeness—and myself to yr. remembrance.

Ever and entirely yrs.
N BN

[TO A PRUSSIAN OFFICER][1] *April 1, 1824*

Sir,—I have the honour to reply to your letter of this day. In consequence of an urgent, and, to all appearance, a well-founded complaint, made to me yesterday evening, I gave orders to Mr. Hesketh to proceed to your quarters with the soldiers of his guard, and to remove you from your house to the Seraglio; because the owner of your house declared himself and his family to be in immediate danger from your conduct; and added, that that was not the first time that you had placed them in similar circumstances. Neither Mr. Hesketh nor myself could imagine that you were in bed, as we had been assured of the contrary; and certainly such a situation was not contemplated. But Mr. Hesketh had positive orders to conduct you from your quarters to those of the artillery brigade; at the same time being desired to use no violence; nor does it appear that any was had re-

[1] Gamba says he was a Russian officer, but Byron said distinctly that he was Prussian. See April 3, 1824, to Barff.

course to. This measure was adopted because your landlord assured me, when I proposed to put off the inquiry until the next day, that he could not return to his house without a guard for his protection, and that he had left his wife and daughter, and family, in the greatest alarm; on that account putting them under our immediate protection; the case admitted of no delay. As I am not aware that Mr. Hesketh exceeded his orders, I cannot take any measures to punish him; but I have no objection to examine minutely into his conduct. You ought to recollect that entering into the auxiliary Greek corps, now under my orders, at your own sole request and positive desire, you incurred the obligation of obeying the laws of the country, as well as those of the service.

I have the honour to be, &c.

N B

[TO SAMUEL BARFF] *April 3d. 1824*

Dear Sir—I received yr. letter by Sr. Trikupi.—With the Sciot you will or ought to receive a long letter—and one also from Capt. Parry. —I trust that you have also received my letter explaining *why* I have declined accepting Mr. Dunn's bill—as I wish the statement to be repeated to him.—We have the Turkish Squadron blockading the port—a third Greek Deputy Sr. Zaimi in the town on his way to England—and a quarrel (not yet settled) between the Citizens and some of Karriaskaki's people[1]—which has already produced some blows;—I keep my people quite neutral—but have ordered them to be on their Guard;—some days ago—we had an Italian private Soldier drummed out for *thieving*—the German Officers wanted to *flog* him—but I flatly refused to permit the use of the stick or whip—and delivered him over to the police.—*Since* then a Prussian *Officer* rioted in his lodgings—and I put him under arrest according to the Code—this it appears did not please his German Confederation—but I stuck by [my intent?]—and have given them plainly to understand—that those who do not choose to be amenable to the laws of the Country

1 A nephew of George Karaiskakis, a Greek chieftain at Anatolico, was wounded in a quarrel with some Missolonghiot boatmen, and 150 of the chieftain's followers came to seek revenge. They occupied the fortress of Vasilaidi at the mouth of the harbour at a time when the Turkish fleet was blockading it. Mavrocordatos feared that it was a plot and that Karaiskakis had betrayed the town to the enemy. Byron's coolness and energy, according to Millingen, brought an end to the siege. Gunboats frightened the rebels away and they returned to Anatolico.

and service—may retire—but that in all that I have to do—I will see them obeyed by foreigner or native.——I wish something was heard of the arrival of part of the loan—for there is a plentiful dearth of every thing at present.——

yrs. ever
N Bn

P.S.—The Weather has been and is such that neither Mavrocordato nor any one else could go to Salona—The roads are quite impassable and the rivers too.

[TO SAMUEL BARFF] *Missolonghi, April 6th, 1824*

Dear Sir,—Enclosed are some Bills of Mr. Millingen which I guarantee by request of the Committee, as far as I understand their directions. Since I wrote, we have had some tumult here with the citizens and Kariascachi's people, and all are under arms, our boys and all. They nearly fired on me and fifty of my lads, by *mistake*, as we were taking our usual excursion into the country. To-day matters seem settled or subsiding; but, about an hour ago, the father-in-law of the landlord of the house where I am lodged (one of the Primates the said landlord is) was arrested for high treason.[1]

They are in conclave still with Mavrocordato; and we have a number of new faces from the hills, come to *assist*, they say. Gunboats and batteries all ready, etc.

The row has had one good effect—it has put them on the alert. What is to become of the father-in-law, I do not know: nor what he has done, exactly: but

"'T is a very fine thing to be father-in-law
To a very magnificent three-tail'd bashaw,"

as the man in *Bluebeard* says and sings.[2]

I wrote to you upon matters at length, some days ago; the letter, or letters, you will receive with this. We are desirous to hear more of the Loan; and it is some time since I have had any letters (at least of an interesting description) from England, excepting one of 4th February, from Bowring (of no great importance). My latest dates are of 9bre,

[1] Constantine Volpiotti, father of the wife of Byron's landlord, who lived in the house, was suspected of intriguing with Kolokotrones and Karaiskakis. At the request of Mavrocordatos Byron had him arrested and turned over to the town guard.

[2] George Colman the Younger, *Bluebeard; or Female Curiosity,* Act II, scene 3.

or of the 6th 10bre, four months exactly. I hope you get on well in the Islands: here most of us are, or have been, more or less indisposed, natives as well as foreigners, Cap. Parry included; but the fine weather may bring them about again.

Yours ever,
N B

[TO SAMUEL BARFF] *April 7th. 1824*

[At end of letter of Lega Zambelli to Barff]

Dear Sir—The Greeks here of the Govt. have been boring me for more money.—as I have the brigade to maintain—and the Campaign is apparently soon to open—and as I have already spent nearly 30000 dollars in three months upon them in one way or another—and more especially as their Public Loan has succeeded—so that they ought not to draw from individuals at that rate—I have given them a refusal—and as they would not take *that—another* refusal in terms of considerable sincerity.—They wish now to try in the Islands for a few thousand dollars on the ensuing loan—if you can serve them—perhaps you will (in the way of information at any rate) and I will see that you have fair play—but still I do not *advise* you except to act as you please.——Almost every thing depends upon the arrival—and the speedy arrival of a portion of the loan——to keep peace amongst themselves—if they can but have sense to do this—I think that they will be a match and better for any force that can be brought against them for the present.—We are all doing as well as we can—and I am

yrs very truly
N Bn

[TO SAMUEL BARFF] *April 9th. 1824*

[At end of a copy of a letter from Ransom & Co. to Byron]

Dear Sir—The above is ye Copy of a letter from Messrs Ransom received this morning.—I have also to acknowledge yrs. and one from Mr. Barry of Genoa (partner of Messrs Webb & Co. of Leghorn and Genoa) who had forwarded the same to you for my address.—I agree with you in opinion—and shall continue to draw directly on England—as upon the whole the safest (and perhaps least expensive method) instead of having dollars up from Genoa or Leghorn.—This will be the preferable course as long as the Exchange is fair in the Islands.——

Will you instruct me how to regulate myself about the order of first and second &c. of Exchange as indicated in the 2d. paragraph of the letter copied—as I am not very accurate or intelligent in *technical* matters of business of this sort—and wish to be quite correct.—Have you any further news of the Greek Loan? is it really settled—and how? for my advices are not recent enough to treat of this fully—some say one thing and some another *here*.—Bowring's letter to me is sanguine —but others are less decisive—though not discouraging to the Greeks. ——I hope that you have received various letters of mine—as you do not state having received any since the 30th.—I mention this accordingly——Lega will state the various dates of the expedition of letters. ——The letter of Credit is for 4—instead of 3000 £—(as mentioned in yr. letter of this morning, perhaps by mistake—) but the number is of no material difference—(as you are sufficiently aware—) when I draw directly upon my London Correspondents.——

Ever and truly yrs.

N BN

[TO CHARLES F. BARRY] *April 9th. 1824*

[At end of letter of Pietro Gamba to Barry]

Dear Barry—The Account up to 11th. July—was 40-541-&c. Genoese livres in my favour—since then I have had a letter of Credit of Messrs Webb for 60.000 Genoese livres—for which I have drawn—but how the account stands *exactly*—you do not state—the balance will of course be replaced by my London Correspondents—referring more particularly to the Hon[oura]ble Douglas Kinnaird who is also my Agent—and trustee—as well as banker—and a friend besides since we were at College together—which is favourable to business—as it gives confidence—or ought to do so.—

I had hoped that you had obtained the price of the Schooner from Ld. Blessington—you must really tell him that I must make the affair public—and take other steps which will be agreeable to neither—unless he speedily pays the money—so long due—and contracted by his own headstrong wish to purchase.—You know how fairly I treated him in the whole affair.——Every thing except the best (i.e. the Green travelling Chariot) may be disposed of—and that speedily—as it will assist to balance our account.——As the Greeks have gotten their loan—they may as well repay mine—which they no longer require —and I request you to forward a copy of the agreement to Mr. Kinnaird and direct him from me to claim the money from the Deputies.—They were welcome to it in their difficulties—and also for Good and all—supposing that they had not got out of them—but as it is—they can afford repayment—and I assure you—that besides *this*—they have had many "a strong and long pull" at my purse—which has been (and still is) disbursing pretty freely in their cause—besides—I shall have to *re-expend* the same monies—having some hundred men under orders—at my own expence for ye G[ree]k Government and National service.——Of all these proceedings here, health—politics—plans—acts and deeds—&c. good or otherwise Gamba or others will tell you—truly or not truly according to their habits—

yrs. ever

N Bn[1]

[1] This and the letter to Barff of the same date are apparently the last letters Byron wrote. Later that day he went for a ride in the rain and the soaking he got brought on the fever that resulted in his death ten days later.

LETTERS IN THE SCROPE DAVIES TRUNK

In 1976 a trunk was discovered in the vaults of Barclays Bank, successor to Morland Ransom & Co., of which Byron's friend Douglas Kinnaird was senior partner. This trunk contained the papers of Scrope Berdmore Davies, one of Byron's closest friends. Scrope left it in Kinnaird's care when he precipitately departed for the continent in January, 1820, to escape his creditors. There it remained for more than a hundred and fifty years, for Scrope spent the rest of his life abroad, in exile, first in the Low Countries and then in Paris where he died in 1852.

When the trunk was opened, it was found to contain what some people called "the literary find of the century" (see *The Times*, Dec. 20, 1976). As well as a fair copy in Byron's hand of *Childe Harold*, Canto III, a transcript in Mary Shelley's hand of *The Prisoner of Chillon*, with corrections and additions in Byron's hand, a draft in Shelley's hand of his "Hymn to Intellectual Beauty" and transcripts in Mary Shelley's hand of "Mont Blanc" and of two hitherto unknown Shelley sonnets, the trunk contained numerous letters to Scrope Davies from friends of Byron, and these fifteen from Byron himself (fourteen to Scrope and one to Charles Skinner Matthews) all hitherto unknown and unpublished. They show the closeness of their relationship and the facetious and playful good nature of their intercourse.

Scrope, born in 1782 at Horsley in Gloucestershire where his father Richard Davies, a classical scholar, was a country vicar, had some distinguished relations. His unusual names came from his mother's family, the Scropes and the Berdmores. His uncle Scrope Berdmore was Warden of Merton College, Oxford, and was Vice-Chancellor of the University in 1796. His mother's cousin, Samuel Berdmore, was Master of the Charterhouse from 1769 to 1791. Another cousin, Thomas Berdmore (1740–1785), had been dentist ("Operator for the Teeth") to George III and was the "Chirurgeon and Dentist to Royalty" mentioned in Byron's letter to Hobhouse of 16th January 1809. One of Scrope's great uncles, the Rev. William Berdmore, was a Canon Residentiary of York Minster and a friend of Laurence Sterne, and participated in events which inspired *Tristram Shandy*. (For further biographical details, see Vol. 1, p. 184, note 1, but it is now known that the year of Scrope's birth was 1782 and his escape to the continent was in January 1820, as here stated.)

[TO SCROPE BERDMORE DAVIES] *Falmouth, June 22. 1809*

Dear Davies,—Since your epistle I have received a codicil from Hanson, which I trust will prevent the sad catastrophe of the triple suicide, yours, Mrs., & Miss Massingberd's.[1]——We are shortly to sail, & I hope by this time Hanson has prepared the cash requisite to suspend your "ensuing insanity" (at least for the present) and I further trust that a few months will make you free, the old woman like Æson[2] with renovated youth, and me independent.—Pray let me hear from you, your letters are always amusing particularly the tragical ones, I hope I shall not behold any catastrophical paragraphs in the "Malta Mercury".—Seriously, dear Scrope, you are one of the few things in England I leave with regret & shall return to with pleasure. I hope God or the Devil (it matters not which if the end is the same) will prosper you at Newmarket, at the Union, at Racket's, at the *Cocoa* Tree.[3] I am sure in my absence you will laugh when you think of me, I wish I may be able to do the same and to furnish you with many Oriental anecdotes wherewithal to astonish your gregarious audience at the various clubs of which you form so distinguished an ornament.——

Nothing of moment has occurred at this port, except a pleasing spectacle yesterday morning, viz—the corporal punishment of a female peculator, who had appropriated her neighbours Assets to her own worldly emolument, and pertinaciously contemned the Corporation, telling them to be damned! and using like contumelious phrases to the discomfiture of their worships albeit unused to epithets of Opprobrium.—The people here are as ⟨handsome⟩ pretty as their town is filthy. I never saw so many handsome youth of both sexes in my life.——Adieu Davies! expect advices by all sorts of conveyances, & believe me in all parts of the terraqueous globe

yours most truly
BYRON

[1] Davies had acted as guarantor in 1807 and 1808 when Byron borrowed certain sums from usurers through the Massingberds, who acted as agents or go-betweens. See Jan. 16, 1812, to Hanson, Vol. 2, p. 154 (where the guarantor is conjectured to be Dorant but is more probably Davies). And for an account of Byron's complicated dealings with Mrs. Massingberd, see Doris Langley Moore, *Lord Byron: Accounts Rendered*, p. 155 ff. Now that Byron had come of age and was going abroad, the money lenders were pressing Davies. Byron asked Hanson to make a codicil to his will acknowledging the debt to protect Davies in the event that he did not return safely. In the meantime he foolishly expected Hanson to take care of the demands of the money-lenders.

[2] Father of Jason and half-brother of Pelias. According to Ovid, Æson survived the return of the Argonauts and was made young again by Medea.

[3] Places where Davies gambled.

[TO SCROPE BERDMORE DAVIES] *Patras, Morea. July 31st. 1810*

My dear Davies,—Lord Sligo, who travelled with me a few days ago from Athens to Corinth, informs me that previous to his departure he saw you in London.—Though I do not think you have used me very well in not writing after my very frequent requests to that effect, I shall not give you an opportunity of recriminating, but fill this sheet to remind you of my existence and assure you of my regard, which you may accept without scruple, as, God knows, it is no very valuable present.—As I do suppose that before this time my agents have released you from every responsibility,[1] I shall say nothing on that head, excepting, that if they have not, it is proper I should know it immediately, that I may return for that purpose.——Since I left England, I have rambled through Portugal, the South of Spain, touched at Sardinia, Sicily, and Malta, been in the most interesting parts of Turkey in Europe, seen the Troad and Ephesus, Smyrna, &c. in Asia, *swam* on the 3d. of May from *Sestos* to Abydos, and finally sojourned at Constantinople, where I saw the Sultan and visited the interior of the Mosques, went into the Black Sea, and got rid of Hobhouse. I determined after one years purgatory to part with that amiable soul, for though I like him, and always shall, though I give him almost as much credit for his good qualities as he does himself, there is something in his manner &c. in short he will never be any thing but the "*Sow's Ear*".——I am also perfectly aware that I have nothing to recommend me as a Companion, which is an additional reason for voyaging alone.—Besides, I feel happier, I feel free. "I can go and I can fly" "freely to the Green Earths end"[2] and at present I believe myself to be as comfortable as I ever shall be, and certainly as I ever have been.—My apparatus for "*flying*" consists of a Tartar, two Albanian soldiers, a Dragoman, and Fletcher, besides sundry sumpter horses, a Tent, beds and Canteen.—I have moreover a young Greek in my suite for the purpose of keeping up and increasing my knowledge of the modern dialect, in which I can swear fluently, and talk tolerably. —I am almost a Denizen of Athens, residing there principally when not on the highway.—My next increment from hence is to visit the Pacha at Tripolitza, and so on to headquarters.—

Hobhouse will arrive in England before this, to him I refer you for all marvels, he is bursting to communicate, hear him for pity's sake.—

[1] Actually Byron did not repay Davies until 1814, when the debt with interest had mounted to more than £6,000. He was able to do so only after receiving an advance from Thomas Claughton, who had contracted to purchase Newstead.

[2] Milton, *Comus*, line 1014: "Quickly to the green earth's end."

He is also in search of tidings after that bitter "miscellany", of which we hear nothing, Seaton to be sure compared him in a letter to Dryden, and somebody else (a Welch physician I believe) to Pope, and this is all that Hobby has yet got by his book.—I see by the papers 15th May my Satire is in a third Edition, if I cared much about the matter, I should say this was poor work, but at present the Thermometer is *125*!! and I keep myself as cool as possible.—In these parts is my Lord of Sligo with a most innavigable ship, which pertinaciously rejects the addresses of Libs, Notus, and Auster,[3] talking of ships induces me to inform you that in November last, we were in peril by sea in a Galliot of the Pacha of Albania, masts by the board, sails split, captain crying, crew below, wind blowing, Fletcher groaning, Hobhouse despairing, and myself with my upper garments ready thrown open, to swim to a spar in case of accidents; but it pleased the Gods to land us safe on the coast of Suli.—My plans are very uncertain, I may return soon, or perhaps not for another year.—Whenever I do come back it will please me to see you in good plight, I think of you frequently, and whenever Hobhouse unlawfully passed off any of your *good things* as his own, I immediately asserted your claim in all cabins of Ships of war, at tables of Admirals and Generals, Consuls and Ambassadors, so that he has not pilfered a single pun with impunity.—I tell you with great sincerity that I know no person, whom I shall meet with more cordiality.—Address to me at Malta, whence my letters are forwarded to the Levant.—When I was at Malta last,—I fell in love with a married woman, and challenged an officer,[4] but the Lady was chaste, and the gentleman explanatory, and thus I broke no commandments.—I desire to be remembered to no one, I have no friends any where, and my acquaintances are I do suppose either incarcerated or made immortal in the Peninsula of Spain.—I lost five guineas by the demise of H. Parker.[5]—Believe me

yours most truly
BYRON

P.S.—I believe I have already described my suite, six and myself, as Mr. Wordsworth has it "we are seven".—Tell Mr. E. Ellice[6] that Adair has a letter for him from me to be left at Brookes's.—Adio! I place my name in *modern* Greek on the direction of this letter for your edification.—

[3] South and west winds.

[4] See Sept. 15, 1812, to Lady Melbourne (Vol. 2, p. 198).

[5] Unidentified.

[6] Edward Ellice (1781–1863) married the widow of Byron's cousin, Captain George Bettesworth. See Vol. I, p. 209 n.

[TO CHARLES SKINNER MATTHEWS]

Reddish's Hotel St. James's Street July 31st. 1811

My dear Matthews,—I have this day been informed that you are at Cambridge where you have possibly heard that I have been some fourteen days in England.—Of these, two were passed with Cam of the Cornish Corps, who is exiled to Ireland with his Miners, of course I grieve, & so will you.—The rest of my time has been spent on business & in acquiring a Gonorrhea, which I regret as I was only just cured of a severe one contracted in Greece, of all places!

"Such things we know are neither rich nor rare
But wonder how the Devil they got *there*.—["][1]

If you bend your steps hitherward, I shall be happy to see you before I leave town for Notts, I am going down to Newstead & afterwards to Rochdale for the purpose of arranging my affairs, in spring I shall probably return to the East, being sick of your climate already.——I have to thank you for a long & entertaining epistle, which saved my life in an Ague at Malta;—your pugilistic qualifications have made you of marvellous celebrity in that department as I hear from Jackson and other deep mouthed Thebans, I meant to have attended lectures myself, but this Clap has laid an Embargo on all exertion.—Believe me

yrs. very truly

BYRON[2]

[TO SCROPE BERDMORE DAVIES] *Newstead Abbey. Septr. 2d. 1811*

My dear Davies,—I should have thought by this time that the Dragon of Harrowgate [sic] had as little chance of containing you as the Dragon of Wantley,[1] & under that supposition I sent you a letter forwarded here by *Tom Stepney* or Tom Thumb or Thomas d'Aquinas or some other uncouth correspondent, without adding a word of mine own.—I am detained here by the Ins. no—the ["]I*nd*olence of Office"[2] (an Attorney's) & the "Law's["] or rather the Lawyer's "delay" for my worldly Director will not come before 14th. & I must be patient, for I like *fair* means as well as any body when *foul* are not likely to be so useful, as they always are agreeable.——I shall attend to your hint

[1] Pope, *Epistle to Dr. Arbuthnot*, lines 171–172.

[2] Written only a few days before Matthews was drowned in the Cam. See Aug. 10, 1811, to Hobhouse. (Vol. 2, p. 69.)

[1] See July 25, 1813, to Moore, note 1. (Vol. 3, p. 79.)

[2] *Hamlet*, Act III, scene 1: "the law's delay, The insolence of office."

in the Postscript, but what can I do? you might as well preach moderation to the mad or maudlin, as caution to an embarrassed man.—You know my situation, indeed you have a right to know it, you know too how completely I am in trammels, & all the advantages I am ever likely to derive from that property, is the sad satisfaction of knowing it to be lucrative, & never being able to make it so.—If my affairs are not in some order very soon I have made up my mind to the step I shall take, what that is, I think you will guess, & all things considered it would not be the worst.——I will not live to be the Shuttlecock of Scoundrels.—In the mean time I *hope* & *laugh* in Spite of *Johnny Stickles*.[3]—I mean to accept your Invitation to Cambridge.—I am also invited by Bold Webster, who is reconciled with as little reason as he was angry;[4] I am invited by a friend in Lancashire, I am invited by you, & (now for an Omega) I am invited by *Wm Bankes*[5] to *"One of my places in Wales"*!!! but which of all these places this Deponent knoweth not, do you think Lewellyn[6] ever invited any body to one of *his* places in such a manner? one would think Corfe Castle had perched itself upon Penmanmaur.—I have heard of purse-pride & birth-pride & now we have Place-pride.—Good Even.—I won't detain you from your Rubbers.

yrs. ever
BYRON

[TO SCROPE BERDMORE DAVIES]

8 St. James's Street January 14th. 1812

Dear Davies,—On arriving in town last night I found your letter and immediately set off to my Solicitor's with it, who will take measures accordingly and write to you today as I left a frank for that purpose.—I have been doing every thing to raise money by mortgage on Newstead for these last three months to no purpose. I have been disappointed in every expectation and as these people will not allow time, we must have recourse to legal measures.—If they thought proper to wait a little longer until my arrangements could be completed, this might have been avoided, but as the business now stands

[3] John Stickles, an evangelical preacher, who remarked of some snickering sceptics in his audience: "No hopes for them as laughs." See note to line 382 of *Hints from Horace*.

[4] Byron had quarrelled with James Wedderburn Webster over the purchase of a carriage. See July 31, 1811, to Webster, note 1. (Vol. 2, p. 64.)

[5] Byron's Cambridge friend, later an M.P. and an Eastern traveller.

[6] Unidentified, but possibly a reference to Llewellyn the Great.

there is no other course.—For me to take the annuities on myself as they now stand would be madness, when they only require exposure to be quashed, but if the parties would accept proper interest and fair terms I should have no objections to the measure.—You will recollect that the money was paid in my presence to me and the disputes I had with Riley and Thomas at their house on their own exorbitant charges for the papers, I am sure I was present at the payment of *all* either at Thomas's or my lodgings in Brompton, this you can prove without difficulty.—My Solicitor will explain more fully the course to be taken, it is an unpleasant one, but, unless they will give time, the only means of extrication at present.—Nothing has been wanting on my part to hasten the arrangement,—I have returned to England, journeyed here and there, and suffered every possible anxiety on this subject, and I still hope to adjust it, without much delay.—To yourself on my own part I am at a loss how to express myself, your friendship has been put to so severe a test; I wish to preserve it if possible and at all events can never be your enemy, you can have no conception how I am harrassed, pray let me hear from you immediately; and believe me

yrs. very truly
BYRON

[TO SCROPE BERDMORE DAVIES (*a*)] [*1814?*]

Dear Scrope—I have not my own box tomorrow—but have taken another *No. 3 South Side private box door* where I shall be very happy to see you——

ever yrs.
BN

[TO SCROPE BERDMORE DAVIES (*b*)] [*1814?*]

My dear Scrope—I need not say that I should have been glad to *have seen* you oftener—but today I am obliged to go out early—& stay late—tomorrow or Friday I am yours any time before *3*.—Pray present my respects to Mr. M[1]—& say everything for me which you know *we* both feel but no one can express better or so well as yourself when you like.

ever yrs.
B

[1] Henry Matthews? See March 25, 1814, to Davies, p. 162.

[TO SCROPE BERDMORE DAVIES] *March 24th. 1814*

Dear Sir/—I have to request the favour of a memorandum of the sum on bond due from me[1] to you with ye interest & expences incurred upon the same.—An early answer will oblige

yr. very obedt. Servt.
BYRON

P.S.—As I am preparing to liquidate it (tomorrow I hope) you will perhaps get it ready for delivery——

[TO SCROPE BERDMORE DAVIES] *March 25th. 1814*

My dear Scrope—My Bankers (Messrs Hoares) will discount some bills of Mr. Claughton's today to the amount required & I *peremptorily* hope the whole will be adjusted tomorrow & transferred to you.——Hobhouse has informed me of some unintentional sin of omission on my part towards you in regard to an appointment made to meet Col. Matthews the brother of our late friend—I can only say—that the whole thing had entirely escaped my memory—and I trust it will not live in yours; had I been at all aware that you had been the least annoyed by this or any other apparent negligence on my part—I should long ago have said—what I say now—that I am sorry for it.—In the ignorance of my innocence—I had imputed this estrangement to any cause but the real one—I thought that a sudden passion for ye Prince Regent—the columns of the Courier—or—to be serious—pleasanter pursuits than visiting an abstemious friend might have made this hitch in our acquaintance—but of any real cause of difference between us I had as little suspicion—as I now have hesitation in saying that I wish I had known it before.——Hobhouse & I have a kind of a dual Club once a week at the Cocoa—to which we are allowed to ask one visitor—who must be a *Cocoan*—will you dine with us on Monday next? at 6.—We are restricted to fish all the year—except Lent when *flesh* is

[1] An undated letter in the Murray MSS, from Davies to Byron says: "The bond debt is £4633." This was the amount due to the usurers when Byron reached his majority. It is possible that Davies paid the debt himself and later took Byron's bond for repayment, or more probably that he had given his bond to the money-lenders. Some time previous Byron had paid to Davies £244. 10s. to cover interest (D. L. Moore, *Lord Byron: Accounts Rendered*, p. 182), and £1,500 in November, 1812 (Vol. 2, p. 241). On March 27, 1814, he paid the balance of principal and interest, £4,800 (Vol. 3, p. 255).

strictly enjoined—the season is luckily in your favour for greater variety of viands as a guest—pray come.—

ever yrs. very affectly

Biron

[TO SCROPE BERDMORE DAVIES] *Venice—March 7th. 1817*

My dear Scrope—Though I regard your not writing as a baseness—yet I cannot longer refrain from enquiring how you are—in health & fortunes—& whether you have yet seen a "Boa Constrictor".[1]—Hobhouse has been at Rome some time with his Indian relations—but reasons physical & moral retained me at Venice—where I have passed the Carnival—and am at present, it being Lent, a little incommoded with a lowish fever or a high cold—which—I don't know & have not asked.—Dr. Polidori—as you know was congé-ded by me previous to passing the Alps—& you may have probably heard that he was subsequently forwarded to Florence by the Milan government for a squabble with a Hungarian man of war.———He wrote to me lately from Pisa—his present project is—to go [to] the Brazils to teach (not "the Dutch English") but the Portuguese—Medicine which they are fond of to distraction.[2]——

Bailey[3] was met by us at Vicenza & did not appear to be so much declined into the vale of years as you had given me to understand.—We were but a few minutes together—he being for Bologna and we for Venice—but these minutes were sufficient to suscitate a slight discrepancy between Hobhouse & him—upon the most approved mode of treating Postboys.—I should be glad to know your opinion between the respective answers to the Quarterly of Wedderburne Webster & Hobhouse[4]—I have yet seen neither—but my friendship for Hobhouse would naturally balance in his favour—now you are impartial—or I fear rather inclining to Webster—but pray let me know.———Hobhouse will not be pleased to hear that W. W. has been running the same

[1] When Davies was at Geneva with Byron in 1816 he insisted that he wanted to see a boa constrictor.

[2] Goldsmith, *Vicar of Wakefield*, Chap. 20.

[3] "Long" Baillie, a friend of Hobhouse and Scrope Davies.

[4] Webster wrote a reply to the harsh criticism of his *Waterloo and other Poems* which had appeared in the *Quarterly Review* for Jan., 1816. His letter was published in the *Morning Chronicle* for Dec. 19, 1816. Webster had attacked the editor, William Gifford, but the review was by Croker. In the same number of the *Quarterly* Hobhouse's *Letters written by an Englishman resident at Paris during the last reign of Napoleon* was severely handled by Croker.

career of respondency—so pray don't tell him—at least till I am present to hear you & mediate.—Kinnaird's deposition has been intimated to me—but the causes are still a mystery—but I suppose that—in short I don't know what to suppose.——If you see Dr. Clarke at Cambridge, will you make my remembrances.—I do not send you any descriptions—which you will find better in the Road book—or in H[obhouse]'s future Elephantine quarto.——I have been acquiring the Armenian Alphabet—& have lately translated into scriptural English—Chapter & verse an epistle *to* St. Paul—and an epistle *from* St. Paul to the Corinthians—which is in the Armenian version of the Scriptures—& not in ours;—this I mean to send on soon to Mr. Murray.——I have also sent the said Jno. Murray Esqre. *two acts* transcribed of a sort of metaphysical dramatic poem (written in Switzerland last autumn most of it) & I will send him the third in a few days[5]—pray tell him so—& ask if he has received it or them—I have also been in love these three months.—The post presses—

ever & very truly & sincerely yrs.

[Scrawl]

[TO SCROPE BERDMORE DAVIES] *Venice—April 10th. 1817*

My dear Scrope—The Doctor Polidori is here on his way to England with the present Lord Guilford—having actually embowelled the last at Pisa & spiced & pickled him for his rancid ancestors.——The said Doctor has had several ⟨patients⟩ invalids under his proscriptions—but has now no more patients—because his patients are no more—the following is the Gazette extraordinary ⟨of his⟩ according to his last *dispatches*—

Ld. Guilford—killed—inflammation of bowels—
Mr. Horner—killed—diseased lungs—
Mr. T[homa]s Hope's son—killed—Scarlet fever—

Rank & file—killed—45 paupers of Pisa—wounded & missing (the last supposed to be dissected) 18 in the hospitals of that city.—

Wounded

Lady Westmoreland—incurable—her disease not defined. But the Doctor himself is alive & well & still bent upon the Brazils—Frederic

[5] The poem was *Manfred*, the revised third act of which Byron sent to Murray on May 5, 1817, from Rome.

North that was & the disconsolate widow of his embalmed brother—have bodkined him homewards;—& I shall advise him to pay his court to the jointure.——He brings me news from Rome of Hobhouse & Bailey—who are as inseparable as their exceeding disproportion will admit.[1]——Hobhouse's brother's wife has brought forth a son—Hobhouse himself is several months gone with book ⟨& feels th⟩ but has probably felt fewer qualms than his future readers. Polidori left him over Dionysius of Halicarnassus—& other folios which he must read (at least the tops of the pages) with a ladder.——All this portends another battle between him and the Quarterly.——Kinnaird & others have given me a doleful account of the issue of poor Maturin's tragedy[2]—it is all luck in this best of possible worlds—and the fate of Drury Lane has been decided by an Irish Clergyman.——I am as sorry as an author can be for another—more especially as I am not on the "same lay"—but Sotheby (whom Kinnaird—say so to him—treated with atrocious cruelty—adding injury to insult—banter to rejection—& procrastination to contumely) Sotheby—I say—will be damned glad—and damned without being glad if ever his own play or plays are performed.[3]——Scrope!—I have had a fever—slow & quick—"days & nights were thirty one"[4] but not being at Pisa or Rome—I recovered, & am really very well bating an earache—& very low spirits—which you would not suspect from this buffooning perhaps—if you did not know human nature well enough to be aware that when people are most melancholy they are often most addicted to buffooning.—Polidori has put me out of humour with a parcel of rumours—much the same as those of last year from Geneva—about harlotry women—which were rife among the dirty English at Rome & Florence—it is very odd that they will not let me alone—I see none of them—I harm nobody—I make love but with one woman at a time & as quietly as possible & they lie through thick & thin—& invent every kind of absurdity—and all about "P P Clerk of this parish."—Murray tells me that you carried off two acts of "Manfred" which I think would suit you admirably—he being something like your favourite "Boa Constrictor"—to be sure—I must have been mad when it was written—but you & I are so now & then.——

[1] Baillie was tall and Hobhouse was short.

[2] Maturin's second tragedy *Manuel* was produced at Drury Lane on March 8, 1817, with Kean in the leading role, but it failed and was withdrawn after five nights. His first tragedy *Bertram*, recommended by Byron, had been successful.

[3] Sotheby's tragedy *Ivan* was accepted at Drury Lane on Byron's recommendation in September, 1815, but later rejected by the managers.

[4] *Macbeth*, Act IV, scene 1.

Is it serious that you & Kinnaird are out-coming? is it true that W. Webster is writing upon the suspension of the "Habeas corpus"?[5]—and Jackson—how is Jacky? "before G–d Sir"—I hear that the fancy has had a sad reality in somebody being killed in a fight—which will turn the pugilistic uniform to Sackcloth.——When shall you & I at two in the morning (or it may be *three*) sit in fierce defiance of imploring friends—& insist upon another bottle (or bowl—with broiled bones) & weep over the woes of humanity—& the shameful unbelief in the "day of Pentecost"?—The wines of these parts might do very well for the Gauls & Teutones & Cimbri—who knew no better—but one bottle from your binn is worth all the vineyards from ⟨this⟩ hence to Otranto.—Good Even.—

yrs. alway
BN

[TO SCROPE BERDMORE DAVIES] *Venice June 6th. 1817*

My dear Scrope—Many prodigies besides your own promise have announced a letter from you—but it tarries like the wheels of Sisera's chariot[1]—howbeit I make great allowances for the meetings & other interruptions to your intentions if you ever had any.——From Hodgson I received not long ago a diuretic letter of the most urinary tenderness —which I by no means propose as a model for yours;—after describing his insipid happiness in a Derbyshire vicarage—he exclaims "Oh! my Friend! inveni *portum*" which being interpreted I presume to mean *port-wine*—that being the *only* port at least which I ever knew him to find or seek in the course of the last twelve twelve-months.——I am just returned from Rome where I went to see the Pope and Hobhouse; —of things remarkable in Rome I can tell you nothing not described elsewhere—except that we saw three delinquents guillotined a short time before leaving the city.——Hobhouse is gone to Naples—I returned to Lombardy—& mean to pass my summer villegiatura a few miles from Venice at a Palazzino (in Italy every house with a facing or front is called a *palace*—little or great) on the banks of the Brenta—the situation is not very unlike Newington Butts—as the Venetians like the Cockneys seem to think that they can never build too

[5] Murray wrote to Byron on March 20, 1817 (*Memoir*, I, 383): "Wedderburn Webster is again at work; he is composing a pamphlet on the subject of the recent suspension of the Habeas Corpus Act."

[1] *Judges*, Chapter 4.

close to the road;—I have sent off my horses—(which in the interior of the country I have lately ridden a good deal—) & luggage—& tomorrow or next day I propose being there myself.——

I have lately written twice to Kinnaird—& I should feel greatly obliged to *you* if you would press upon him the expediency & indeed necessity of his enforcing Hanson to bring Newstead once more to the hammer & that immediately & selling it for whatever it may bring,—my expectations are greatly lowered upon that point—I have made up my mind to take almost any price for it.——I well know the answer will be the times &c. &c. But I must even take the times as they are—& whatever price the land may bring,—all further delay must be ruinous—& I do beg & entreat of you as my friend—to represent this to Kinnaird—& to request him most earnestly to act as he has full power to do for me in compelling the sale—that is the *putting up* to sale—there was a Mr. Wilson who offered eighty thousand two years ago—& I heavily regret the advice which prevented my taking that sum for it;—see what is to be done—& if possible about Rochdale also—I wish so much to part with both this summer—about *me* there can be little difficulty;—I am disposed to take the market price—in short what is offered,—it is of much greater consequence to me to have no further delay—than to have a greater future sum—for every month would be an increasing loss.——

Recommending these points most earnestly to you—I will only add that no consideration short of health & absolute necessity will induce me to return to England—& that no consideration at all will or could make me reside there—so that an additional obligation will be conferred on me by doing this in my absence;—Hanson will act much more readily at Kinnaird's representation than mine—I am not a man of business—& he (Kinnaird) is—surely it is simple—bring the estate to the hammer—& knock it down to the highest bidder——that is all I require—or request—but I shall never be easy till this is done.——If you ask me my plans I can only say that I have *none*—except *not* to ⟨live⟩ reside in England;—I am perfectly serious—& have been so much more happy & tranquil since I passed the Alps—that you need hardly wonder at a resolution justified by experience;—& when you recollect what I have encountered since my funeral with Miss Milbanke & in consequence of that interment you will perhaps be disposed to commend my intention.——There is one motive which might & may bring me to England—but as it is purely personal—I regard it less seriously.—[seventeen lines crossed out] All this erasure & blotting will puzzle you but it alluded to a subject which—as I should have to take your opinion & advice upon it when we meet—I shall not anticipate[2]—〈& if we do not meet—it would be useless〉—because what I have to do—will probably require to be done in your presence, at any rate at present I will postpone what I meant to say.—

yrs. ever truly & affectly

B

[TO SCROPE BERDMORE DAVIES] *Venice August 3d. 1818*

Dear Scrope—You are requested to read & deliver the enclosed letters to our little friend Hobhouse—who has been writing to me a smart letter—but I will give it him—although he has been speaking upon a dinner table—like Grildrig to his Majesty—I suppose you picked him out [of] the butter boat in which he nearly perished.[1]——I am not near enough—I pray you—avenge me [upon] him by making him *retract "retract Sir"* believe me

ever & most affectionately yours

B

P.S.—Take the Poker to him—do.

[TO SCROPE BERDMORE DAVIES] *Venice. Decr. 7th. 1818*

My dear Scrope,—You forget that as a Peer I cannot directly nor indirectly interfere in an Election (unless I were proprietor of a Borough) so as to be of service to our friend Hobhouse.[1]—You forget that my arrival would probably have the very reverse effect by reviving every species of Calumny against *me* for the Electioneering purpose of injuring *him* by the reflection, and that so far from his connection with me being of use to him on such an occasion—it may possibly even *now* be a principal cause of his failing in the attainment of his object.—I wish him every success, but the more I limit myself

[2] Byron for some years intended if he came back to England to challenge Henry Brougham to a duel for spreading slander about him, and he wanted Davies to act as his second.

[1] Byron was irritated by Hobhouse's failure to answer his letters and made sport of his making political speeches at banquets by taunting him for his diminutive size (Gulliver in the land of the giants).

[1] In November, 1818, on the death of Sir Samuel Romilly, Hobhouse tried for the vacant seat of Westminster in the House of Commons, but when the votes were counted the following March, George Lamb had won. The following year, however, Hobhouse succeeded in winning the Westminster seat. Scrope Davies had urged Byron to return to aid Hobhouse in the election.

to wishes only—the better I shall serve him or any one else in that Country.———You can hardly have forgotten the circumstances under which I quitted England, nor the rumours of which I was the Subject—if *they were true* I was unfit for England, if *false* England is unfit for me. ———You recollect that with the exception of a few friends (yourself among the foremost of those who staid by me) I was deserted & blackened by all—that even my relations (except my Sister) with that wretched Coxcomb Wilmot[2] and the able-bodied Seaman George,[3] at their head, despaired of or abandoned me—that even Hobhouse thought the tide so strong against me—that he imagined I should be "assassinated";—I am not & never was apprehensive on that point—but I am not at all sure that I should not be tempted to assassinate some of the wretched woman's instruments, at least in an honourable way—(Hobhouse's parliamentary predecessor, one of them, having already proved the existence of Nemesis by cutting his own throat)[4] and this might not much forward his Election.———

That sooner or later I must return to England—if I live—seems inevitable—as I have children—connections—property—and interests political as well as personal to require my presence—but I shall not do so willingly—& nothing short of an imperious duty will recall me,—it is true the service of a friend is the most imperious of duties, but my return would *not* serve our friend Hobhouse in this instance—and this conviction is so strong that I should look upon my presence as an actual injury.—With regard to my more personal & private feelings—you are well aware that there is nothing here nor elsewhere that can make me amends for the absence of the friends I had in England—that my Sister—and my daughter;—that yourself and Hobhouse and Kinnaird and others have always claims & recollections that can attach to no subsequent connections of any description—that I shall always look upon you with the greatest regard, & hear of your welfare with the proudest pleasure.—But having said this much,—& feeling far more than I have said; my opinion upon other points is irrevocable—nothing can ever atone to me for the atrocious caprice—the unsupported—almost unasserted—the kind of *hinted* persecution—and *shrugging* Conspiracy—of which I was attempted to be made the

[2] Robert Wilmot had won Byron's hatred by acting as a biased mediator in the Separation negotiations in 1816.

[3] Byron's cousin George Anson Byron took Lady Byron's side in the Separation proceedings.

[4] Sir Samuel Romilly, after holding a general retainer for Byron, became a chief legal adviser to Lady Byron and thus earned Byron's eternal enmity. He committed suicide in November, 1818, supposedly for grief over the death of his wife.

victim,—if the tables were to be turned—if they were to decree me all the columns of the Morning Post—and all the tavern-Signs of Wellington, I would not accept them—or if I could tread upon the necks of those who have attempted to bow down mine—I would not do it—not because I do not abhor them—but there is a something inadequate in any species of revenge that I can figure to my imagination—for the treatment they tried to award me.———

We will talk of something else.———Pray report to me the progress of H[obhouse]'s contest—he is in the right to stand—as even if unsuccessful—it is something to have stood for Westminster—but I trust that he will be brought in.—I have heard from all hands that he speaks uncommonly well, Lord Lauderdale told me so in particular very recently.—He is gone to England—& has [a] whole Cargo of my Poesy addressed to Hobhouse's care for Murray[.][5] *Hanson* has been here too—he *bears* a letter (about *himself*) addressed from me to *Kinnaird* & *Hobhouse jointly* to which I hope they will *attend*—that is when they have *leisure*—you will see *why*, by the Contents—if the Attorneo delivers them safely.———Will you remember me to every body—& assure H[obhouse] of my best wishes, and all our friends of my regards—believing me

ever and most affectionately yours

B

P.S.—When I sent Hobhouse the parcel by Lord Lauderdale—I knew nothing of the Suicide and Nomination—of course he cannot nor would I wish him to attend to such trifles now, Murray will get one of his literati perhaps—or if not the M. S. S. will take their chance.———Pray beg *Kinnaird* to be sure to get my letter to *him*, from *Hanson*.—We have all here been much pleased with Hobhouse's book on Italy[6]—some part of it the best he ever wrote—and as good as anything can be.———

[TO SCROPE BERDMORE DAVIES] *Venice. January 26th. 1819*

My dear Scrope—Yesterday I received through Hobhouse the decision of your Æreopagus or Apollophagus—or Phœbopagus;[1]—

[5] The cargo of poetry consisted of the first canto of *Don Juan*, *Mazeppa*, and the *Ode on Venice*.

[6] Hobhouse's "book on Italy" was ***Historical Illustrations of the Fourth Canto of Childe Harold***, which contained a chapter on Italian literature written, but not acknowledged, by Ugo Foscolo.

[1] This might roughly be translated: "your solemn judges or Apollo consumers—

and by the same post I growled back my reluctant acquiescence (for the present) of which I have repented ever since—and it is now four & twenty hours.—What I meant to call was a Jury—(not ⟨a Jury⟩ of *Matrons*) and not a Coroner's Inquest.—That Hobhouse the politician & Candidate should pause—I marvel not—his existence just now depends upon "the breath of Occupation"[2]—that Frere the poet and Symposiast of the Coteries should doubt was natural—but that you a man of the world and a wit,—and Douglas Kinnaird—my friend—my Power of Attorney—and banker—should give in to the atrocious cant of the day surprizes me.——The motto "domestica facta" in any case —whether fully published—or simply printed for distribution, must be erased—there is no occasion for a motto at all.[3]—What I meant by "domestica facta" was "*Common life*"—& not one's own adventures—Juan's are no adventures of mine—but some that happened in Italy about seven or eight years ago—to an Italian.—If the bitch Inez resembles any other bitch[4]—that's fair—nature is for the poet & the painter.—The lines on Castlereagh must be omitted[5]—(as I am not now near enough to give him an exchange of shots—)—& also the words *Bob* at the end of the third stanza—which leave "high & dry" decent & pointless rhymes.[6]——

I have finished another canto in 206 stanzas—with less love in it—and a good deal of Shipwreck—for which I have studied the Sea, many narratives—and some experience, at least of Gales of Wind.—If we are to yield to this sort of cant—*Johnson* is an immoral writer—for in his first imitation—*London* he has "cures a Clap"—and again—

["]——swear
He gropes his breeches with a Monarch's air".—

Surely far grosser—& coarser than anything in Juan.—Consult

or judges of the sun." All of Byron's friends had objected to the publication of *Don Juan* on the grounds that its frankness and its obvious satire on Lady Byron would damage his reputation.

[2] *Corialanus*, Act IV, scene 6: "you that stood so much / Upon the voice of occupation and / The breath of garlic-eaters!"

[3] Byron changed his mind, however, for when the first two cantos were published anonymously on July 15, 1819, they bore the motto: "Difficile est proprie communia dicere. Horace, *Epist. ad Pison.*"

[4] Donna Inez, Don Juan's mother, is in some parts obviously drawn from the character of Lady Byron, but as a fictional character she has many other traits, even some of Byron's mother.

[5] The whole of the "Dedication" containing the lines on "The intellectual eunuch Castlereagh" was omitted because, Byron said, "I won't attack the dog so fiercely without putting my name".

[6] In the third stanza of the Dedication was a ribald reference to Southey (a "dry-Bob" in Regency slang meant coition without emission).

"*London*".—I will try what I can do against this disgusting affectation —and whether I succeed or not—the experiment will be made.——It is my intention to write a preface stating that the poem is printed against the opinion of all my friends and of the publisher also,—& that the whole responsibility is mine—& mine only.——H[obhouse] talks to me about the woman—& of the thing being forgotten—is it so?—*I* have *not* forgotten—nor *forgiven*.——And Ellice talks of my standing "*well & high*"—who cares how I stand—if my standing is to be shaken by the breath of a bitch—or her infamous Setters on?——If she was Scylla with all her dogs—I care not—I have swum through Charybdis already.—I write in haste and in very bad humour—but in all hurry and in every Mood always

yrs. truly & affectly

B

P.S.—I have written in such haste, as to omit the most essential of All—"the *Monies*"—I should like to know what is to make me amends for the "*ducats*" I should have received—fairly & hardly earned—am I neither to have them nor "my pound of flesh nearest the heart?"—I will have both.——

[On cover] Take for the Motto "No Hopes for them as laughs"—Stickles's Sermons.[7]—You will recollect the passage.——

[7] See Sept. 2, 1811, to Davies, note 2, p. 159.

ADDITIONAL LETTERS

Among the letters, the manuscripts of which have come to light recently and been made available to me, are several which were published in earlier volumes from printed sources or from quotations in catalogues. Where there is only a slight difference in punctuation, I have not reprinted them here, but have only given the volume and page number of my earlier publication. The present location of the manuscript is given in the List of Sources. Where there are significant differences between the printed version and the manuscript, I have given the full manuscript text.

[TO MRS. MASSINGBERD] *Little Hampton, Aug. 26th. 1806*

[In Volume 1, p. 100, from Sotheby catalogue, with slight variations from MS.]

[TO JOHN EDLESTON?] *May, 1807*

[Note in cipher]

D–R–T [Dearest?]—Why not? With this kiss make me yours again forever[1]

BYRON

[TO BEN CROSBY] *Trin[ity] C[ollege] Cambridge Decr. 1st. 1807*

Sir,—I have been rather surprised by an epistle from Mr. Ridge,[1]

[1] This note in cipher together with a key (a complete alphabet of cipher characters with their equivalent letters written over them) occupies two note sheets in the Lovelace Papers. On a separate sheet in Lady Byron's hand are the words "Cyphers —by B—". At the bottom of the note in cipher is written "*May* 1807" in what could be Byron's handwriting. The letters of the alphabet in the accompanying key do not resemble Byron's writing. Perhaps this is a copy by Lady Byron of a draft of the original. The conjecture that it was addressed to Edleston is based on the fact that it was written a short time before Byron left for Cambridge on June 27, 1807, and on the evidence of his feeling for Edleston in the letters of June 30 and July 5, 1807, to Elizabeth Pigot. (Vol. 1, pp. 122–126.)

[1] John Ridge, a printer of Newark near Nottingham, who published Byron's first volume of poems, *Hours of Idleness* (two privately printed volumes had preceded it)

announcing his intention of publishing a second Edition of poems, which I [supp?]osed to be quietly reposing, with many other volumes of *equal value*, either on your *upper* shelves, or in the less dignified, but not less useful depository of some Pastry-Cook.—Seriously, I think Mr. Ridge [mor]e enterprising, than prudent in publishing a second Edit[ion] [before?] the [sa]le of the first; this I ha[zard as?] he mentions you as his [adviser. I] will be obliged to you to inform me why you have encouraged Mr. R[idge] in his premature undertaking, the Book [hasn']t been out above five months, & I never heard much of it's popularity.—If Walter Scott's poem[2] is out, I beg you will send it, as to any reviews of my *precious* Publication, you may keep them, for I have [seen?] at least a score of one description or another, magazines & c.—some very favourable, as the Critical, others severe but just enough, one in particular (the Eclectic) quits the work, to criticise the author, & expresses a doubt whether I am not a *Mussulman*, or a *Pagan*, being [persuaded that I?] have never been *baptized*. [With all this?] praise & Dispraise, I am tired of my state of authorship, & was in hopes, I & my work might repose together in a happy [sta]te of oblivion, when Mr. Ridge's Intimation discomposed me not a little, as I see no occasion, for such extraordinary Dispatch. If you can persuade him to wait till the first is disposed of, or give a satisfactory reason for his proceeding, you will much oblige

&c. &c.
BYRON

[TO WILLIAM HARNESS]

Dorant's Hotel. Albemarle Street February 11th. 1808

My dear Harness,—As I had no opportunity of returning my verbal thanks, I trust you will accept my written acknowledgement, for the compliment you were pleased to pay some productions of my unlucky Muse, last November.—I am induced to do this not less from the pleasure, I feel in the praise of an old School-fellow, and Brother Author (if *I* dare assume the name) than from Justice to you, for I had heard the Story with some *slight* variations.—Indeed, when we met this morning, Wingfield had not undeceived me, but he will tell you

in June, 1807, had proposed the new edition earlier, so that it was not news to the poet. (See Nov. 20, 1807, to Ridge, Vol. 1, p. 138.) Crosby was Ridge's London agent. He was a bookseller and publisher of *The Monthly Review*, which puffed *Hours of Idleness*. Despite his protestations Byron went ahead with the preparation, and the second edition, with the title *Poems, Original and Translated*, was published in March, 1808.

[2] Scott's *Marmion* came out in 1808.

that I displayed no resentment in mentioning what I had heard, though I was not sorry to discover the truth.—Perhaps, you hardly recollect some years ago a short, though for the time, warm friendship, between us, why it was not of longer duration, I know not, but I have a *gift* of yours in my possession, that must always prevent me from forgetting it.—I also remember being favoured with the perusal of many of your compositions, and several other circumstances very pleasant in their day, which I will not force upon your memory, but entreat you to believe me, with much regret at their short continuance, and a hope that they are not irrevocable

yours very sincerely
BYRON[1]

[TO———] *Newstead Abbey. Nottinghamshire Sept. 15th. 1808*

[Fragment] a similar suit—made on the same model—...is not returned immedia[tely]...—tains any danger, I...the fullest compensation,...willing to pay any thin[g]...the *dramatic line.*—...feel much obliged if...procure the dress...[re]main

your very obedt. Sert.
BYRON[1]

[TO FRANCIS HODGSON] [*Novr. 27, 1808*]

To Mrs. M. C.[1]

1

When Man expelled from Eden's bowers
A moment lingered near the Gate,
Each Scene recalled the vanished hours
And bade him curse his future fate.—

2

But wandering on to distant Climes
He learnt to bear his load of Grief,
Just gave a sigh to other Times
And found in busier scenes Relief.—

[1] Published by Moore with some omissions and variations. (See Vol. 1, p. 154.)

[1] This was written when Byron was trying to procure costumes for some amateur theatricals at Newstead. See Sept. 14, 1808, to John Becher (Vol. 1, p. 170).

[1] Mary Chaworth.

3

Thus Mary! shall it be with me
And I must view thy charms no more
For while I linger near to thee
I sigh for all I knew before.—

4

In flight I shall be surely wise
Escaping from Temptation's Snare;
I cannot view my *Paradise*
Without a wish to *enter there*.—

[Note in margin] You perceive the last lines are a little too much on the "Double Entendre" [for?] English *poesy*.[2]

[TO MRS. MASSINGBERD?[1]] [*1809?*]

Madam—Mr. Hanson has directions to wait upon you with the Money for the ensuing quarter & before the next becomes due the whole will be settled. I remain

yr very obedt. S[erva]nt.
BYRON

[TO WILLIAM HARNESS]

Reddish's Hotel. St. J[ames]'s St. February tenth 1809

My dear Harness,—I write merely to claim your promise to the same effect, and to assure you that had I been aware of your residence in town I should have been most happy to have seen you elsewhere than at the place where we casually met.——You mentioned to me during our last interview that you had written to me when at Brighton in the summer, though I regret the loss of your letter, I am so far glad that my silence cannot be imputed to any neglect on my part.——I do not know how you and Alma Mater agree, I was but an untoward

[2] This was the poem mentioned in the letter to Hodgson dated Nov. 27, 1808, as being "on the opposite page". It was written after Byron and Hobhouse had visited Mary Chaworth, then married, and was first published (anonymously) in Hobhouse's *Imitations and Translations* (1809), with the title "The Farewell, to a Lady". In later Murray editions of Byron's poems the last line was changed to "Without a wish of dwelling there".

[1] As a go-between for the money lenders Mrs. Massingberd was continually making demands on Byron, who placated her with small sums.

Child myself, and I believe the good Lady and her Brat were equally rejoiced when I was weaned, and if I obtained her benediction at parting, it was at best equivocal.——Excuse the brevity of my letter, and forgive the interruption of your studies by my writing at all, when you have leisure I shall be happy to have it answered, I am obsolete amongst Harrow men, or I should desire you to present some remembrances, if I knew any person who would accept them, but I believe you are the sole Cantab contemporary of

your very sincere and affectionate
BYRON

P.S.—When do you come to town?[1]

[TO FRANCIS WERRY[1]] *Athens. Dec. 10h. 1810*

Dear Sir,—I have to thank you for a packet of letters by the hands of Mr. Hume.—As it appears that most of my letters are forwarded to Smyrna, I have sent a boat to receive any others which may now be in your possession, and to request that if there be none at present, whenever they arrive you will be kind enough to forward them by a caicque to Athens, and I will with great pleasure pay all the necessary expences.—If you have any news, or a tattered newspaper, it will be a very grateful present to myself and the rest of my countrymen now at Athens.—I beg leave to present my best respects to Mrs. Werry, and with a warm recollection of your kind hospitality I have the honour to be dear Sir

yr. obliged & very obedt. Sert.
BYRON

P.S.—Be good enough to forward my letter to Hobhouse by the first ship.

[TO SAMUEL BOLTON] *Newstead Abbey, Augst. 12th. 1811*

[In Vol. 2, p. 71, from Moore, with slight variations from the MS.]

[1] Part of this letter is in Vol. 1, p. 193, from a sale catalogue.

[1] Byron and Hobhouse stayed for more than a month with Werry, British Consul-General in Smyrna, on their way to Constantinople (see Marchand, Vol. I, pp. 234–6). When they left, Mrs. Werry cut off a lock of Byron's hair. Hobhouse wrote: "I saw her cry at parting—pretty well at 56 years at least."

[TO FRANCIS HODGSON] *London. Decr. 8th. 1811*

Dear Hodgson—I sent you a sad tale of three friars the other day, & now take a dose in another style.—I wrote it a day or two ago on hearing a song of former days.—

1

Away, Away ye notes of Woe,
  Be silent thou once soothing strain,
Or I must flee from hence, for oh!
  I dare not trust those sounds again,
To me they speak of brighter days,
  But lull the chords, for now, Alas!
I must not think, I may not gaze
  On what I *am*—on what I *was*.

2

The voice that made those sounds more sweet
  Is hushed, and all their ⟨power is⟩ charms are fled
And now their softest notes repeat
  A dirge, an Anthem on the dead.
Yes, Thyrza, yes, they breathe of thee,
  Beloved dust, since dust thou art,
And all that once was Harmony
  Is hideous discord to my heart.

3

'Tis silent ⟨now⟩ all—but on my ear
  The well remembered Echoes thrill,
I hear a voice I would not hear,
  A voice that now might well be still,
But oft my doubting Soul 'twill shake,
  Ev'n Slumber owns it's gentle tone,
Till Consciousness will vainly wake
  To listen, though the Dream is gone.

4

Sweet Thyrza, waking as in Sleep,
  Thou art but now a lovely dream,
A Star, that trembled oer the deep,
  Then turned from Earth it's tender beam,
But he that through Life's dreary way
  Must pass, when Heaven is veiled in wrath,
Will long lament the vanquished Ray
  That scattered Gladness oer his path.—

I have gotten a book by Sir W. Drummond printed but not published entitled Œdipus Judaicus, in which he attempts to prove the greater part of the Old testament an Allegory, particular[l]y Genesis and Joshua, he professes himself a theist in ye preface, and handles the literal interpretation very roughly. I wish you could see it. Mr. Ward has lent it to me, and I confess to me it is worth 50 Watsons.—You and *Harness* must fix on the time for your visit to Newstead, I can command mine at your wish unless anything particular occurs in ye Interim.—Master William Harness & I have recommenced a most fiery correspondence, I like him as Euripides liked Agatho, or Darby admired Joan, as much for the past as the present.—Bland dines with me on Tuesday to meet Moore;—Coleridge has attacked the "Pleasures of Hope" and all other pleasures whatsoever. Mr. Rogers was present & heard himself indirectly rowed by the Lecturer, we are going in a party to hear the new Art of Poetry by this reformed schismatic, & were I one of these poetical luminaries, or of sufficient consequence to be noticed by the Man of Lectures, I should not hear him without an answer, for you know, "an' a man will be beaten with brains, he shall never keep a clean doublet." Campbell will be desperately annoyed. I never saw a Man (& of him I have seen very little) so sensitive, what a happy temperament!—I am sorry for it, what can *he* fear from Criticism—I don't know if Bland has seen Miller, who was to call on him yesterday.——

To-day is the Sabbath, a day I never pass pleasantly but at Cambridge, and even there the Organ is a sad remembrancer.—Things are stagnant enough in town, as long as they don't retrograde 'tis all very well.—Hobhouse writes & writes & writes & is an Author.—I do nothing but eschew tobacco.—I wish parliament was assembled, that I may hear, & perhaps some day be heard, but on this point I am not very sanguine.—I have many plans, sometimes I think of the East again, and dearly beloved Greece.—I am well but weakly, yesterday Kinnaird told me I looked very ill, & sent me home happy.—You will never give up wine, see what it is to be thirty, if you were six years younger, you might leave off anything.—You drink & repent, you repent & drink.—Is Scrope still interesting & invalid?—And how does Hinde with his cursed Chemistry?—To Harness I have written, & he has written, & we have all written, & have nothing now to do but write again, till Death splits up the pen & the Scribbler.—The Alfred has 354 Candidates for six vacancies. The Cook has run away & left us liable, which makes our Committee very plaintive. Master Brook our head Serving man has the Gout, & our new Cook is none of ye best, I speak from report, for what is Cookery to a leguminous eating Ascetic? So now you know as much of the matter as I do, books and quiet are still there, and they may dress their dishes in their own way for me.—Let me know your determination as to Newstead, & believe me

yrs. ever

Μπαιρῶν[1]

[TO SAMUEL ROGERS (*c*)] *11 on ye Clock* [*1812?*]

[In Vol. 2, p. 152, from facsimile in catalogue.]

[TO SAMUEL ROGERS] *Fy. 29th. 1812*

My dear Sir,—Your epigrammatic example has set Moore & me scribbling, I send you the fruits of *my* midnight buffoonery, forgive me.—I don't know whether you have seen M[oore]'s *parody*,[1] it is without exception the best thing of ye kind I ever heard or read.—Believe me

yrs. ever

B

[TO EDWARD DANIEL CLARKE] *M*[*arc*]*h 8th. 1812*

[As in Vol. 2, p. 169, except for punctuation.]

[TO SAMUEL ROGERS] *April 12th. 1812*

Dear Sir,—I have dozed too long to obtain my book in time for you, but I will send for it immediately.—In the mean time will you hear my ribaldry on the late nuptials between Conceit & Chemistry.[1]—

"Apreece[2] with her Davy resolved an alliance
A little for love & a good deal for Science,

[1] In Vol. 2, pp. 139–141, with variations from the MS. See footnotes in that volume.

[1] Probably one of the satires which Moore collected and published in 1813 as *The Twopenny Post-bag*.

[1] Sir Humphry Davy.

[2] In 1812 Davy married a rich widow, Jane Apreece (née Kerr). She was socially ambitious and invited many distinguished people to her breakfasts and dinners. Byron was a frequent guest and saw there Mme. de Staël and Maria Edgeworth.

And the *Strength* of her *parts* has already been shewn
For last night she found out the "*Philosopher's Stone.*"

yrs. alway
B

[TO MR. LONGMAN] *June 30, 1812*

[In Vol. 2, p. 181, as in MS., except for punctuation.]

[TO EDITOR OF THE MORNING CHRONICLE] *Oct. 13, 1812*

To the Editor—Though I am not one of those who formed some undefined notion of a faultless monster in the Drury-lane Address, nor a disappointed competitor ready to decry a successful rival, yet I confess, I should participate in the public disappointment and surprize which it has excited were I not able to account in some degree for the inferiority it unquestionably exhibits. It is a hurried performance, and therefore inferior to the other productions of its noble author; it is not a selected one, and therefore inferior to the reasonable expectations of the Public. I believe it will be found that the Triumvirate who were to decide discovered something objectionable in every one of the Addresses regularly transmitted; many were probably condemned by an over-scrupulous delicacy on the part of Mr. Whitbread in prohibiting all praises of himself; many were unquestionably appropriate without being poetical, and as many were poetical without being appropriate. In this emergency, I have reason to believe that his Lordship was applied to subsequently to the 10th of September, with some intimation of the wishes of the acting persons of the Committee as to the tendency of the productions required. Thus restricted in the range of his Muse, hurried in the execution, and perhaps a little agitated by the universal attention which his Poem would excite, it is less wonderful that it should evince, as it indisputably does, marks of obscurity, harshness, and mediocrity. Certain it is, by his Lordship's own explicit testimony, that at the period limited by the advertisement for the reception of Addresses, he had declined writing. Why he was applied to afterwards, and why he departed from his previous resolution, I do not pretend to know, but what I have stated, may perhaps serve to extenuate his faults, and diminish the disappointment of the public. We are not so aristocratical as our forefathers in literary matters. A

Lord has owned "the happy lines," but we do not find that "the wit brightens," or, "the sense refines;"[1] on the contrary, we are disposed to criticise them with additional severity, and it is to counteract this undue rigour, that I have been induced to trouble you with this explanatory communication.

I am Sir, yours, &c.

CANDIDUS[2]

[TO JOHN CAM HOBHOUSE] *Decr. 26th. 1812*

My dear Hobhouse—I wanted to take a house for the Season not to purchase *hares* nor entire *mansions* which would amongst other things militate against our travelling schemes besides the weightier objection you justly guess at.—This you will have the goodness to say to your friend—if he will let it for the winter—I shall be glad to treat.[1]—I wish you had come down here for you would not have got away in a hurry as the roads are impassable but I believe I shall try them in ye beginning of January—but pray write again.—Your friend Lady Jane is in excellent health & voice & will I dare say [sing?] "your own songs" to all the tunes you prefer on her return.[2]—Ly O[xford] returns your remembrances & regrets that you did not honour her with yr. presence.—I am in great force & fullness of habit (which I shall reduce on my return) but still pestered with Phryne[3] who has been playing the fool at Brocket Hall and —sdeath!—how you will laugh! *burning me* in *effigy* (instead of Guy Faux I presume) but all this absurdity is literally true—& she vows all kinds of ridiculous vengeance. I can have no intelligence to send you from this wilderness —but I wish you would *row* Murray for not sending me the Quarterly according to promise—if you step that way.—When will you be out?[4]

yrs, ever

B.

[1] Pope, *Essay on Criticism*, ll. 420–421:

"But let a Lord once own the happy lines,
How the wit brightens! how the style refines!"

[2] Candidus is probably Byron. The letter appeared in the *Morning Chronicle* of Oct. 17, 1812. See Oct. 14, 1812, to Lord Holland. (Vol. 2, p. 225.)

[1] Byron was then at Eywood, Presteign, established as the Cavalier Servente of Lady Oxford. He wanted to rent a house near the Oxfords.

[2] Lady Jane Harley was the young daughter of Lady Oxford. Although she was only thirteen at the time, Hobhouse was romantically interested in her.

[3] One of the fanciful names that Lady Caroline Lamb adopted for herself.

[4] Hobhouse was working on his *Journey through Albania* which was finally published on May 23, 1813.

[TO MATTHEW GREGORY LEWIS] [*1813?*]

My dear L[ewi]s—I will call about 6—we have *both* an offer of places from Ly. M[elbourn]e in Ld. Egremont's box—but I think we shall have more of the audience—(always more amusing than the performers on a *first* night) in the seats you have taken.—We can go to which you please.[1]—

ever yrs.
BIRON

[TO CHARLES HANSON] *March 28th. 1813*

[In Vol. 3, p. 33, from Parke-Bernet Catalogue, with slight omission ("immediately" omitted after "Rochdale").]

[TO HENRY GALLY KNIGHT]

4 Bennet Street. St. James's. May 5th. 1813

My dear Sir—I am glad you like the fragments[1] because independent of other qualifications none but a traveller can judge correctly of the *costume* of one's Orientalisms.———Pano Canarioti[?][2] is very good *poetical*—but not—matter of fact authority—it is however of no consequence to your purpose—both Hobhouse & myself had our account from an eye witness & performer in *their* scene.———Your plan is new & excellent—if you should tire of the regular measure which after all is the best—why not compose a tale in each—the Spenser—the lyric—and any —except perhaps blank verse? which is not a good *publishing* measure. You must & will get over your qualms—& I would wish to recommend Murray as a publisher who will do justice to your work[3]—I should esteem it as a favour if you would allow him to *deal* (I must talk in technicals) with you on this occasion.———At all events I trust nothing will deter you from adding to your own reputation & to our pleasure—

[1] In Volume 3, pp. 4–5 from catalogue, which omitted the last sentence.

[1] *The Giaour* was a disconnected tale to which Byron added sections in each succeeding edition. He once referred to it as "this snake of a poem, which has been lengthening its rattles every month".

[2] Unidentified.

[3] Murray did become Knight's publisher, turning out his *Ilderim, a Syrian Tale* (1816), and *Phrosyne, a Grecian Tale*, and *Alashtar, an Arabian Tale* (1817). Byron later ridiculed Knight's tales as insipid and wrote satirical verses on him.

you want nothing but confidence in your own powers.———Your friend Mr. Douglas is about I understand to publish an essay on Greece which I have not seen[4]—but have heard it "applauded to the very echo"[5] and that by persons not much accustomed to praise.———The more we have upon the East the better—it is a subject to which the world has betaken itself with great good humour—& one upon which you must feel still more interested than myself—inasmuch as you have seen more of it.—How is your health?—it will give me sincere gratification to know that while your poem is proceeding—*that* has not retrograded.—Believe me with great truth

faithfully yrs.
BYRON

P.S.—Though I am no critic—I suppose you would not allow me to have a peek—I should of course keep sacred & return any extract.———

[TO LORD AND LADY GREY] *Albany May 20th. 1813*

Ld. Byron presents his compliments to Lord and Lady Grey.[1] Ld. B will have the honour of fulfilling his engagement on Monday next—& feels always too much gratified in ye prospect of meeting Lord and Lady Grey to run any risk of forgetting their kind invitation.

[TO JOHN MURRAY (*a*)] *[June, 1813?]*

"Should seek & share her narrow bed"[1]

the 4 lines you have to FINISH this *paragraph*

[TO JOHN MURRAY (*b*)] *[June, 1813?]*

D[ea]r Sir—I hope the Catalogue of the books &c. has not been

[4] The Hon. Frederick Sylvester North Douglas, only son of Lord Glenbervie, published an "Essay on Certain Points of Resemblance between the Ancient and Modern Greeks" in 1813.

[5] *Macbeth*, Act V, scene 3: "I would applaud thee to the very echo."

[1] The 2nd Earl Grey, later Prime Minister (1830–34) and promoter of the Reform Bill of 1832, was a liberal Whig whom Byron admired and respected.

[1] In the first edition of 41 pages of *The Giaour*, p. 37, line 2.

published without my seeing it[1]—I must reserve several—& many ought not to be printed.—The advertisement is a very bad one—I am not going to the *Morea*—& if I was—you might as well—advertise a man in Russia as going to *Yorkshire*.——

ever yrs.

[TO T. OR J. CLARKE] *July 15th. 1813*

Sir—If Mr. S. thinks proper to wait till the Purchaser of Newstead has fulfilled his contract his demand will be liquidated—if not—he must pursue his own remedy.—Mr. J. Hanson—65[6] Chancery Lane is the address of my attorney.—I shall forward your letter to him this day & am

yrs. &c.
BYRON[1]

[TO THE DUCHESS OF SOMERSET[1]] *August 15, 1813*

I leave London so soon that it will not be in my power to have the honour of seeing you before my departure.

Your Grace is one of the few whom I would not willingly see for ye *last* time—and though my regrets are not numerous I must not add so melancholy a reflection to ye account.

I trust at some future period you will permit me to renew an acquaintance which does me such honour—and should be more grieved for its present interruption—but for the idea that you will now have less to remember to my disadvantage—if indeed you condescend to

[1] When Byron was preparing to leave England in June, 1813, he arranged with R. H. Evans, the auctioneer, to sell his books. The catalogue stated that they were "the property of a nobleman about to leave England on a tour of the Morea", and the sale was advertised for Thursday, July 8th, and the following day. (See Dallas, *Recollections of the Life of Lord Byron from the Year 1808 to the end of 1814*, Philadelphia, 1825, pp. lxiii–lxiv.) Byron did not go abroad then and his books were not sold until Evans auctioned them on April 5 and 6, 1816.

[1] In Vol. 3, p. 76, from catalogue, unsigned and with variations.

[1] Charlotte, second daughter of the 9th Duke of Hamilton, married the 11th Duke of Somerset in 1800. She had the reputation of being somewhat sparing in her domestic economy and in the entertainment of the guests of the Duke, who devoted himself to science and mathematics and was a patron of men of science and letters.

remember me at all.—With my best wishes for your health and welfare—I have ye honour to be most respectfully

Yr. obliged & faithful Servant

Byron

[TO JOHN MURRAY (*a*)] [*Septr. 1813?*]

The circumstances related in the following letter[1] I have kept back for reasons which will be sufficiently obvious—and ⟨had no other testimony than so⟩ indeed till no very long time ago I was not aware that the occurrence to which it alludes was known to the writer—and when once aware of it—it will not perhaps appear unnatural that I should feel desirous to be informed of "the tale as it was told to him"[2] on the spot & in a country where oral tradition is the only record—& where in a ⟨few years⟩ short time facts are either forgotten or distorted from the truth.——

Here print the letter.—

As a picture of Turkish Ethics—and having in some degree a reference to the fiction of the foregoing poem—the perusal may not perhaps displease the reader—the writer of the letter was the only countryman of mine who arrived on the spot for some time after the event to [which] he alludes—he relates what he heard—it is not requisite for me to subjoin either assent or contradiction.—

[TO JOHN MURRAY (*b*)] [*Sept., 1813?*]

D[ea]r Sir—Will you find out for me about the *Storeship*.[1]—

ever yrs.

B

[1] Lord Sligo's letter, written at Byron's request explaining what he had learned in Athens about Byron's rescue of a Turkish girl about to be drowned for infidelity, was supposedly the basis of the story of *The Giaour*. Byron apparently intended this as a note to a new edition of the poem, but Sligo's letter was not published until Moore included it in Byron's *Life* in 1830. Byron hinted in his journal and elsewhere that the letter did not tell the whole truth and for that reason he wanted to circulate it to satisfy public curiosity and to counter rumours too near the fact. Sligo's letter (12 lines were heavily crossed out in the MS.) is printed in *LJ*, II, 257–258n.

[2] Scott, *The Lay of the Last Minstrel*, Canto I, stanza 22:

"I cannot tell how the truth may be;
I say the tale as 'twas said to me."

[1] Byron was looking for passage in a storeship to the Mediterranean. See Vol. 3, p. 88.

[TO JOHN MURRAY] [*November, 1813?*]

[In Vol. 3, p. 156, with slight variations.]

[TO ?] *Novr. 20th. 1813*

Sir/—There are 2 portraits—both by Mr. Phillips now at Mr. Sharpe's for the purpose of engraving—and one at Mr. Westall's[1] in W. Charlotte Street—which possibly your artist may prefer—as no plate has been taken from it.—So much of my time has been passed in different parts of the world—that I can hardly refer to any friend sufficiently acquainted with "the data" requisite—which are confused even in my own memory.——Mr. Dallas—(a letter addressed to him at Messrs Longman will reach him) is very well acquainted with my family—and with some of the particulars of which you may wish to be informed—& would I am sure willingly communicate all that are necessary.——I have to thank you very sincerely for thinking such enquiries worth your trouble—and am

very truly yr. obliged & obedt. Svt.
BYRON

[TO JOHN HAMILTON REYNOLDS] *Fy. 20th. 1814*

[In Vol. 4, pp. 68–69, from *The Athenaeum.* There are slight variations in punctuation from the MS.]

[TO JOHN MURRAY] [*April 18, 1814?*][1]

Dear Sir/—If Mr. Valpy[2] sends for ye Ode[3]—let him have it at *my* cost—and if published within any reasonable time *one* of the copies with the new Stanza.—I enclose ye proof & some verses the Ode have procured me—very pretty—& meant to be sarcastic.—

yrs. ever
B

[1] Both Phillips and Westall painted portraits of Byron in 1813.

[1] Probably the same date as the letter to an unknown correspondent [Mr. Valpy] addressed on that date. See Vol. 4, p. 98.

[2] See Vol. 2, p. 133, second note 1.

[3] Byron's *Ode to Napoleon Buonaparte* was published by Murray on April 16, 1814. A second edition with added stanzas was published soon after.

[TO FRANCIS JEFFREY] *February 28th. 1815*

Whatever pride I may have felt in your praise of works which I will not affect to undervalue, since they have been sanctioned by your judgment, is, nevertheless, far inferior to the pleasure I should derive from the power of exciting, and the opportunity of cultivating, your personal friendship. My former letter, in 1812, was written under circumstances of embarrassment; for, although you had not allowed my rashness to operate upon your public sentence,[1] I was by no means sure that your private feelings were equally unbiassed. Indeed, I felt that I did not deserve that they should be so, and was, besides, not a little apprehensive of the misconstruction which might be put upon my motives by others, though your own spirit and generosity would acquit me of such to yourself. I shall be now most happy to obtain and preserve whatever portion of your regard you may allot to me. The whole of your conduct to me has already secured mine, with many obligations which would be oppressive, were it not for my esteem of him who has conferred them. I hope we shall meet before a very long time has elapsed; and then, and now, I would willingly endeavour to sustain your good opinion.

[TO SAMUEL TAYLOR COLERIDGE] *Piccadilly March 31st.* 1815

[In Vol. 4, pp. 285–286, from Moore, with slight variations from the MS.]

[TO HENRY GALLY KNIGHT] *April 4th. 1815*

Dear Knight—I have read "Alashtar" with attention and great pleasure.—It appears to me preferable to the Yaniote but that may be owing to the measure which is a favourite of mine.——I have seen nothing to make me change the opinion already expressed—very little to alter—& hardly anything which is not—or may not be made very good.—I have always thought both the *risk* & the *reward* of publication (I don't mean *pecuniary* reward but fame & so forth) very much overrated—& half imaginary—but I have seldom seen less ground for ap-

[1] Jeffrey reviewed the first two cantos of *Childe Harold* in the *Edinburgh Review* (Vol. XIX, pp. 466–477, Feb., 1812) with generous praise, though Byron had attacked him bitterly in *English Bards and Scotch Reviewers,* wrongly thinking that he was the author of the caustic review of *Hours of Idleness,* which in fact was written by Henry Brougham.

prehension on the part of an author than in the poem before me.——
Believe me

very truly yr. obliged & affecte St.
BYRON

[TO DOUGLAS KINNAIRD] *July 17th. 1815*

My dear K.—I will be your postman—pray lend me your *Goldoni*[1] for a day or two!——I will visit you tomorrow at 4—

yrs. ever
B

P.S.—My hand shakes so I can hardly scrawl.—

[TO—ALLSOP] *13 Piccadilly Terrace.—August 21st. 1815*

Sir—Your letter states that Mr. Maby paid "Eighty pounds of the sum charged out of pocket at my solicitation"—this is not correct—nor do I understand that part of the statement—to whom was this paid?—& when & where was such solicitation made on my part?—Whatever Mr. M is "fairly entitled to" he shall have—but I wish for the particulars of his account—which I have never yet received.——I believe that the gentleman to whom I am addressing myself is the friend of Mr. Walker—who was recently in London—& saw Mr. Hanson.—Mr. Hanson told me that Mr. Walker had some disposition to take the Manor of Newstead for the ensuing season[1]—provided it were to be let—this is not my present intention—but if Mr. W. is fond of sporting he is very welcome to shoot there whenever he pleases—& should such permission be agreeable to him—you would oblige me by telling him so with my compliments.——I am Sir

yr. very obedt. Sert.
BYRON

[TO SAMUEL ROGERS] *Fy. 16th. 1816*

[In Vol. 4, pp. 61–62 (to Rogers (*b*)) as Feb. 16, 1814, from *LJ*, III, 38, with slight variations in punctuation.]

[1] Carlo Goldoni (1707–1793), the Italian writer of comedies. Byron knew his work as early as 1811 (see Vol. 2, p. 104), and later saw many of his comedies in Venice.

[1] Walker's interest in Newstead was such that in 1814 Byron thought he might buy it after Claughton defaulted in his contract to purchase. See Vol. 4, pp. 186, 188.

[TO PRYSE LOCKHART GORDON] [*July? 1816*]

Reinagle is a better poet and a better ornithologist than I am; eagles and all birds of prey attack with their talons, and not with their beaks, and I have altered the line thus—

"Then tore, with bloody talon, the rent plain.

This is, I think, a better line, besides its poetical justice.[1]

[TO JOHN MURRAY] *Florence—April 23d. 1817*

If Mr. G[iffor]d thinks this good—it may be published[1]—you will see that it is the consequence of a visit to Ferrara.——I am thus far on my way to *Rome*—but mean to return to Venice directly—so address your answer to *Venice*, as usual.——I have done nothing at the 3d. act of Manfred—but will—by and bye.——

yrs. [scrawl]

P.S.—On this day year the *23d.*—I left London—& on the 25th. England.——

[TO JOHN MURRAY] *Rome.—May 9th. 1817*

Corrections Canto 3d.[1]—

Stanza *103*—you have printed in line first *love* instead of "learn that *Lore*"—which you may easily see by the ultimate rhyme of "*more*" as well as by the *sense* that it should be—I remember in the *M.S.*—taking particular pains to make the *r* legible—anticipating some such cursed blunder of Mr. Davison.—

Stanza 85.

[1] Byron had visited the field of Waterloo with Gordon and afterwards wrote his impressions in two stanzas which later appear in the third canto of *Childe Harold*. Before leaving Brussels he copied them into Mrs. Gordon's album. A few weeks later, Gordon wrote, "the well-known artist, R. R. Reinagle, a friend of mine, arrived in Brussels." Gordon asked him to make a drawing to go with these lines:

"Here his last flight the haughty eagle flew,
Then tore, with bloody beak, the fatal plain."

Mr. Reinagle "sketched with a pencil a spirited chained eagle, grasping the earth with his talons." When Gordon told Byron of the liberty the artist had taken, he received the above reply.

[1] The poem was *The Lament of Tasso*. Murray published it on July 17, 1817.

[1] These printer's errors are in the first edition of the third canto of *Childe Harold*, published by Murray in December, 1816.

Line 2d.—it was not "*wide* world" but "wild world".——I sent you a long letter last night.——

yrs.

[TO RICHARD BELGRAVE HOPPNER] *Venice. Nov. 20, 1817*

[In Vol. 5, pp. 274–275, from Bixby, with variations in punctuation.]

[TO RICHARD BELGRAVE HOPPNER] *January 18th. 1818*

I wish you Joy and hope that the young Venetian and his Mother are both doing their best.—

His father's Sense, his Mother's Grace,
In Him I hope will always fit so
With (still to keep him in good case)
The Health and Appetite of *Rizzo*.[1]—

yrs ever

[TO DOUGLAS KINNAIRD] *Venice. May 3d. 1818*

Dear Douglas—A Son of a friend of Mr. Rose's—noble Venetian by birth—young in years & unfortunate by circumstances—has been strongly recommended to me to recommend to others—for a situation in some banking house—for which if his qualifications are adequate—his honesty can be vouched for.——The young man is named *Giorgi*[1] —his family Patrician—his age seventeen or eighteen.—This letter will be delivered by himself.—If you can help him to what he seeks in your own—or by recommendation to other banking houses—or rather house—you will do good—and oblige me, and I make it my earnest & particular request that you will as far as in you lies do what you can for him.—

ever yrs & truly affectionately
BYRON

[1] Hoppner's newborn son, probably named for Count Francesco Rizzo Patarol, a Venetian nobleman.

[1] See April 7, 1819, to Kinnaird (Vol. 6, p. 109).

[TO SIGNORE D'ORVILLE[1]] *Bologna. August 21st. 1819*[2]

Sir,—I wrote some time ago to Edgecombe desiring him to bring my daughter Allegra directly to me at Bologna—and informing him that you would authorize from *me* Messrs Siri & Willhalm to furnish the necessary sum for his journey.——I am impatient to see my child —and wish her to be sent immediately—with all proper regard to her health & pleasure on the journey.—I cannot admit of any further delay.—When I return to Venice—(which may be soon or late according to circumstances) she will accompany me—but in the mean time I wish to have her with me.——I received yr. letter of the 14th. and am very much obliged by the trouble you are taking in my con[c]erns—excuse this further one—and believe me

very truly yr. obliged & obedt. Sert.

BYRON

P.S.—I dare say the child may be very comfortable with the [Gehnis?]—but I must have her with me—and I am a good deal surprized at Edgecombe's delay—did he receive my letter?——

[TO JOHN MURRAY] *Bologna. Septr. 7th. 1819*

[In Vol. 6, pp. 223–224, from *LJ*, IV, 353–354, where the date is given as Sept. 17, 1819. Slight variations from the MS.]

[TO MICHELE LEONI] [*May 8–10? 1820*]

[Written for Byron by Teresa Guiccioli]

Pregiatissimo Signore—Il far piacere a Lei—ed il contribuire in qualche maniere ad onorare la memoria del nostro immortale S[hakespeare?]—sono cose che io valuto moltissimo—e per le quali supererei ogni ostacolo—anzi mi si convertirebbe in diletto qualunque fastidio. Ma p[er] mio dispiacere più che per suo certamente—vi è forza dirle che il solo limite che poteva arrestare in questo caso la mia volontà— è quello appunto che ora mi si presenta *il rifiuto dato a vari miei Amici che mi hanno interressato* [*sic*] *p*[*er*] *simili cose in addietro.* Secondondo

[1] Byron regularly spelled the name Dorville when referring to him in his letters and also in the address of a letter to him of Aug. 9, 1819, but in the address of this letter it is clearly written D'Orville.

[2] The first two sentences of this letter were published in Volume 6, p. 198, from a Sotheby catalogue, where the date was erroneously given as August 2, 1819.

dunque ora i miei e di Lei desideri—io non potrei che incontrare e ben giustamente i loro rimproveri. Mi confido che Ella non avrà queste ragioni p[er] pretesti—ma che anzi conoscendole buone mi perdonerà. Mi sarà però ben grato associarmi p[er] due copie—il cui prezzo io anticiperò anche ⟨ben⟩ volontieri—se Ella me ne indicherà la direzione.

Io non mi meraviglio punto delle Vessazioni da Lei incontrate p[er] la Versione colla quale ha onorato il 4 o Canto del mio Childe Harold—bene mi sarei meravigliato del contrario; solo mi duole che sieno cadute sopra di Lei. Per la ristampa poi di questa Versione—che Ella pensa commettere in Inghilterra—se io osassi lusingarmi che le fosse grato un mio consiglio ne la disuaderei. E ciò solamente p[er] ⟨suo vantaggio⟩ le grandissime spese della stampa—e p[er] la maggiore difficoltà in seguito dell'esito. In ogni modo Ella farà ciò che più le aggrada—mi basta solo che in ogni maniera riconosca in me quella stima che mi fa dichiarare

Il suo Devo[tissi]mo Servitore
LORD BYRON

[TRANSLATION] [*May 8–10? 1820*][1]

[Teresa's note at top: "Written by me at Lord Byron's request"]

Dear Sir—To please you—and to contribute in some way to honour the memory of our immortal S[hakespeare?]—are things that I value very much—and for which I would overcome every obstacle—in fact, it would convert any annoyance into a pleasure for me. But for my displeasure more than for yours certainly—it is unavoidable that I tell you that the only restraint that in this case could have checked my willingness[2]—is precisely that which now occurs to me—*the refusal given to several of my friends that had applied to me for similar things in the past*. Therefore, if I were to accede to your wishes and my own now—I could not but encounter, and very justly, their reproaches. I am counting on the fact that you will not take these reasons as pretexts—but on the contrary, knowing them to be good [reasons] you will excuse me. I will however be very glad to subscribe for two copies—the price of which I will pay in advance—also willingly—if you will advise me as to the management of it.

I am not surprised at all at the vexations that you have encountered

[1] This is apparently a reply to Leoni's letter quoted in Byron's letter to John Murray of May 8, 1820. (See Vol. 7, p. 97.)

[2] Byron was unwilling to have any of his poems translated into Italian, as Leoni asked his permission to do.

for the translation with which you have honoured the 4th Canto of my *Childe Harold*—I would have been very surprised by the opposite; I am pained only that they [the vexations] have fallen upon you. As for the reprinting of this translation that you think of commissioning in England—if I dare flatter myself that you might be grateful for my advice—I would dissuade you from it.[3] And this only for the tremendous expense of the printing—and for the great difficulty afterwards of the sale. Anyhow, you will do that which is most agreeable to you—it is enough for me only that you might, in any case, recognize in me that esteem which makes me declare myself

Your most devoted servant
LORD BYRON[4]

[RICHARD BELGRAVE HOPPNER] *Ravenna, July 20th, 1820*

[In Vol. 7, pp. 135–6, from *LJ*, V, 55–57, with slight variations from MS.]

[TO RICHARD BELGRAVE HOPPNER] *Ravenna August 31st. 1820*

My dear Hoppner/—I thank you for the termination of the Mocenigo.[1]—The Spoons are sent by Vincenzo[2] with some books.—No Novels have been sent lately by Murray—not even the Monastery. ——An Advocate Fossati writes about Merryweather[3] wanting me to sign a paper.—He says—that I ⟨said⟩ declared to Mingaldo[4]—"that I would release him—" *previously* to his arrest.—To Mingaldo I never spoke on the subject in my life—I have not even seen him for these last fifteen months.—I ⟨said⟩ wrote to you to let him out—but this was *after* he was *in*—and as you showed no great alacrity and the fellow had behaved like a damned rascal—there was no violent hurry ⟨shown⟩ manifested on my part.—I will do whatever you think proper about it —I never meant to *keep* him in—but it seems to be the law—& not the

[3] Leoni's translation of the Fourth Canto of *Childe Harold* was confiscated in spite of the fact that some passages the censor objected to were omitted. He wanted to have the whole translation printed in England.

[4] Transcribed and translated by Ricki B. Herzfeed.

[1] Byron finally, through Hoppner, gave up the lease on the Palazzo Mocenigo in Venice, after much squabbling with the owners about reparation of damages, etc.

[2] Vincenzo Papi, Byron's coachman, who was later the assailant of Sergeant Masi in Pisa in 1822. (See Vol. 9, p. 139.)

[3] See Vol. 6, p. 213, note 1.

[4] See Vol. 6, p. 51, note 3.

creditor at present which does so. As to signing papers—one should think twice first—and *he* should have thought twice—before he bilked his bail[5]—and then defied me at law for two years—however I have no objection to let him out again.——Allegra has been unwell—but is getting better in the country—where the air is much purer,—the heat has been tremendous.—Take care of your little boy—my best respects to Madame Hoppner—believe me

ever yrs most truly
BYRON

P.S.—My Paris papers come direct—but the Calais paper goes round by Venice.—I got all right by Vincenzo—who—however *had eaten double* wages—taking here & there his pay.—Have you never got a hint of the Napoleons—how many were there?—I will remit them, or will you draw on *me* through *Siri* & Willhalm and I will honour the draft.——I don't write politics—on account of the post.[6]—

[TO COUNT GIUSEPPE ALBORGHETTI] *Ravenna, May 25th, 1821*

[In Volume 8, p. 124, with slight variations from the MS.]

[TO THE GOVERNOR OF PISA] [*March 27, 1822?*]

Eccellenza,—Mi è stato recato questo documento, che io credo doversi aggiungere all rapporto da me presentato; e perciò mi pregio di farlo presente a V[ostro] E[ccellenza]. Ill relatore è pronto a confermare in ogni modo ciò che ha veduto e qui descritto. Sono di V. E.

Umilissimo Dev[otissi]mo Servitore,
NOEL BYRON, Pair d'Angleterre

[TRANSLATION] [*March 27, 1822?*]

Excellency,—There has been brought to me this document[1], which I believe should be subjoined to the report which I have submitted; and therefore I take the liberty of having it presented to Your

[5] This seems to throw light on Byron's lengthy quarrel with Merryweather. He apparently lent him money to pay bail when the merchant was in trouble with the law, and Merryweather either jumped bail or refused to pay it back.

[6] A fragment of this letter was published from a quotation in a catalogue in Vol. 7, p. 167.

[1] The deposition was that of Dr. James Crawford, an English resident of Pisa, concerning what he had witnessed of the Masi affair. The Italian text and Medwin's partial translation is given in *LJ*, VI, 404–5, 406.

Exellency. The reporter is ready to confirm in every way what he has seen and has here described. I am Your Excellency's

Most humble devoted servant,
NOEL BYRON, Peer of England[2]

[TO ?]

[*Lerici*] *Octr. 2d. 1822*

Sir—I have been very unwell and confined to my bed for four days, but am up today again—and ⟨will⟩ it is my intention (if the weather serve) to start early tomorrow.——A place in the felucca is at your service—or if you prefer it—I have a small Schooner of my own in the harbour on board of which you may embark at pleasure—though there will be this difference—that the felucca can *row* and the Schooner must *sail* so that the Wind must determine the matter.——I have the honour to be

yr. obedt. humble Svt.
N B

EXCERPTS FROM MOORE'S MANUSCRIPT JOURNAL[1]

(Passages deleted by Moore from Byron's letters when he published them in his *Letters and Journals of Lord Byron with Notices of His Life.*)

JOURNAL OF MARCH 3, 4, 1842:

No date given by Moore. "You say nothing of * * [Rogers]—how is the old fellow? Has he written nothing more *posthumous* since Jacqueline?"[2]

Septr. 19, 1818. "I should have preferred Medea to any woman that

[2] Editor's translation.

[1] These excerpts were sent to me by Professor Wilfred S. Dowden, of Rice University, who is now editing Moore's journals from the original manuscripts. They were omitted by Lord John Russell when he published Moore's *Memoirs, Journal, and Correspondence* (1853–56).

[2] *Jacqueline* was published in a volume with Byron's *Lara* in 1814.

ever breathed. You may perhaps wonder that I don't in that case *take to my wife. But she is a poor mawkish, moral Clytemnestra (and no Medea) who likes to be vindictive according to law, and to hew me down as Samuel sawed Agag, religiously.*[3] I would have forgiven the dagger and the bowl. . . ."

No date given by Moore. "Three on the clock—I must 'to bed—to bed' as Mother Siddons [as Lady Macbeth] (that tragical friend of the mathematical Blue Devil, my wife) says."

No date given by Moore. Speaking of Rogers he [Byron] says "The Countess Albrizzi showed me a head of him done by Denon at Paris—as like and large as death.—"

Moore wrote: "He called Queen Caroline, the *Quim*, and has several coarse jests thereon."

No date given by Moore. "P. S.—What do you think of 'Manfred'? considering all things, it must astonish *you.* But—always a but—I can't express myself, in writing—however you will understand me."

Feby. 2d. 1818. "I have a great love for my little Ada, though perhaps she may torture me like *the mathematical Medea, her mother, who thinks theorems and speaks problems; and has destroyed, as far as in her lay, her husband, by only shaking her head, like Lord Burleigh, in the Critic.*"[4]

No date given by Moore. Moore writes: "In speaking of Murray he says, it is hardly possible for tradesmen to continue long gentlemen." And he quotes Byron: "They may start like a free-booter, into a sudden fit of grandeur, but they are sure to relapse."

JOURNAL OF MARCH 3–4, 9, 10.

No date given by Moore. Moore writes: "In one of his letters to me he talks of having endured so long Rogers's 'liver-complaint, or if you choose to latinize it, *livor.*'"[5]

No date given by Moore. Speaking of the ninth canto of *Don Juan,* Byron says, ". . . with much sarcasm on those butchers in large business, your mercenary soldiery, it affords also a good opportunity of gracing the Proem with that disgrace to his country, the pensioned imposter, Wellington."

[Sept., 1822?] "H[obhouse] has been here, and is gone to Florence—do you remember your saying that you would rather *praise* him than *live* with him? For my part I say nothing."

[3] The omitted passage is in italics.
[4] The omitted passage is in italics.
[5] Envy, spite, malice.

Moore writes: "The following is of Rogers, written in 1814"—"Lately I have seen him much—with that chin of his like the Dew Drop—it never falls without some character hanging by it to dislocation. It is a good man—but they tell me he loveth me not. Whether he does or no, I make great efforts to like him. This says moreover he likes not the success of another.—Do you believe in such things? I don't. I suppose it is what in time we shall all come to."

Letter of 1816. "Sam [MS. damaged] depend upon it—Who would dare to cut off his head, as [MS. damaged] follow [MS. damaged] decapitated the Gorgon? I suppose you think it is rolling down the Brenta or Po, muttering the Pleasures of Mummery."[6]

No date given by Moore. Moore writes: "Having asked him on some occasion whether he knew any one who would undertake a review of Sismondi, he says, in his answer, 'If I thought you meant it to me, I should swear you were not shamming, but *Sam*-ming me—comprenez vous?—i.e. trying to make me do a foolish thing for the pleasure of seeing a particular friend fail.'"

Moore writes: "In one of his many tirades against Wordsworth, and the Lakers, he states '[Wordsworth] that pedlar-praising son of a bitch'. Another of the erased passages about * * is as follows—'You may say what you please, but please *think* as I do about him.—damn him. I believe him to be [MS. damaged] of unhappiness!'. The very day of his quitting Pisa, I heard of the death of [MS. damaged]."[7]

[6] Samuel Rogers published *The Pleasures of Memory* in 1792.

[7] Possibly Castlereagh, who died about this time.

Appendix I

LIST OF LETTERS AND SOURCES

Date	*Recipient*	*Source of Text*	*Page*
		1823	
Aug. 3	Edward Blaquiere	MS. Murray	15
Aug. 4	Teresa Guiccioli	MS. Biblioteca Classense, Ravenna	15
Aug. 10	Teresa Guiccioli	MS. Biblioteca Classense, Ravenna	15
Aug. 10	Charles F. Barry	MS. Murray	16
Aug. 11	Teresa Guiccioli	MS. Biblioteca Classeuse, Ravenna	18
Aug. 20	Teresa Guiccioli	MS. Biblioteca Classense, Ravenna	18
Aug. 23	Teresa Guiccioli	MS. Biblioteca Classense, Ravenna	18
Aug. 26	Capt. Wright Knox	Text: Kennedy, *Conversations on Religion with Lord Byron*, pp. 388–389	19
Sept. 4	William Fletcher	MS. Murray	20
Sept. 9	Col. Charles Napier	MS. Robert H. Taylor Coll., Princeton University Library	20
Sept. 11	Teresa Guiccioli	MS. Biblioteca Classense, Ravenna	21
Sept. 11	John Cam Hobhouse	MS. Murray	21
Sept. 12	D. Grant & Co.	Text: City Book Auction, Nov. 24, 1945	25
Sept. 15	John Cam Hobhouse	MS. Murray	26
Sept. 18	Capt. Clifford, R.N.	MS. Scripps College Library	27
Sept. 27	John Cam Hobhouse	MS. Murray	27
Sept. 28	Journal in Cephalonia	MS. Murray	29
Oct. 1	Alexander Mavrocordatos	MS. Benaki Museum, Athens	36

Date	*Recipient*	*Source of Text*	*Page*
		1823 (continued)	
		Vol. VII, f. 17)	63
Nov. 25	Col. Leicester Stanhope	MS. Stark Library, University of Texas	64
Nov. 29	John Bowring	MS. Roe-Byron Coll., Newstead Abbey	64
Nov. 29	Teresa Guiccioli	MS. Biblioteca Classense, Ravenna	66
Nov. 30	General Govt. of Greece	MS. National Library, Athens	66
Dec. 2	Alexander Mavrocordatos	MS. Benaki Museum, Athens	70
Dec. 7	John Bowring	MS. Henry E. Huntington Library	72
Dec. 10	John Bowring	MS. Carl H. Pforzheimer Library	73
Dec. 10–11	Douglas Kinnaird	MS. Murray	74
Dec. 11	Charles F. Barry	MS. Murray	75
Dec. 13	John Bowring	MS. Stark Library, University of Texas	76
Dec. 14	Teresa Guiccioli	MS. Biblioteca Classense, Ravenna	78
Dec. 15	London Greek Committee	MS. National Library, Athens	79
Dec. 23	Douglas Kinnaird	MS. Murray	80
Dec. 23–24	Charles F. Barry	MS. Murray	81
Dec. 26	John Bowring	MS. Stark Library, University of Texas	82
Dec. 26	Dr. James Kennedy	Text: *Englische Studien*, Vol. 51, 385–387 (1918)	84
Dec. 27	Thomas Moore	Text: Moore, II, 700	84
Dec. 27	John Cam Hobhouse	MS. Murray	85
Dec. 27	Douglas Kinnaird	Text: *Notes and Queries*, 4th ser., Vol. 4, p. 250, Sept. 25, 1869	85
Dec. 31	Col. Leicester Stanhope	Text: Moore, II, 705–706	86
		1824	

Date	*Recipient*	*Source of Text*	*Page*
		1824 (continued)	
Jan. 2	Henry Muir	MS. Stark Library, University of Texas	87
Jan. 2	Charles Hancock	MS. Harrow School Library	89
Jan. 7	Lord Sydney Osborne	MS. Pierpont Morgan Library	90
Jan. 13–14	Charles Hancock	MS. Harrow School Library	91
Jan. 17	Charles Hancock	MS. Harrow School Library	94
Jan. 19	Charles Hancock	MS. Harrow School Library	95
Jan. 19	George Stevens	MS. Stark Library, University of Texas	96
Jan. 23	Yusuff Pasha	MS. National Library, Athens	97
Jan. 24	Barff & Hancock	MS. Benaki Museum, Athens	99
Jan. 27	Greek Captains of Privateers	MS. Biblioteca Classense, Ravenna; Text: Gamba, *A Narrative of Lord Byron's Last Journey to Greece, p.* 136	99
Jan. 27	Samuel Barff	MS. Benaki Museum, Athens	100
Jan. 27	Teresa Guiccioli	MS. Biblioteca Classense, Ravenna	101
Jan. 27	Capt. Yorke	MS. British Library (Zambelli Papers—Add. 46878)	101
Jan. 28	John Bowring	MS. National Library of Scotland	101
Jan. 30	Andreas Londos	MS. Ivan Londos	103
Feb. 1	Edward Blaquiere	Text: F. Naylor (London), No. 32, Oct. 1877	104
Feb. 5	Alexander Mavrocordatos	MS. Benaki Museum, Athens	104
Feb. 5–9	Charles Hancock	MS. Harrow School Library	106
Feb. 9	Douglas Kinnaird	MS. Murray	110
Feb. 11	Samuel Barff	MS. Benaki Museum, Athens	110
Feb. 11	Teresa Guiccioli	MS. Biblioteca Classense, Ravenna	111
Feb. 15	Note on Suliotes	MS. Murray	111

Date	*Recipient*	*Source of Text*	*Page*
		1824 (continued)	
Feb. 15	Journal	MS. Murray	113
Feb. 17	Suliotes and Artillery Corps	MS. Gennadius Library, Athens	115
Feb. 19	Samuel Barff	MS. Benaki Museum, Athens	115
Feb. 21	Samuel Barff	MS. Benaki Museum, Athens	115
Feb. 21	Douglas Kinnaird	MS. National Historical Museum, Athens	116
[Feb. 21]	Mr. Mayer	Text: Gamba, pp. 181–182	118
[Feb. 22?]	Samuel Barff (*a*)	MS. Benaki Museum, Athens	118
Feb. 22	Samuel Barff (*b*)	MS. Fales Coll., New York University Library	119
Feb. 23	Barff & Hancock	MS. Benaki Museum, Athens	119
Feb. 23	Augusta Leigh	MS. British Library (Add. 31037)	120
Feb. 24	Teresa Guiccioli	MS. Biblioteca Classense, Ravenna	121
Feb. 24	Andreas Londos	MS. Ivan Londos	122
Feb. 25	John Murray	MS. British Library (Ashley 4753)	123
March 4	Thomas Moore	MS. Henry E. Huntington Library	125
March 4	James Kennedy	Text: Moore, II, 743–744	126
March 4	London Greek Committee	MS. Carl H. Pforzheimer Library	127
March 5	Samuel Barff	Text: *LJ*, VI, 340	128
March 8	Sir Frederick Stoven	Text: Maggs Cat. 317, Nov.–Dec., 1913	129
March 9	John Bowring	MS. National Library, Athens	129
March 9	Samuel Barff	MS. Benaki Museum, Athens	130
March 10	Samuel Barff	MS. Benaki Museum, Athens	130
March 10	James Kennedy	Text: Moore, II, 748–750	131

Date	Recipient	Source of Text	Page
		1824 (continued)	
March 10	Charles Hancock	MS. Harrow School Library	133
March 11	Signor Demetrius Parucca	MS. Facsimile, Gamba, *Narrative*	134
Mar. 12–13	Douglas Kinnaird	MS. National Historical Museum, Athens	135
March 13	Douglas Kinnaird	MS. Lord Kinnaird	136
March 17	Teresa Guiccioli	MS. Biblioteca Classense, Ravenna	137
March 17	Samuel Barff	Text: Copy by J. Victor Barff	137
March 19	Col. Leicester Stanhope	MS. Gennadius Library, Athens	137
March 19	Samuel Barff	MS. Benaki Museum, Athens	138
March 19	John Bowring	Text: Stanhope, *Greece in 1823 and 1824*, p. 127n	139
March 22	Samuel Barff	MS. Benaki Museum, Athens	139
Mar. 26–28	Samuel Barff	Text: *LJ*, VI, 359–362; MS. P.S. only, Benaki Museum, Athens	141
March 30	Douglas Kinnaird	Text: *LJ*, VI, 362	143
March 30	John Bowring	MS. Robert H. Taylor Coll., Princeton University Library	145
March 31	The Earl of Clare	MS. British Library (Add. 33964)	148
March 31	The Countess of Jersey	MS. Pierpont Morgan Library	149
March 31	John Cam Hobhouse	MS. Vigo County Library, Terre Haute, Indiana	149
April 1	A Prussian Officer	Text: Gamba, *Narrative*, pp. 235–236	149
April 3	Samuel Barff	MS. Benaki Museum, Athens	150
April 6	Samuel Barff	Text: *LJ*, VI, 370–372	151
April 7	Samuel Barff	MS. Benaki Museum, Athens	152
April 9	Samuel Barff	MS. Benaki Museum,	

Date	*Recipient*	*Source of Text*	*Page*
		Athens	152
April 9	Charles F. Barry	MS. Murray	153
June 22, 1809	To Scrope Berdmore Davies	MSS. All in	156
July 31, 1810	,, ,, ,,	British	157
July 31, 1811	To Charles Skinner Matthews	Library	159
Sept. 2, 1811	To Scrope Berdmore Davies		159
Jan. 14, 1812	,, ,, ,,		160
[1814?] (*a*)	,, ,, ,,		161
[1814?] (*b*)	,, ,, ,,		161
March 24, 1814	,, ,, ,,		162
March 25, 1814	,, ,, ,,		162
March 7, 1817	,, ,, ,,		163
April 10, 1817	,, ,, ,,		164
June 6, 1817	,, ,, ,,		166
Aug. 3, 1818	,, ,, ,,		168
Dec. 7, 1818	,, ,, ,,		168
Jan. 26, 1819	,, ,, ,,		170

ADDITIONAL LETTERS

Date	*Recipient*	*Source of Text*	*Page*
Aug. 26, 1806	Mrs. Massingberd	MS. Mugar Memorial Library, Boston University (In Vol. 1, p. 100, from Sotheby Cat.)	173
May, 1807	[John Edleston?]	MS. Lovelace Papers, Bodleian Library	173
Dec. 1, 1807	Ben Crosby	MS. Humanities Research Center, University of Texas	173
Feb. 11, 1808	William Harness	MS. Dyce Coll., Victoria and Albert Museum (In Vol. 1, from Moore)	174
Sept. 15, 1808	[?]	MS. Carl H. Pforzheimer Library	175

Date	*Recipient*	*Source of Text*	*Page*
Nov. 27, 1808	Francis Hodgson	MS. Harry S. Dickey Coll., Milton S. Eisenhower Library, The Johns Hopkins University	175
[1809?]	[Mrs. Massingberd?]	Text: Copy in letter of the Marchioness of Tweeddale, Murray MSS.	176
Feb. 10, 1809	William Harness	MS. Harry Oppenheimer (Part in Vol. 1 from Sotheby, July 21, 1970)	176
Dec. 10, 1810	Francis Werry	MS. Carl H. Pforzheimer Library	177
Aug. 12, 1811	Samuel Bolton	MS. Brigadier D. E. Taunton (In Vol. 1 from Moore)	177
Dec. 8, 1811	Francis Hodgson	MS. Arents Tobacco Coll., N.Y. Public Library (In Vol. 2 from fac. of first page and *LJ*, V, 82–87)	178
[1812?]	Samuel Rogers (*c*)	MS. Francis Lewis Randolph (In Vol. 2, from Cat.)	180
Feb. 29, 1812	[Samuel Rogers]	MS. Watson Library, University College London	180
March 8, 1812	E. D. Clarke	MS. Widener Coll., Harvard University Library (In Vol. 2 from Cat. of Walter H. Hill, April, 1910)	180
April 12, 1812	[Samuel Rogers]	MS. Watson Library, University College London	180
June 30, 1812	Mr. Longman	MS. University of Delaware Library (In Vol. 2, from Maggs Cat. 425, Summer, 1922)	181
Oct. 13, 1812	Ed. of *Morning Chronicle*	Text: *Morning Chronicle*, Oct. 17, 1812	181
Dec. 26, 1812	John Cam Hobhouse	MS. G. M. Clive	182
[1813?]	M. G. Lewis	MS. Carl H. Pforzheimer Library	183
March 28,	Charles Hanson	MS. Milton S. Eisenhower	

Date	*Recipient*	*Source of Text*	*Page*
1813		Library, The Johns Hopkins University (In Vol. 3, p. 33, from Parke-Bernet Cat.)	183
May 5, 1813	Henry Gally Knight	MS. Fitzherbert Papers, Derbyshire Record Office	183
May 20, 1813	Lord and Lady Grey	MS. Christie's sale, April 2, 1975	184
[June, 1813?]	John Murray (*a*)	MS. D. Tolstoy	184
[June, 1813?]	John Murray (*b*)	Text: Sotheby Cat., Feb. 18, 1975	184
June 15, 1813	T.[J?] Clarke	MS. Gene De Grusen (In Vol. 3, from Parke-Bernet Cat. 318, Nov. 26, 1941)	185
Aug. 15, 1813	The Duchess of Somerset	Text: Helen Gwendolen Ramsden, *Correspondence* of *Two Brothers*, 1906, p. 117	185
[Sept., 1813?]	John Murray (*a*)	MS. The Mitchell Library, the Library of N.S.W., Sydney, Australia	186
[Sept., 1813?]	John Murray (*b*)	MS. Nottingham Archives, M5590	186
[Nov., 1813?]	John Murray	MS. Robert A. Wilson (In Vol. 3, from copy in Murray MSS.)	187
Nov. 20, 1813	[?]	MS. Roger W. Barrett	187
Feb. 20, 1814	J. H. Reynolds	MS. Anonymous (In Vol. 4, from *Athenaeum*, Dec. 31, 1831)	187
[April 18, 1814?]	John Murray	MS. T. Cottrell Dormer	187
Feb. 28, 1815	Francis Jeffrey	Text: Lord Cockburn, *Life of Lord Jeffrey*, I, 416–417	188
March 31, 1815	Samuel Taylor Coleridge	MS. Texas Christian University Library (In Vol. 4, from Moore)	188

Date	*Recipient*	*Source of Text*	*Page*
April 4, 1815	Henry Gally Knight	MS. Fitzherbert Papers, Derbyshire Record Office	188
July 17, [1815?]	Douglas Kinnaird	MS. C. E. P. Clarabut	189
Aug. 21, 1815	Allsop	MS. Carl H. Pforzheimer Library	189
Feb. 16, 1816	Samuel Rogers	MS. Watson Library, University College London. (In Vol. 4, p. 61 as 1814)	189
[July? 1816]	Pryse Lockhart Gordon	Text: *Personal Memoirs*, II, 327	190
April 23, 1817	John Murray	MS. Carl H. Pforzheimer Library	190
May 9, 1817	John Murray	MS. Murray	190
Nov. 20, 1817	R. B. Hoppner	Text: Bixby; Fac. of last page in Rendell Cat. 118 (In Vol. 5, from Bixby)	191
Jan. 18, 1818	R. B. Hoppner	MS. Buffalo and Erie County Public Library	191
May 3, 1818	Douglas Kinnaird	MS. Carl H. Pforzheimer Library	191
Aug. 21, 1819	Signore D'Orville	MS. The Rt. Hon. Lord Brocket	192
Sept. 7, 1819	John Murray	MS. Fac. in *The Complete Works of Lord Byron*, 1 Vol. Brussels, 1830 (In Vol. 6, p. 233, as Sept. 17 from *LJ*, IV, 353)	192
[May 8–10, 1820?]	Michele Leoni	MS. Carl H. Pforzheimer Library	192
July 20, 1820	R. B. Hoppner	MS. Carl H. Pforzheimer Library	194
Aug. 31, 1820	R. B. Hoppner	MS. Pierpont Morgan Library	194
May 25, 1821	Count Giuseppe Alborghetti	MS. Carl H. Pforzheimer Library	195
[March 27, 1822]	Governor of Pisa	Text: Tribolati, *Saggi*, p. 179	195

Date	*Recipient*	*Source of Text*	*Page*
Oct. 2, 1822	[?]	Christie's sale, April 16, 1980	196

ADDITIONS TO ALREADY PUBLISHED LETTERS TO MOORE

1814	Thomas Moore	Text: Moore's MS Diaries, Longman Group Ltd.	page 198
1816	,,	,,	198
Feb. 2, 1818	,,	,,	197
Sept. 19, 1818	,,	,,	196
Sept. 1822	,,	,,	197
The other excerpts are undated		,,	196–8

Appendix II

FORGERIES OF BYRON'S LETTERS

Dec., 1823: "My dear Madam". MS. British Library.

March 9, 1824: To John Murray. In the James Root sale at Charles F. Libbie's, April 22–23, 1879, page 11, item 51.

April 5, 1824: To S. Barff. Schultess-Young, Letter XLVII, pp. 232–233.

ADDITIONAL FORGERIES

March 2, 1814: To John Murray. Milton S. Eisenhower Library, The Johns Hopkins University.

March 2, 1814: To Webster. Bixby.

Appendix III

BIBLIOGRAPHY FOR VOLUME 11

(*Principal short title or abbreviated references*)

Bixby—*Poems and Letters of Lord Byron.* Ed. from the Original Manuscripts in the Possession of W. K. Bixby of St. Louis by W. N. C. Carlton, M. A. Published for the Society of Dofobs, Chicago, 1912.

Blaquiere, Edward: *Narrative of a Second Visit to Greece. Including Facts Connected with the Last Days of Lord Byron....* London, 1825.

Cockburn, Lord: *Life of Lord Jeffrey.* 2 vols. London, 1852.

The Complete Works of Lord Byron. Brussels, 1830.

Correspondence of Two Brothers, Edward Adolphus, Eleventh Duke of Somerset, and His Brother, Lord Webb Seymour, 1800–1819, and After. London, 1906.

Dictionary of National Biography.

Englische Studien, vol. 51 (1918), Leipzig.

Finlay, George: *History of Greece.* 7 vols. London, 1877 (vols. 6 and 7).

Gamba, Count Peter (Pietro): *A Narrative of Lord Byron's Last Journey to Greece.* London, 1825.

Gordon, Thomas: *History of the Greek Revolution....* 2 vols. 2nd Ed. Edinburgh, 1844.

Keats-Shelley Journal, Vol. XIX, 1970.

Kennedy, James: *Conversations on Religion with Lord Byron.* London, 1830.

LBC—*Lord Byron's Correspondence*, ed. by John Murray. 2 vols. London, 1922.

LJ—*The Works of Lord Byron. A New, Revised and Enlarged Edition. Letters and Journals*, ed. Rowland E. Prothero. 6 vols. London, 1898–1901.

Maggs, Sotheby, and Christie's sale and auction catalogues.

Marchand, Leslie A.: *Byron: A Biography.* 3 vols. New York, 1957; London, 1958.

Millingen, Julius: *Memoirs of the Affairs of Greece.* London, 1831.

Moore, Doris Langley: *The Late Lord Byron.* London, 1961.

———*Lord Byron: Accounts Rendered.* London, 1974.

Moore—*Letters and Journals of Lord Byron, with Notices of His Life.* By Thomas Moore. 2 vols. London, 1830.

Morning Chronicle, Oct. 17, 1812.

Nicolson, Harold: *Byron, the Last Journey, 1823–1824*. London, 1924.
Notes and Queries, 4th. ser., Vol. 4, Sept. 25, 1869.
Origo, Iris: *The Last Attachment*. London, 1949.
Parry, William: *The Last Days of Lord Byron*. London, 1825.
Poetry—The Works of Lord Byron. A New, Revised and Enlarged Edition. Poetry, ed. Ernest Hartley Coleridge. 7 vols. London, 1898–1904.
St. Clair, William: *That Greece Might Still Be Free*. London, 1972.
———*Trelawny: The Incurable Romancer*. London, 1977.
Smiles, Samuel: *A Publisher and His Friends: Memoir and Correspondence of the Late John Murray*, 2 vols., London, 1891.
Stanhope, Col. Leicester: *Greece in 1823 and 1824*. London, 1824.
Trelawny, Edward John: *Recollections of the Last Days of Shelley and Byron*. London, 1858.
———*The Letters of Edward John Trelawny*, ed. H. Buxton Forman. London, 1910.

Appendix IV

BIOGRAPHICAL SKETCHES OF PRINCIPAL CORRESPONDENTS AND PERSONS FREQUENTLY MENTIONED

(*See also sketches in earlier volumes*)

SAMUEL BARFF (1793–1880)

Charles Hancock's partner, Samuel Barff, had settled at Zante as a banker and merchant in 1816. Along with his partner he handled all of Byron's business, and much in addition to his banking, in the islands. Gordon (*History of the Greek Revolution*, Vol. II, p. 104, note) called him "one of the steadiest friends of the cause [Greek] . . . [who] sacrificed every year considerable sums in relieving distressed refugees and needy Philhellenes, besides the loss of business at Constantinople". Byron relied on his judgment, not only in money matters but also in many other things including the evaluation of the merits of Greek leaders and Philhellenes. When the first two instalments of the Greek Loan (amounting to £80,000) arrived in Zante in his care after Byron's death, he impounded them pending the appointment of a new commissioner. Barff remained in Zante for many years and died in 1880 at the age of 87. Some of his descendants still reside on the island.

LUKAS CHALANDRITSANOS (1809–1832?)

Byron had brought from Ithaca to Cephalonia in August, 1823, a Moreote family named Chalandritsanos, consisting of three young girls and an invalid mother. They had been well to do in Patras, but were made destitute refugees by the revolution. He provided them a house and maintenance in Argostoli. Lukas, then a handsome boy of fifteen in the service of the chieftain Kolokotrones in the Morea, having heard what was being done for his family, came over to Argostoli, hoping to find service with the generous English Lord. Byron took to him immediately and engaged him as a page (a post not requiring menial service) when he left for Missolonghi. In fact he formed a romantic attachment for him much as he had with Edleston, the choir boy at Cambridge. But unfortunately he faced a new experience, for his affection for the boy was not returned. Though he heaped presents of money (supposedly for his family), gilded pistols, and gold-embroidered clothes on him, he got in return only indifference. He realized that he had indeed "grown aged in this world of woe". It was a sorrow and a frustration that he could not confess even to his intimate friends, but it found expression in the last three poems he wrote in Greece, notably the verses written on his thirty-sixth birthday. This added to the pathos of his last days. The situation has been best and most sympathetically described by Doris Langley Moore in *The Late Lord Byron*, pp. 175–183. Lukas apparently died not long after Byron, how is not known. The meagre fact was reported in a letter in Greek from his sisters appealing to Byron's daughter for assistance in 1832.

Charles Hancock (1793–1858)

Charles Hancock was born in London of a family that had been for several generations members of the Society of Friends. Some time before 1820 he joined in partnership with Samuel Barff, a merchant who had established himself in Zante in 1816 after the English had assumed the Protectorate of the Ionian Islands. While Barff remained in Zante, Hancock settled in Argostoli on the island of Cephalonia, where Byron met him after he arrived in August, 1823. Following some unsatisfactory dealings with Greek bankers and merchants, Byron put all his business, including the cashing of bills of exchange, in the hands of Barff and Hancock. He established a very friendly personal relationship with Hancock before he left for Missolonghi and wrote some of his most frank and confidential letters to him during his last months among the Greeks. Hancock returned to England in 1828 and furnished Moore with letters and much information about Byron. His reminiscences written in the Ionian Islands, which undoubtedly contained many details and anecdotes of Byron's life there, were lost by Moore.

Dr. James Kennedy (? –1827)

Dr. Kennedy got his medical education at the University of Edinburgh. He had been a medical officer in the British forces in the Mediterranean for several years before he met Byron in Cephalonia in August, 1923. He was a serious Christian of the evangelical stripe who wished to convince his brother officers of the truth of Christianity, and got Dr. Muir, the health officer at Argostoli, to gather a group at his house to listen to his presentation. Byron joined the group. Unlike Muir and some of the other sceptical officers, Byron, without abating his detestation of cant and hypocrisy, had a serious interest and curiosity in the arguments which Kennedy put forward. He had wrestled with theological and cosmological problems in *Cain,* in *Heaven and Earth,* and in *Don Juan,* and had read enough of theological arguments to meet Kennedy on his own ground. He soon discovered that Kennedy's dogmatism could not be moved by rationalist objections, but at the same time he respected his Methodistical sincerity, and never scoffed openly at his opinions. The seriousness of his discussions gave Kennedy the hope of converting him. Byron's facetious remarks to Muir and other friends in Argostoli, however, indicate that Kennedy had not shaken his scepticism. Nevertheless Byron continued to value the doctor as an honest and good man. When he wanted to find a temporary refuge for the little Turkish girl Hatagée, he appealed to Kennedy and his wife to undertake the care of her and her mother. Kennedy returned to England in 1826 and wrote some of his reminiscences of Byron, but he died in Jamaica in September, 1827. His wife published his memoir as *Conversations on Religion with Lord Byron* in 1830.

Prince Alexander Mavrocordatos (1791–1865)

The Prince (the courtesy title of a Greek who had been in the Service of the Turks as Hospodar or local ruler in Wallachia and Moldavia) had followed other Greeks into exile, his Greek patriotic activities having made him persona non grata to the Turks. He came of a long line of Phanariots (Greeks in Turkish administrative posts). Educated at Constantinople, he had devoted his earlier years to the study of Oriental languages. During his exile he became proficient in French and Italian and understood English. He had settled at Pisa in 1818, and was closely associated with Shelley and his circle in 1820 and 1821 before Byron arrived. Mary Shelley took Greek lessons from him in exchange for English instruction, and Shelley dedicated his poem *Hellas* to the Prince.

Mavrocordatos returned to Greece after the outbreak of the revolution and, following the establishment of a central Provisional Government by the National Assembly at Epidaurus, he was elected President. But quarrels with the military chieftains such as Kolokotrones caused him to resign and flee to the island of Hydra. Byron's loan of £4,000 to activate the Greek fleet brought Mavrocordatos to Missolonghi as Commander-in-chief and governor of Western Greece, where Byron joined him in January, 1824.

Byron soon recognized the virtues and weaknesses of the Prince. He was predisposed to respect and trust him more than any other Greek leader, partly because of his education and breeding, and partly because Col. Napier and Count Delladecima had recommended him for his honesty and unselfish patriotism. He was a small man with squinting dark eyes peering through the small frames of his glasses and looked more like a scholar than the statesman and warrior he aspired to be. Dr. Millingen (*Memoirs*, pp. 65–67) described him as "a clever, penetrating, ambitious man. His large Asiatic eyes full of fire and wit, were tempered by an expression of goodness." But Millingen continued: "Incapable of a plain, bold, open conduct, it has been said, that he could only advance by crooked ways, and obtain his ends by trick and cunning. The untractable, suspicious, and deceitful character of those he had daily to deal with, might render this necessary." Byron was often exasperated by him but still found him the most honest of the Greeks, all of whom he conceived suffered from the heritage of centuries of slavery, and survived by cozening their masters.

Julius Michael Millingen (1800–1878)

Julius Millingen had offered his services as a physician to the London Greek Committee. He came to see Byron in Cephalonia in the autumn of 1823 and later joined him in Missolonghi. He was the son of James Millingen, archaeologist. In his youth he had been in France and had gone to school in Rome. In his holidays he went on walking tours in Germany and is said to have visited Goethe in Weimar. In 1817 he started medical studies in Edinburgh University and received a diploma from the Royal College of Surgeons of Edinburgh in 1821. In Missolonghi he was put in charge of a clinic established for the artillery corps.

After Byron's death in 1824 Millingen had a variety of unusual experiences. On recovering from a severe attack of typhoid fever, he was appointed surgeon in the Greek army, and on their surrender to the Turks was taken prisoner by Ibrahim Pasha. On his release he went to Smyrna in 1826 and settled in Constantinople in 1827 where he was attached as a physician to the Dutch Legation. Later he became court physician to five successive Sultans.

In 1831 he published in London his *Memoirs of the Affairs of Greece, with Anecdotes relating to Lord Byron.* This was Volume I of a more extended memoir. Volume II remained in manuscript and was destroyed by fire in Constantinople in 1870. Millingen's account of Byron in Missolonghi is generally sympathetic, though he was thought by some to have been harsh on the Greeks. He ministered, along with Dr. Bruno, to Byron in his last illness, and like Bruno insisted on the bleeding that probably hastened the patient's death. Millingen participated in the autopsy and gave some details not in Bruno's report.

William Parry

When Parry, the fire-master, arrived in Missolonghi in February, 1824, on the storeship *Ann* with mechanics and artificers sent by the London Greek Committee to set up an arsenal for the Greeks, he found much confusion. Byron took to him immediately as a practical man who could get things done. He wrote to Hancock: "Parry seems a fine rough subject." He gave him every assistance and a free hand in his work, and living quarters in his own house. Parry was a ball of energy and a great contrast to the indecisive Mavrocordatos and the "Typographical Colonel" Stanhope. Byron was not repelled by the lack of education and rough exterior of the fire-master and found him more congenial than others around him. Before long he used him as paymaster and even amanuensis. Several letters written by Parry and signed by Byron give some evidence of his illiteracy. It is true that they drank brandy together, but they also had long and serious conversations about Greece and Byron's hopes and frustrations. There is no doubt that Byron trusted him more and more, and in his last illness it was Parry that he leaned on more than the doctors, who were urging him to be bled.

After Byron's death Parry returned to England and published in 1825 *The Last Days of Lord Byron*, a frank and unvarnished account of the difficulties encountered in Missolonghi and of Byron's opinions of some of his associates there, including some unflattering remarks about Stanhope and the Benthamites. The book was recognized as a biographical masterpiece, but his authorship was called in question. An article in the *Examiner* of April 2, 1826, called Parry "a slanderer, a sot, a bully, and a poltroon", and concluded that "he cannot write ten words in English". Parry brought action for damages in 1827, and the trial was riotous and widely reported. Parry won the case and was awarded £50. William St. Clair, who has examined the evidence, concluded that the material in the book was Parry's, but that it was skilfully ghosted by Thomas Hodgskin (1787–1869) a radical thinker and prolific writer. (See *Keats-Shelley Journal*, Vol. XIX, 1970, pp. 4–7.) Parry spent his last days in a lunatic asylum in Middlesex.

Colonel Leicester Stanhope (1784–1862)

The Hon. Leicester Stanhope was the third son of Charles Stanhope, third Earl of Harrington, whose title he later inherited (1851) on the death of his elder brother. He entered the army in 1799 and served in India in the Mahratta War. He had risen to the rank of Lt.-Colonel before he was placed on half pay in June, 1823. He had become a doctrinaire Benthamite who had more faith in republican institutions and printing presses than in military strength as a means of assisting the Greeks in their war for independence. He was sent out by the London Greek Committee to act with Byron as its agent in Greece. Byron tried to cooperate with him in every way he could, even contributing to the establishment of his press, though he thought it would do more harm than good. But he could not but compare him with the practical soldier and administrator Colonel Napier. In moments of irritation he referred to him as "the Typographical Colonel". Stanhope did, however, do much of the routine labour of correspondence at Missolonghi and reported regularly to John Bowring, the Committee secretary in London, who shared his Benthamite thinking. While in Missolonghi he established a Greek paper called the *Hellenica Chronica*, and an Italian one, the *Telegrafo Greco.* On February 21, 1824, he left for Athens, and like Trelawny was won over by Odysseus, who flattered him by humouring his propensity to establish schools and presses. Stanhope did, however, have a genuine admiration for Byron's zeal for the Greek cause, as is reflected in his letters and reminiscences in his *Greece in 1823 and 1824* (1824).

Appendix V

ADDITIONS AND CORRECTIONS

VOLUME 1

Page

2 line 24—*for* Dibden *read* Dibdin.

5 line 13—*for* Francis *read* Frances.

8 line 2—*for* Guicciolo *read* Guiccioli [first printing].

10 line 8 foot of text—*for* only a by strange *read* only by a strange.

11 line 2—*delete* is.

25—*for* temerity *read* timidity [first printing].

17 line 32—*for* not *read* nor.

29 line 11 foot—*for* are given *read* is given.

43 head of letter of [Sept. 15? 1803] to Mrs Byron—*for* Mrs Cuthering Gordon Byron *read* Mrs Catherine Gordon Byron.

47 note 2, line 3—*for* Prince Regent *read* Prince of Wales.

68 P.S. line 4—*for* [innovation?] read innovation [immolation?] [first printing].

86 line 11—*for* or your *read* of your.

94 note 7, line 5: *insert* to *after* Presented.

101 note 3, line 2: *for* (stanza 91) *read* (stanzas 91–92).

107 line 8—*for* Ætsculapius *read* Æsculapius [first printing].

109 line 1 to Long, Feb. 23, 1807: for *Vulgas* read *Vulgus.*

111 line 25—*for* large *read* larger.

113 line 3—for *firot* read *profit.*

123 line 13—*for* Mr. B. *read* Mrs. B.

124 line 21—*for* Corneilan *read* Cornelian.

138 to Ridge, line 6—*insert* in *before* completing.

144 line 6 foot of text—*for* Though *read* Through.

147 lines 1–2—*for* [devoted?] *read* [donated?].

154 note 1, line 4—*for* Christ Church *read* Christ's College.

161 note 1, lines 6–7—*read* . . . and Paul Whitehead, satirist and secretary of the Club.

179 line 3—". . . a lengthened chain." *Add note:* Goldsmith, *The Traveller*, line 10: ". . . a lengthening chain". See also page 240, line 1.

181 line 13—*for* unfortunately *read* unfortunate.

184 note 1, line 1—*for* (1783–1852) *read* (1782–1852); note 1, line 2 foot—*for* 1819 *read* 1820.

Page

186 line 24—*insert* & Co. *after* Sidmouth.

190 line 7 foot of text—*for* humourous *read* humorous.

192 note 3—*for* Unidentified *read* Scott, "Cadyow Castle".

198 lines 14–15—". . . paper bullets . . ." *Add note: Much Ado About Nothing*, Act II, scene 3.

208 note 1—This note applies also to quotations on page 177, line 12, and page 186, line 9.

226 line 19—*insert* a *before* single article.

240 lines 1–2—". . . jolly miller". *Add note:* Isaac Bickerstaffe, *Love in a Village*, Act I, scene 3. See also Vol. 2, page 48, line 2.

262 last line—*insert* MS. *before* Nottingham Public Libraries.

273 title—*for* Augusta Leigh *read* The Hon. Augusta Leigh.

285 (index)—*delete* B. as middle initial of Keats [first printing].

286 (index)—*transfer from* Murray, John *to* Murray, Joe pp. 142, 143 [first printing].

(index)—*for* O'Hare *read* O'Hara.

VOLUME 2

13 note 9—*for* Unidentified *read* Fielding, *Joseph Andrews*, Book II, chapter 5.

15 first note 1—*substitute*: Byron's parody is on the lines beginning "In the worst inn's worst room" in Pope's lines to Allen Lord Bathurst (*Moral Essays*, III, 299–314), referring to the 2nd Duke of Buckingham, who died in 1687 [first printing].

16 note 2—*for* Unidentified *read* Thomas Macgill, who had published a book on Turkey, lived at Malta.

note 6, line 4—*for* does not displease us *read* does not always displease us. line 3—*for* déplait *read* déplaît.

23 line 25—"Ld. Grizzle". *Add note:* In Fielding's *Tom Thumb.*

29 note 9—as corrected in page 16, note 2 above.

33 note 6—*add:* See "William Haygarth: Forgotten Philhellene", by William Randel, *Keats-Shelley Journal*, Vol. IX, part 2 (1960), pp. 86–90.

43 line 6 "rix dollars". *Add note:* German-Dutch coins worth about a dollar.

to Hobhouse, line 10—*delete* [?] *after* Limae. *Add note:* Horace, *Ars Poetica*, 291, 388–89.

45 note 5—*delete* Mr. Bent is unidentified. *Add:* Jeffrey Hart Bent (b. 1780) went to Trinity College, Cambridge, and was called

Page

to the bar in 1806. In 1814 he became the first judge of the new Supreme Court of New South Wales and remained in Sydney until 1817.

47 note 8, line 4—*for* They will be carried to *read* I will carry them to.

48 lines 1–2—"jolly Miller". See correction for Vol. 1, page 240.

55 lines 11–12—"Castalian State". *Add note:* Pope, *Epistle to Dr. Arbuthnot*, lines 229–30.

56 line 12 foot—"a *Non* Intermittendo". *Add note:* Byron doubtless had in mind the proverbial Latin phrase, "lucus a non lucendo" (a grove is so called because it excludes the light), commonly used of any ridiculous derivation or non sequitur.

70 line 11——*add note:* Ben Johnson, *Every Man in his Humour*, Act I, scene 2.

86 line 3 foot—*for* "Alternative" *read* "Alterative" [first printing].

87 note 1, lines 3 and 6—*for* Alternative *read* Alterative [first printing].

89 note 2—*for* die young *read* dies young.

92 note 2—*substitute*: The Vauxhall pleasure gardens offered light musical entertainment.

94 line 13—*for* shoot of move *read* shoot or move.

97 line 2 foot of text—*for* Breslau *read* Breslaw.

112 note 2, line 3—*for* prophecying *read* prophesying.

126 note 6, line 2—*for* Valleta *read* Valletta.

134 line 7—*for* diverted *read* directed.

143 line 9—Matthews. *Add note:* probably Henry Matthews, brother of Charles Skinner Matthews who drowned in the Cam in August, 1811.

153 3rd note 1—*for* Andreas Saraci *read* Spiro Saraci.

154 line 6 foot of text—*for* D[orant?] *read* D[avies?]; also in line 5 foot of text and line 2 foot of text.

170 Moore line 2—*for* Ye. *read* Yr.

line 5—*for* apprehensions *read* apprehension.

line 7—for dose read *dose.*

174 second note 1, line 2—*for* the Late John Skinner *read* the late John Skinner.

179 note 3—*insert* Cambridge *after* St. John's College.

182 Scott line 16—*Svbstitute* semicolon for comma *after* Lake.

line 17—*for* James's no *read* James's as no.

183 line 8—*for* if the *read* if that.

185 to Lady C. Lamb, line 3—*delete* nervous.

Page

187 line 13—*for* [Daily? Dandy?] *read* [Derby? Donkey?].

189 Aug. 23, 1812, to Hanson, line 2—*insert* [sic] *after* titled.

194 lines 1–2—"burthen is light". *Add note:* St. Matthew, 11: 30.

200 line 4—"James the Fatalist". *Add note:* Diderot, *Jacques le Fataliste.*

206 line 10—*for* players and play *read* players and plays.

222 notes—*transpose* the two notes numbered 1.

227 note 2—*substitute:* This is an instance of Byron's familiarity with the 18th-century plays and of his retentive memory of quotable lines that caught his fancy or amused him. In Colley Cibber's *The Careless Husband* (Act V) Lord Foppington says to Lady Betty Modish: "I have lost a thousand women in my time, but never had the ill manners to be out of humour with any one for refusing me, since I was born." [first printing].

228 to Murray, (*b*) line 2—*for* moment *read* amount.

238 to Hanson, (*b*), line 4—*for* [act?] read [write?].

240 line 12 foot—"never laughed at P—" *Add note:* The initial refers to Princess Caroline. See p. 263.

241 line 3—*for* sussessor *read* successor.

251 to Hobhouse, line 8—*for* a taken seat *read* taken a seat.

254 first note 1—*for* shop on *read* shop in.

259 line 27—*for* merit if Novelty *read* merit of Novelty.

263 note 2—*substitute:* Byron must have been thinking of the Duke of Cumberland who married Mrs. Holton secretly.

265 note 1, line 3—*delete* Road.

289 (index)—*for* Blackett *read* Blacket.

297 (index)—Strabo. *for* Geography *read Geography.*

298 (index)—*for* Vergil *read* Virgil.

Volume 3

6 line 8—*for* authorize *read* authorise.

11 note 1, line 2—*for* Vol. II *read* Vol. I.

14 line 21—*for* one way of the other *read* one way or the other.

22 Note 2—*substitute:* William Tomline, M.P. for the borough of Truro from 1811. He was the son of George Pretyman Tomline, tutor and friend of the younger Pitt, and later Dean of St. Paul's and Bishop of Lincoln.

33 line 2—"Mr. R.P.K." *delete* Unidentified. *Add note:* Probably Richard Payne Knight.

Page

39 April 15, 1813, to Hanson, line 3—*for* Now *read* None.

42 lines 4–5—"... plead in vain". *Add note:* See Pope, *Rape of the Lock*, IV, 132: "Who speaks so well should ever speak in vain."

45 note 2—*substitute for last sentence:* Byron's acquaintance was Prince Peter Kozlovsky (1783–1840), who was Russian minister in Turin and later in Stuttgart. He was a nephew of Prince Feodor.

52 line 18——*for* worst positive *read* worst possible.

58 note 2—*substitute:* The Romaika, as Byron called the traditional Greek dance, was described by Galt in his *Letters from the Levant* (1813), page 190. He saw a group of musicians who were joined by "about twenty young fellows, drunk, holding each other by the hand. These were the dancers. The leader was shaking a handkerchief over his head, admiring at the same time his feet, which were cutting strange capers."

61 note 1—*substitute for last sentence:* The "abominable poems" still exist in a private case in the British Library.

62 note 4—*for* Roger's *read* Rogers's.

71 note 1—*add after second sentence:* His mother was a mistress of the Prince Regent.

73 line 5—*for* nonchalent *read* nonchalant.

78 *for* Henry Fox *read* Henry C. Fox, at head of letter and in note, and also on page 82 and pages 85 and 86. This correction also applies to page 263, July 22 and Aug. 6.

79 note 4—*substitute for last sentence:* Byron was thinking of a current joke of a man who marred a joke in telling it.

80 note 7—*for* Edmund Malone *read* Edmond Malone. This note also applies to Vol. 6, p. 4, note 6 and p. 286 (index).

85 note 3—*substitute:* The cousin was perhaps going to be a nun. By "Waistcoat" Byron meant a straightjacket used to restrain lunatics.

95 line 17—*for* marvelous *read* marvellous.

96 note 8—*add source: LJ*, II, 250n.

101 lines 12–13—"disparaged your parts". *Add note:* Wycherley, *The Country Wife*, Act II, scene 1; Act V, scene 4.

102 note 3—*Place dates in second line after* Lady Le Despenser *in first line.*

107 note 5—*add:* The undutiful father-in-law was the Emperor of Austria who had abandoned Napoleon.

109 line 26—"craving void". *Add note:* Pope, *Eloisa to Abelard*, line 94.

Page	
115	second note 1—*for* "Gentlemen" *read* "Gentleman".
116	note 2—*substitute:* Lord Bury was the 2nd son of the 4th Earl of Albemarle. Augustus Frederick, the 1st son and heir, styled Viscount Bury, died in 1804 at age 11, when the title passed to the 2nd son.
133	note 2—*for* Unidentified *read* Perhaps the father of George Agar Ellis, later Baron Dover, who wrote *The True History of the Iron Mask.*
145	note 2—*for* note 3 *read* note 4 (Vol. 3, p. 136).
155	P.S., line 10—*place* ["] *after* N[ewstead].
168	line 3—*for* sequal *read* sequel.
171	line 18—*for* persuation *read* persuasion.
172	line 4 (Webster)—*for* ye. security *read* yr. security.
	7 (Webster)—for *wordly* read *worldly.*
178	line 19—*for* caprious *read* capricious.
190	note 1—*for* 1913 *read* 1813.
190	note 2—*add:* As Vicar of Harrow, Cunningham later prevented a plaque from being placed in the church to the memory of Byron's illegitimate daughter Allegra.
198	line 11—*for* our *own words read* your *own words.*
207	line 13—for *word things* read *words things.*
	note 4—*add:* Byron elsewhere ascribed the phrase "words are things" to Mirabeau (Vol. 4, p. 74).
210	line 11—"O-hone-a-rie!" *Add note:* Scott, *Glenfinlas; or, Lord Ronald's Coronach.* "O hone a rie" is an expression of lament.
212	line 12—*for* absinence *read* abstinence.
213	note 2—*substitute:* "Ak-Deniz", literally "white sea" is the Turkish word for Mediterranean (as opposed to "Kara-Deniz", Black Sea).
214	note 3, line 3—*for* was being discussed *read* were being discussed.
220	line 3—*for ὁι πολλοι read οἱ πολλοι.*
	note 1, line 1—for *Laisons* read *Liaisons.*
	note 1, line 1—after *Les Liaisons Dangereuses* add: Pierre Ambroise François Choderlos de Laclos.
223	note 1, line 4—*for* (1789) *read* (1739).
229	lines 26–27——*add note:* Guarini, *Il Pastor Fido,* III, i, i.
243	Nine o'clock, line 11—Locke. *Add note:* William Locke (1767–1847) was an amateur painter, a friend of Fuseli.
246	note 2—*for* Hanlet *read* Hamlet.

Page

256 line 17—"Sylla"—*Add note:* A variant spelling of Sulla, the Roman dictator. See also Vol. 9, p. 41, No. 83.

267 Nov. 29 Clark—*insert* MS. *before* Trinity College Library.

269 *for* April 29, 1813, *read* April 27, 1813.

Volume 4

13 lines 10–11—"Gods—men—nor columns". *Add note:* Horace, *Ars Poetica*, line 373. (See also Vol. 3, p. 199, line 7.)

16 P.S., line 5—for *listness* read *listless.*

16 first note 1—*for* "Thou act not false" *read* "Thou art not false".

21 note 2—*for* Unidentified *read* See page 61, note 2. (See also Vol. 3, p. 30, line 6 foot.)

25 note 1—*substitute:* In Maria Edgeworth's *Patronage* the praise of the Lord Chief Justice is not meant for Lord Ellenborough but for the Irish lawyer, Charles Kendal Bushe.

36 line 5 foot—"*Remember him*" *Add note:* The lines recalled Byron's romance with Lady Frances Webster.

51 note 3, line 2—*insert after* fragment No. 23: in Elegy and Iambus.

61 to Rogers (*a*)—*change date to* Fy. 16th 1816 (See Additional Letters, Volume 11.)

63 to Dallas, line 4—*for* G[aiou]r *read* G[iaou]r.

74 note 3, line 1 *insert after* P. M. O'Donovan: [Peacock?].

79 line 1—"The night almost at odds with morning". *Add note: Macbeth* Act III, scene 4.
last line——"white stone"——*add note:* Emblem of an important or happy day.

82 line 9—*insert after* Runci: [Runes?].

93 note 5, line 2—*for* Annias *read* Annius.
note 9, line 1—*for* Inchiquen *read* Inchinquin.

98 April 18, 1814—*for* [To ————————] *read* [To the Rev. Dr. Valpy].

107 line 7—*for* G[aiou]r *read* G[iaou]r.
note 3, line 2—for *Abydes* read *Abydos.*

110 note 3, line 1—for *Anastasia* read *Anastasius.*

120 to Moore, line 2—*for* convenient *read* inconvenient.

122 second note 2—*delete* Southey? Sotheby?

124 note 3—*for* Unidentified *read* Lady Gertrude Sloane Stanley (née Howard), daughter of Lord Carlisle and one of Augusta's closest friends.

Page

125 to Charles Hanson—*change date to* 1814.

151 note 3—*add at end:* a term used in the Navy.

152 line 7—"surgit amari" *Add note:* Lucretius, *De Rerum Natura*, IV, 1134.

154 to Murray, line 6—*for* that is the print *read* that is the point.

182 to Milbanke (*b*), line 10—*for* it is a yesterday *read* it is as yesterday.

187 second note 1—*for* Unidentified *read* William Penn (1776–1845), of St. John's College, Cambridge, wrote for the *Gentleman's Magazine* and the *Anti-Jacobin*. He was a great grandson of the founder of the Pennsylvania colony.

217 second note 1—*transfer* (Vol. 1, p. 113) *to third note 1.*

224 line 19——"ears polite"——*add note:* Pope, *Moral Essays*, IV, 150.

226 note 1—*substitute*: Presumably the important word in Chesterfield's dictionary is "graces". The quibble would be on the senses of "favour" and "attainments".

235 note 1—for *the last of the Goths* read *the Last of the Goths.*

240 note 2—*for* Unidentified *read* Probably the wife of William Locke, the painter mentioned several times by Byron.

259 to Hobhouse, line 21—*for* Carnal *read* Carvel.
note 4—*substitute:* "Hans Carvel", a fabliaux verse tale by Matthew Prior. The underscoring of *Hans* indicates that Byron referred to Hanson, who had borrowed £2,800 to buy some property.

273 first note 1—*substitute:* Turkish word meaning inn.

278 note 1—*substitute:* Lord John Townshend.

288 to Burges, line 2—*for* erronious *read* erroneous.

292 first note 1—*add:* (See Vol. 10, p. 119, note 1.)

294 to Hunt, line 1—*for* as I shall to be see you *read* as I shall be to see you.

315 first note 1—*add:* It furnished the libretto for Rossini's *La Gazza Ladra* (1815).

316 note 1, line 2—*for* Whittinham *read* Whittingham.

317 2nd note 1, line 1—*for* debtors *read* creditors.

320 note 2—for *De Arte Poetica* read *Ars Poetica.* (Also in note 3.)
note 3—*for* anum *read* annum.

322 to Moore, line 6—". . . done the wrong". *Add note:* Dryden, *Conquest of Granada,* Part II, Act I, scene 2.

333 first note 1—*for* debtors *read* creditors.

Page

337 first note 1—*substitute:* Thomas Davison Bland, Lady Byron's uncle and trustee.

339 [Jan. 8] to Murray—*insert* MS. *before* Robert H. Taylor Coll.

342 March 3, to Moore—*for* MS. Moore *read* Text: Moore.

345 [July 23–24?]—*add beginning bracket.*

353 [Aug. 16]—*for* Univeristy *read* University.

356 Forgeries—*insert after* [1814] to Hanson: March 2, 1814, to Webster. Bixby.

367 (index)—Raymond. *Add* George.

VOLUME 5

5 line 9—*for* are *read* is.

7 May 20—*for* As Basle *read* At Basle.

28 note 1, line 1—*for*]ames *read* James.

28 note 1, line 9—*for*]anuary *read* January.

34 note 3—*add:* Adapted from *Proverbs,* 12:10: "The tender mercies of the wicked are cruel."

36 to Murray (*a*), line 5—*for* Tyrnhill's *read* Tyrwhitt's.

77 line 28—*after Spooney insert* [Hanson].

78 line 29—"Morat". *Add note:* The field of Morat, near Aventicum (Avranche) where the Swiss defeated the Burgundians in the fifteenth century.

84 line 3—"make assurance double sure". *Add note: Macbeth,* Act IV, scene 1.

100 line 9—"agreeable companion in a postchaise". *Add note:* Cf. Johnson's "I would spend my life in driving briskly in a postchaise with a pretty woman."

124 note 7, line 2—*for* Ludivico *read* Ludovico.

127 last line—*for* more even that *read* more even than.

136 note 5—*substitute:* Perhaps a *jeu d'esprit* on Lady Byron or one of his "enemies".

138 to Murray, line 1—"letter from England". *Add note:* One letter mentioning this fact was from Shelley, dated Nov. 20, 1816 (See *Shelley and His Circle,* V, 15–22).

note 1—*add:* It is curious that, without consulting Byron, Murray employed the poet's enemy Romilly to seek the injunction.

147 note 5—*delete second sentence and substitute:* He provided the carriage for Louis XVI and Marie Antoinette in the flight to Varennes in June, 1791.

Page

153 [To?] [1817?]—This "fragment" was mistakenly placed here, It belongs to the letter of Jan. 25, 1819, to Murray (Vol. 6. p. 95).

157 line 12—*insert* not *before* dormant.

159 line 12—"Hath he laid perjury upon his Soul?". *Add note: Merchant of Venice*, Act IV, scene 1.

160 Jan. 13, to Augusta, last line—Ridotto. *Add note:* An Italian social gathering.

162 line 27—"my 'Lucy' & my 'Polly'". *Add note:* Lucy Lockitt and Polly Peachum in *The Beggar's Opera.*

164 to Moore, line 6—*for* filty beer *read* filthy beer.

168 line 23—"Spinning-house Maidenhead". *Add note:* The Spinning-house was the Cambridge University prison where prostitutes were confined.
lines 31–32—"a gap in Nature". *Add note: Antony and Cleopatra*, Act II, scene 2.

172 line 11—"happy few". *Add note: Henry V*, Act IV, scene 3.

182 note 1—*for* Unidentified *read* Demetrius G. Schinas, friend and biographer of Mustoxidi.

198 note 2—*substitute:* The Mrs. K. referred to here and elsewhere in Byron's letters was Maria Keppel, a singer who apparently lived with Kinnaird as a common law wife for a number of years. Byron first mentioned her on Nov. 8, 1811 (Vol. 2, p. 129). About a year after she had gone back on the stage, Kinnaird broke the connection but gave her a settlement. (See Vol. 6, pp. 33–4.)

205 line 8—"kicking against the pricks". *Add note: Acts of the Apostles*, 9:5.
note 6, line 3—*for* Baldwin and Cradock *read* Baldwin, Cradock, & Joy.

210 note 1, line 1—*place* comma *after* Prime Minister.

213 note 1—*add:* That painting, now in the Accademia di Belli Arti in Venice, is known as "La Tempesta".

215 line 1—". . . going to the water—Argal". *Add note: Hamlet*, Act V, scene 1.
line 28—*for* Coterie Nolbachique *read* Coterie Holbachique. *Add note:* A reference to Rousseau's difficulties with the followers of Baron d'Holbach as described in his *Confessions.*
note 2—*add:* According to E. Tangye Lean, Hobhouse "sent a copy to St. Helena inscribed 'Imperatori Napoleon'. It was

Page

impounded by the Governor Sir Hudson Lowe, as an infringement of the rule forbidding the use of the title of Emperor, but another copy got through which was annotated by Napoleon and obsessed his entourage for days." (*The Napoleonists*, p. 31.) note 3—for *af* read *of*.

216 to Hobhouse, line 6—"Guido's innocents". *Add note:* Guido Reni, "Strage degli innocenti", Pinacoteca, Bologna.

217 lines 7–8—"winding Po", "lazy Scheldt". *Add note:* Adapted from Goldsmith's *The Traveller*, line 2.

224 line7—"the Guide-book—which is very accurate". *Add note*: The guide book which Byron mentions here and elsewhere was probably Joseph Forsyth's *Remarks on Antiquities, Arts* . . ., which gave large space to the antiquities of Rome. See pages 233 and 234.

231 note 1—*delete and substitute:* See p. 198, note 2.

243 lines 12–13—"let them look to their bond". *Add note: Merchant of Venice*, Act III, scene 1.

250 line 13—"a reflection on * * * * * * *" *Add note:* The asterisks probably refer to Sheridan. "Fruits and flowers" is an obvious reference to Captain Absolute's flattery of Mrs. Malaprop in *The Rivals*, Act III, scene 3.

253 line 13—"foul is fair". *Add note: Macbeth*, Act I, scene 1.

260 note 10, line 2—*for* Chantrye *read* Chantrey.

262 note 4—*for* Hemens *read* Hemans.

268 note 6—*for* Marlow *read* Marlowe.

270 line 10—"from Germany" *Add note:* The young American was George Ticknor, who had visited Byron in London in 1815.

285 [June?] [Pryse Gordon]—*insert* Text: *before Personal Memoirs.*

297 Shelley, line 21—*for* Bryon *read* Byron.

301 (index)—*for* Casti "animali Parlante" *read* "Animali Parlanti".

308 (index)—*for* Voltaire, *Complétes read Complètes.*

Volume 6

4 note 6, line 2—*for* Edmund Malone *read* Edmond Malone.

10 lines 10–11—See excerpts from Byron's letters in Moore's manuscript journal, Vol. 11, Additional Letters.

20 lines 1–2—"he roared it like any Nightingale". *Add note: Midsummer Night's Dream*, Act 1, scene 2.

24 note 3, line 2—*delete* was not published until 1819 *and substitute:*

Page

was first published under a slightly different title in 1816. A revised and expanded edition was published by Murray in 1819.

26 line 10—*for* Rollo *read* Rolla.

note 4—*substitute:* See Sheridan's *Pizarro,* Act V, scene 3.

32 line 14—"Huncamunca". *Add note:* Huncamunca was the wife of Tom Thumb in Fielding's *Life and Death of Tom Thumb the Great.*

2nd note 1—*substitute:* George Edward Griffiths, publisher of the *Monthly Review.*

45 to Hobhouse, closing—*for* yours faithfully *read* yours faithfoolly.

69 lines 6–7—See excerpts from Byron's letters in Moore's manuscript journal, Vol. 11, Additional Letters.

89 line 17—"a pledge" a *Cazzo. Add note:* Literally "a penis". An Italian vulgarism—meaning "a bother", "a bore", "nonsense".

90 note 2, line 1—*for* Ludivico *read* Ludovico.

95 to Hobhouse, line 2—*for nan*-publication *read non*-publication.

first note 2—*substitute:* See correction for Vol. 5, p. 153.

112 last paragraph, line 1—*for* our unhappiness *read* your unhappiness.

114 note 3—*for* Unidentified *read* Farquhar, *The Recruiting Officer,* Act V, scene 1.

note 4—*for* Unidentified *read Macbeth,* Act III, scene 1: "Rather than so, come fate into the list / And champion me to the utterance."

116 line 22—*for* Sociata *read* Societa.

119 note 1, line 2—*delete* the *before New Monthly Magazine.*

to Fanny Silvestrini, line 1—*for* dici *read* dice.

125 note 2, line 1—*substitute:* In the Preface to the Vampyre is an account of an evening at the Villa . . .

127 note 7—*add:* Elwin (*Lord Byron's Family,* p. 96) identifies her as Elizabeth Hervey, half-sister of William Beckford.

131 note 1—*add:* "buzzerena" is a dialect form of an Italian word "buggerone" (from "bugio" for "hole").

138 to Hobhouse, line 7—"Bill Tibbs". *Add note:* Beau Tibbs in Goldsmith's *Citizen of the World?*

140 to Kinnaird, line 5—*for* eye *read* aye.

to Kinnaird, line 5—"The Redder aye gets the worst lick o' the fray". *Add Note:* The Scottish saying means "The person who intervenes (the redder) always gets the worst."

161 translation, line 6—*for* know *read* known.

Page

168 to Murray, last line—"so cunning of fence". *Add note: Twelfth Night,* Act III, scene 4.

181 line 31—*for* Alderoni *read* Alberoni.

200 second note 1, line 3—*for* Davidson *read* Davison.

211 note 3—*for* Unidentified *read* A well known family in Lancashire.

212 note 2—*substitute:* Medwin, *Conversations* (ed. Lovell), p. 202.

212 note 3—*for* unidentified *read* Possibly José Antonio Paez, Venezuelan revolutionary, who helped Bolivar gain independence for the country of which he became President and dictator.

230 line 5 foot—*for* speaking ill at all *read* speaking ill of all.

258 first line of P.S.—*for* sortito ci casa *read* sortito di casa.

270 Aug. 2, Henry Dorville—*for* Tex: *read* Text:.

273 March 23, 1818, line 2—*for* Charaway *read* Charavay.

286 (index)—*for* Malone, Edmund *read* Malone, Edmond.

287 (index)—*for* Missiaglia, Giorgione Battista *read* Missiaglia Giovanni Battista.

289 (index)—*insert:* Spooney, see Hanson, John.

289 (index)—*for* Warton, Thomas *read* Warton, Joseph.

Volume 7

7 line 7—*for* Feb. 21 *read* Feb. 20.

13 to Teresa (*d*), Italian and translation—*for* [Jan. 1820?] *read* [April?] 1820.

17 line 14—"The gods seem to have made me poetical"—*add note: As You Like It,* Act III, scene 3: "I would the gods had made thee poetical".

29 line 7—*for* ognano *read* ognuno.

30 to Teresa (*b*) (Italian), line 2—*for* poui *read* puoi.

31 to Teresa (Italian), line 2—*for* Se perdessi li denti *read* Se perdessi [sic] li denti.

31 to Teresa (translation), line 2—*for* If you were to lose your teeth *read* If I were to lose my teeth.

32 to Teresa (Italian), line 5 foot—*for* rado *read* raro.

35 to Teresa, line 2—*for* Alassandro *read* Alessandro.

37 to Teresa (*b*) (Italian), line 3—*substitute* comma *for* period *after* Del resto.

38 to Teresa (*d*) (Italian), line 5—"due righe di biglietto". *Add note:* Figaro in Rossini's *Il Barbiere di Siviglia,* Act 1, scene 2.

to Teresa (*a*) (translation), line 6—"[two lines crossed out]"

Page

Add note: See Origo, p. 153, note: "The last words legible are '. . . and rash vows like the evening breeze.'"

40 note 1—*for* Thomas Davidson Bland *read* Thomas Davison Bland.

49 note 1—*for* Habeus *read* Habeas.

53 line 1—*for* Immagionazione *read* Immaginazione.

63 line 22—"*before term ends*"—*add note:* Pope, *Epistle to Dr. Arbuthnot,* line 43.

66 to Teresa (*a*) (Italian), line 9—*for* Credemi *read* Credimi.

70 to Hobhouse, line 9—"Jew King". *Add note:* John King, a famous moneylender who lived as the husband of Lady Lanesborough. See John Taylor, *Records of My Life* (1832), II, 341–5.

87 line 15—*for* Credemi *read* Credimi.

89 line 11—*for* ralazione *read* relazione.

93 line 2—*for* ingiusto *read* ingiuste.

100 line 7—*for* Castlecorner *read* Castlecomer.

note 2—*for* Unidentified *read* Horace Walpole told a correspondent that when the tutor of young Lord Castlecomer broke his leg, the dowager Lady C's only comment was "very inconvenient to my Lord Castlecomer". (See *Horace Walpole's Letters,* ed. by Peter Cunningham, 1891, VI, 154, note 3.)

107 note 1—*for* letter *read* letters.

108 to Teresa (*b*) (Italian), line 6—*for* asvantaggio so *read* asvantaggioso.

125 (Dorville) line 6—*for* request *read* requested.

128 note 1, line 3—*for* their country house at Filetto *read* their country house Filetto.

129 to Teresa (Italian), line 15—*for Vici*-Coco *read Vice*-Coco.

131 line 5—"ricordati di me che son 'la Pia'". *Add note:* Dante's *Purgatorio,* V, 1333. La Pia was a wife killed by her husband who suspected her of infidelity.

132 line 22—*for* Quatering *read* Quartering.

134 line 2—*for* ricordate *read* ricordati.

136 line 2—*for* (of course) *read* (of mine).

150 line 7 foot—il mio "bel paese" *di No. Add note:* Dante, *Inferno,* XXXIII, 80: "Ahi Pisa vitupera delle gente del bel paese là dove *di si* sono."

153 line 20—[Hermogesser?] *Add note:* Perhaps a facetious twist of Hermogenes, the name of a notorious singer and teacher of music mentioned in Horace's *Satires.*

Page

162 The second letter to Murray with the postmark Sept. 14, 1820 belongs to the letter of Aug. 28, 1820 to Murray, pp. 164–5.

168 note 2—*substitute:* See page 225, note 6.

173 to Teresa (Italian), line 9—*for lerej* read *lerci.*

180 note 1—*substitute:* discorrere = to make love; cazzo = penis.

181 to Murray, line 3—"'Egad'—as Bayes says"—*add note:* Buckingham, *The Rehearsal.*

184 line 19—"wild Justice"—*add note:* Bacon's essay "Of Revenge".

190 to Kinnaird, line 14—*add note:* Tiberius Sempronius Gracchus, a distinguished general in the second Punic War.

191 first note 2—*for* Unidentified *read* Johnson said this of his friend Arthur Murphy's tragedy *Zenobia* in which the characters were named Tigranes, Tiridates, etc. See Mrs. Piozzi's *Anecdotes of Dr. Johnson*, p. 280.

192 line 5 from foot of text—*for* Count Monti's *substitute* Count Mosti's.

note 1—*for* Naturae *read* Natura.

198 line 8—"Chancery Bell"—*Add note:* John Bell (1764–1836), who represented Shelley in his Chancery suit for custody of his children.

200 line 7—"brief Chroniclers of the times"—*add note: Hamlet,* Act II, scene 2: "brief chronicles of the times".

211 line 21—"children of the Sun"—*add note:* James Thomson, *The Seasons: Summer*, line 872.

222 line 7—"greatly *daring dine*"—*add note:* Pope, Dunciad, Bk 4, line 318.

226 to Teresa (Italian), line 1—*for* regolo *read* regalo.

228 to Murray, line 11—*for Tus*culum *read Tus*culum. "*Tus*culum questions". *Add note:* A pun on Cicero's *Tusculan Disputations* (*Tusculanae Disputationes*). Cicero's villa was at Tusculum.

232 line 25—"Orson is endowed with reason". *Add note:* In the fifteenth-century story of the twin sons of Bellisant, Orson was carried off and raised by a bear and was called "The Wild Man of the Forest".

233 note 4, line 1—*delete* for.

241 last line—*for* senoche *read* senonche.

282 (index)—*add:* Zinnani [Zinanni?] Countess, 193.

Volume 8

Page

Half-title—line 6 of *Don Juan*, 15, 22—*setting* sun (Italic).

23 note 2, line 2—*for* "Childish Reflections" *read* "Childish Recollections".

37 line 16—*for* future? *read* future[?].

foot—*substitute for three lines of dashes* two dashes, then six lines of alternating seven- and six-dash lines, with indentations, suggesting that what Byron omitted was a verse of poetry.

note 1—*insert* by himself *after* strokes of the pen.

55 line 14—*for* uninterpreted *read* uninterrupted.

68 line 13—"trajects, or common ferries". *Add note: Merchant of Venice*, Act III, scene 4.

72 note 2—*for* Robert Walpole, First Earl of Orford *read* Horace Walpole, 4th Earl of Orford. For *Last Nine Years* read *Last Ten Years*.

73 Feb. 2, 1821, to Kinnaird, P.S., line 1—"High minded Moray". *Add note:* Scott, *Waverley*, Chap. 22. Byron frequently addressed Murray as "Dear Moray". In Scottish history the names were used interchangeably.

85 note 1, line 2—*insert* comma *after* controversy.

175 line 6 foot—*for* county *read* country.

187 verses to Murray—*add note:* a parody of William Cowper's "To Mary".

207 lines 20–21—"quarum [sic] partes fuimus". *Add note:* Byron's adaptation of Virgil's "quorum pars magna fui", *Aeneid*, II, line 6.

208 note 1, line 1—*for* line 843 *read* lines 943–45, quoted inaccurately.

210 line 2 foot—*for* gentlemen *read* gentleman.

244 to Murray, lines 1–2—"write me down an Ass". *Add note: Much Ado About Nothing*, Act IV, scene 3.

Volume 9

35 first note 1—*substitute:* Byron was probably thinking of Gray's "Progress of Poetry", where in the second stanza the poet refers to the Aeolian lyre as an "Enchanting shell", the first lyre according to mythical tradition having been made by stretching cords across an empty tortoise shell.

81 to Moore—*for* [December 13? 1921] *read* [December 13? 1821].

Page

99 lines 23–4—"this 'if' is not intended for a peace-maker". *Add note: As You Like It*, Act V, scene 4. See also Vol. 8, p. 26, last line.

157 note 1—*for* Leone *read* Leoni.

164 line 23—*for* It is a *read* It is.

168 P.S. line 13: *after* "come one come all". *Add note:* Scott, *Lady of the Lake*, Canto V, stanza 10.

176 to Kinnaird, line 5—*for* Brand *read* Bland. See correction for Vol. 4, p. 337.

221 *insert after* [Dec.?] [Douglas Kinnaird] etc.: Dec. 4 Douglas Kinnaird MS. Murray.

225 April 23—Percy Bysshe Shelley—*for* Moore, 591–592 *read* Moore, II, 591–592.

227 line 2 from foot—*delete* Text *before* MS.

244 (index)—*for* Lockhart, John Gibson and Sophie, 87, 154–5; Memoirs ... upon the Affairs of Scotland, 156 and n *read:* Lockhart John Gibson and Sophie, 87, 154–5.
Lockhart, G, Memoir ... upon the Affairs of Scotland, 156 and n.

Volume 10

95 line 1—*for* Cobourne? *read* Colborne and add [3]; and at foot of page add note: 3 Ridley Colborne, a family friend of the Milbankes [Noels] later Lord Colborne.

116 note 3—*substitute:* Probably an adaptation of "the career of his humour", *Much Ado about Nothing*, Act II, scene 3.

126 end of P.S. *add note:* These lines were borrowed from Samuel Johnson's "To Mrs. Thrale on her thirty-fifth Birthday".

148 lines 16–17—"had increased, was increasing and ought to be diminished"—*add note:* See Vol. 9, p. 47, note 1.

161 line 10—*add note:* Byron must not have remembered the figure. Murray had written that he sold 10,000 copies the first day. See Vol. 4, p. 44n.

167 note 2—*substitute:* This drawing is now in the Stark Library at the University of Texas. It is the only known portrait by D'Orsay of Byron with a cap.

170 note 5—*substitute:* A phrase used in the British Army attributed to Col. Watson of the Guards. *See* Stanhope, *Conversations with the Duke of Wellington*, 1888.

207 2nd note 1, line 1—for *Chaussé* read *Chaussée*.

Page

231 (index)—Blessington, Marguerite, line 11: *for* of Napoleon, 197; *read* of Napoleon, 192–3.

232 (index)—Bruno, Dr., line 2: *for* him *read* B.

(index)—Byron, Lady, line 4: *for* 34 *read* 54; line 7: *for* Church 64 *read* Church, 54, 64: etc.

(index)—Byron, Lord, column 2: *The Island*, line 2, *delete* 168.

238 (index)—Sterling, Charles—*for* 212 and n *read* 213 and n.

239 (index)—Whitton, Mr.) *delete* 61.

INDEX OF PROPER NAMES

Page numbers in italics indicate main references and Biographical Sketches in the Appendix. Such main biographical references in previous Volumes are included in this index and are in square brackets.